Edward Everett Hale

The Arabian Nights

A Selection of Stories from Alif Laila wa Laila

Edward Everett Hale

The Arabian Nights
A Selection of Stories from Alif Laila wa Laila

ISBN/EAN: 9783744752374

Printed in Europe, USA, Canada, Australia, Japan

Cover: Foto ©Thomas Meinert / pixelio.de

More available books at **www.hansebooks.com**

THE ARABIAN NIGHTS.

A

SELECTION OF STORIES

FROM

ALIF LAILA WA LAILA

THE ARABIAN NIGHTS' ENTERTAINMENT.

SELECTED AND EDITED BY

EDWARD E. HALE.

———∘o°⚡°o∘———

BOSTON:

GINN & COMPANY, PUBLISHERS.

1888.

TYPOGRAPHY BY J. S. CUSHING AND COMPANY.

PRESSWORK BY GINN AND COMPANY.

PREFACE.

THE Arabian Nights' Entertainments is a book which has been the delight of Europe and America for nearly two hundred years. Before that time, it had been the delight of Western Asia, and of the Mohammedan colonies in Europe and Northern Africa, it would be hard to say for how many centuries more. Since the Frenchman, Galland, first introduced it to readers of his own country, translations of it have been made into every language of Europe. In the English language, there have been. many translations from the original text. The interest in the text has increased in the East, and new manuscripts have been found, and different editions printed from them at Cairo and Calcutta. The literature of the subject is now an important department of literary criticism.

For our readers, young or old, it is perhaps enough to say, that the stories are as popular in the East as they have ever been in their translated forms, and that, at this moment, they may be heard recited wherever a considerable company of Arabs, Turks, or of other Eastern races come together. Nor is the interest which attaches to them in the East or the West difficult to account for. The stories are pure narrative, — narrative without any moral, without any object but that of amusing or pleasing the reader. There is not the slightest pretence that they are instructive, nor that they will lead in particular paths of virtue, nor that they illustrate great or small principles of life or of society. They are simply stories. In this they may be compared with the fairy-tales of our ancestors of France and Germany, and with some other instances in the folk-lore, as it is called, of different countries. But, in general, the folk-lore has some moral to carry with it, almost as definite, in some cases, as that of Æsop's fables. Very critical critics have undertaken to find a similar moral purpose in the Arabian Nights. But it is probably fair to say, that the Arab who listens by a camp-fire, like the school-boy who reads in England or in America, seeks nothing but the story, and finds nothing but the story. Certainly, in the specimens which I lay before the reader, I do not pretend that there is any moral at all. Nor do I wish that anybody shall take this book or read it, excepting with the wish of entering into the joy and delight, with which the simple people who first heard these stories received them.

The machinery of the collection is simple. A great sultan or monarch of India, a person wholly fabulous, whose name is Shahriar, although it is variously spelled in the different renderings, is so much displeased with his wife that he cuts off her head. He even determines that her successors shall not live more than twenty-four hours after marriage, and cuts off their heads after each has held that dangerous position for so short a time. The city is mourning under the loss of its most attractive young women, who suffer under this horrible law which he has laid down, until Scheherazade, the beautiful and accomplished daughter of the grand vizier, offers herself, as another Andromeda, to the fate which has fallen upon so many of her sisters. Her father begs her not to throw away her life. But she is quite confident of the result, and, when the morning after her wedding breaks, she begins to tell to her husband the first of the " Arabian Nights." At sunrise, by some law which seems to reign for them, which does not always govern people at the West, it is absolutely necessary that they shall all rise from bed. It is at this moment, that she says to him, that, if he will be graciously pleased to lengthen her life, she will continue the narrative on another morning. It has been truly said that, in this device of Scheherazade, what is now known as the " serial story " in modern literature was born. So happily did she arrange the moments of crisis, when her story broke off, that her husband, always eager to hear the continuation of the tale, spared her, day after day, till one thousand and one nights had passed. At the end of that time, according to the narrative thought most authentic, she had borne to him three children, and had so won his affection by her love and her power in story-telling that he rescinded the edict which he had laid down, and her life was no longer in danger. The collection of the stories which she told to him in this way, is known in the East as "Alif-laila," and in the West as the "Arabian Nights' Entertainment." Alif-laila means "the chief of stories," Alif being our letter A, and meaning the beginning or the chief; laila meaning stories, as in the infantine babble of children it might mean even in the West.

In making a collection from these fascinating stories, long enough to show the reader of this series what their interest consists in, I have not confined myself to any one of the several English versions. And even for readers who do not care to go much into the literature of the subject, it will be proper to give a brief account of the way in which these stories have been presented to readers in Europe and America.

Antoine Galland [1], who first published them in the West, had been connected with the French embassy in Constantinople. In returning to Paris, he brought with him the manuscript from which he translated, or rather abridged, his version of the Arabian Nights. He published them, somewhat as Scheherazade told them, at short intervals; somewhat as in Paris to-day, some of the best novels of our time have been published in what are called *feuilletons*. They had attained an immense popularity, — more so, it may be said, than any books of the time. It is remembered that the gay young men would gather in groups at night beneath Galland's windows, and sing and shout till he showed himself, when, in the midst of the applause with which they saluted him, they bade him tell them more stories, taking the very phrase with which Scheherazade's

[1] Born 1646, died 1715.

sister was accustomed to wake her, and ask her to renew her narrative. Galland ought to be remembered as a master of good French, although the more acute critics say he was not a master of very good Arabic. He knew Arabic enough to do his work sufficiently well to make, for Western readers, one of the most entertaining versions of the stories which has ever been made. He even introduced into modern language some words which owe their place there to the adaptations which he chose to make of the forms of the text. For instance, the word "djinn," which means a powerful spirit, became, under Galland's pen, the *Genie* who is well known to most young people of England and France, and who carries with him very little of the idea of the French word *genie*. Similar words, really created by Galland, are vizier and Afrite.

Galland severely abbreviated the text. Indeed, the text is so long, and goes into such infinite repetitions and details, that it is not till within ten years that any Western translator has dared present the whole of the Arabic stories to Western criticism. In 1881, however, Captain Sir Richard Francis Burton, who had distinguished himself as a traveller in Arabia, began the publication of a version which should go into every detail of the original language. It included everything which former translators had omitted, and it made the effort, at the same time, to render the poetical passages in English rhymed verse. It must be granted that the verses attempted by Burton and his friends are not very successful. But they are much better, and give a much better idea of the drift and movement of the original than those given in any of the former renderings. Indeed, it has been the general habit of the Western translators to omit the greater part of the verses which abound in the original text.

Whoever were the authors of the original Arabian Nights, they had not the slightest scruple in drawing on all sides for the materials of their stories. Thus the story of Solomon and the Queen of Sheba and the story of Ulysses will be found in more or less

detail in the Arabian Nights as the book exists in the Eastern
manuscripts. Different manuscripts, also, differ in the stories
which they include, and in the order of them. The division into
Nights varies in all the Eastern editions.

If the reader of this volume had the whole collection in his
hands, translated as fully as it is in Captain Burton's rendering, it
would make a series of more than twenty-one volumes of the size
of this. It is rather the office of this series to introduce young
readers into fascinating lines of literature, and to give them their
choice which of those lines they will follow. I satisfy myself, for
the present, with selecting a few of the stories which have, on the
whole, attained the widest reputation. In a single passage, which
I have indicated in foot-notes, I use, for our present purpose, Burton's full translation, as it is published by Lady Burton, in her
edition dedicated to the women of England; but I do not think
that the full detail, excepting for a very enthusiastic reader, adds
to the interest of the story. I have, therefore, taken for the text
of most of the stories, the admirable translation of Mr. Edward
William Lane: this was originally published in London in the
year 1839.

Criticism has exhausted itself to no great purpose on guesses at
the authorship of the Arabian Nights, and on the period in which
they were first written. It is probably safe to say that they originated in the custom of Eastern nations to tell and listen to stories,
where more artificial society writes and reads them. All through
the East, it will be hard to say how far back, there has existed a
company of professed story-tellers, glad to pick up a good story
wherever they could find it, and to tell it, much as the Last Min-
strel sang his lay in the castle-yard of any one who would give him
a welcome. Such stories lived, if they were good enough to live,
and of such stories, the best survive in the Arabian Nights. Somebody took the pains to write them down: who this somebody
was, the boldest critic does not pretend to say.

As to the date, the range of speculation is wide. The Caliph

Haroun Alrashid, and his wife Zobeide, and his vizier Giafar, and his slave Mesrour, are frequently referred to, and many of the stories involve them as actors of minor importance. The book, then, must have been much in its present form after the time of Charlemagne, who was contemporary with Haroun. On the other hand, it has been observed by Sacy that the whole collection alludes to coffee but three times, and in those three passages the allusion is so made that it seems probable that it was added after the original narrative. Now, the use of coffee is so general in the • East on all occasions of hospitality that it can hardly be thought that no allusion to it would have been made, in a book written after the general custom of drinking coffee had come in. The date of the introduction of coffee is itself not absolutely known. It is possible that it may be traced as early as the tenth century. But coffee was not in general use in the East until the fourteenth century. These limits give the dates, such as they are, between which we are to find the origin of the Arabian Nights as a written book. It was probably after the year 900 and before the year 1400 that they were written. The use of tobacco is once or twice alluded to in the book, but it is in exceptional instances, like those in which coffee is referred to, and the critics do not think the references belong to the ancient text. On the other hand, as in the case of coffee, it is impossible to say how early tobacco was used in Asia, although the impression certainly exists that it was introduced from America. In one of the stories a reference is made to the battle of El Hattin, as having taken place recently.

Very fortunately for the world, everybody likes to read the Arabian Nights, sooner or later in his life. A very important minor advantage which they have brought to the Western world, is a certain familiarity with the customs of the Semitic races, or the races of the Arabian peninsula, which proves an assistance in the intelligent reading of the Bible. Whoever will study the Arabian Nights carefully will find many customs alluded to, which make it easier to understand passages describing Eastern life in the Scriptures. Some of these illustrations will be found in the little volume now in the reader's hands.

Some of the stories in the Arabian Nights have become so completely a part of modern literature, that ignorance of them would be considered indicative of dulness. To allude to " Aladdin's Lamp," to allude to "Sindbad the Sailor," to allude to the " Barmecide's Feast," is to refer to narratives of which it is supposed that persons of tolerable education have some knowledge, just as they are supposed to know what is meant by the words, the " Discovery of America," the " Declaration of Independence," or the " Fall of Rome."

Most of the translators into Western languages have abridged those stories at their pleasure. Indeed, some of the Arabic editions, notably the first Boulak edition, have been already abridged ; and Captain Burton speaks as if it were difficult to obtain a complete text. He uses and approves Sir William Hay MacNaughton's of 1839–42. In the book in the reader's hand, I own that I have followed Lane, in leaving out many of the poetical quotations, or versified passages. I have tried to give a fair illustration of one of the best of these in the opening tale of the merchant. But it must be confessed, that to Western readers they are apt to prove a sad drag on the flow of the narrative. Sometimes they are quotations from authors well known in the East, and they seem to be used only to show a ready memory and aptness of citation. But these give Western readers little pleasure, because we know nothing of the originals from which they are taken. I have been content, therefore, to cite as specimens, one or two of Captain Burton's rather elaborate renderings, with one of my own, which follows the original quite closely, but does not attempt to imitate the Eastern rhythm ; and for the rest, I have been satisfied to give one of Captain Burton's ingenious renderings ; and for the rest, I have left Mr. Lane's translations, which do not affect rhyme or rhythm, though they are printed as we print verses.

With the exception of "Abou Hassan the Wag," these stories come from the first two hundred and sixty-nine nights of the Calcutta edition. "Abou Hassan" takes nineteen nights of the Breslau edition, beginning in the 271st and ending with the 290th. But Sir Richard Burton does not follow that text.

Another volume will include the more celebrated stories in the narrations of later Nights.

EDWARD E. HALE.

CONTENTS.

THE ARABIAN NIGHTS.

INTRODUCTION.

In the name of God, the Compassionate, the Merciful.

Praise be to God, the Beneficent King, the Creator of the universe, who hath raised the heavens without pillars and spread out the earth as a bed; and blessing and peace be on the lord of apostles, our lord and our master, Mohammed and his family; blessing and peace, enduring and constant, unto the day of judgment.

To proceed. The lives of former generations are a lesson to posterity; that a man may review the remarkable events which have happened to others, and be admonished, and may consider the history of people of preceding ages, and of all that hath befallen them, and be restrained. Extolled be the perfection of him who hath thus ordained the history of former generations to be a lesson to those which follow.

Such are the tales of a Thousand and One Nights, with their romantic stories and their fables.

It is related (but God alone is all-knowing, as well as all-wise and all-mighty, and all-bountiful) that there was, in ancient times, a king of the countries of India and China, possessing numerous troops, and guards, and servants, and domestic dependents: and he had two sons; one of whom was a man of mature age, and the other a youth. Both of these princes were brave horsemen, but especially the elder, who inherited the kingdom of his father, and governed his subjects with such justice that the inhabitants of his country and the whole empire loved him. He was called King Shahriar: his younger brother was named Shahzeman, and was King of Samarcand. The administration of their governments was conducted with rectitude, each of them ruling over his subjects with justice, during a period of twenty years, with the utmost enjoyment and happiness. After this period the elder king felt a strong desire to see his brother, and ordered his vizier to repair to him and bring him.

Having taken the advice of the vizier on this subject, he immediately gave orders to prepare handsome presents, such as horses adorned with gold and costly jewels, and mamlouks, and beautiful virgins, and expensive stuffs. He then wrote a letter to his brother expressive of his great desire to see him ; and having sealed it and given it to the vizier, together with the presents above mentioned, he ordered the minister to strain his nerves, and tuck up his skirts, and use all expedition in returning. The vizier answered, Without delay, I hear and obey, and forthwith

prepared for the journey : he packed his baggage, removed the burdens, and made ready all his provisions within three days ; and on the fourth day he took leave of the King Shahriar and went forth toward the deserts and wastes. He proceeded night and day ; and each of the kings under the authority of King Shahriar, by whose residence he passed, came forth to meet him, with costly presents, and gifts of gold and silver, and entertained him three days ;

after which, on the fourth day, he accompanied him one day's journey, and took leave of him. Thus he continued on his way until he drew near to the city of Samarcand, when he sent forward a messenger to inform King Shahzeman of his approach. The messenger entered the city, inquired the way to the palace, and introducing himself to the king, kissed the ground before him, and acquainted him with the approach of his brother's vizier; upon which Shahzeman ordered the chief officers of his court, and the great men of his kingdom, to go forth a day's journey to meet him; and they did so; and when they met him they welcomed him, and walked by his stirrups until they returned to the city. The vizier then presented himself before the King Shahzeman, greeted him with a prayer for the divine assistance in his favor, kissed the ground before him, and informed him of his brother's desire to see him; after which he handed to him the letter. The king took it, read it, and understood its contents; and answered by expressing his readiness to obey the commands of his brother. But, said he (addressing the vizier), I will not go until I have entertained thee three days. Accordingly, he lodged him in a palace befitting his rank, accommodated his troops in tents, and appointed them all things requisite in the way of food and drink; and so they remained three days. On the fourth day he equipped himself for the journey, made ready his baggage, and collected together costly presents suitable to his brother's dignity.

THIS is the famous Shahriar, to whom the Arabian Nights' Entertainments were narrated by Scheherazade. Dissatisfied with the wife he left behind, he began the series of beheadings of her successors.

The story goes on thus :—

Now the vizier had two daughters ; the elder of whom was named Scheherazade, and the younger Dinarzade. The former had read various books of histories, and the lives of preceding kings, and stories of past generations ; it is asserted that she had collected together a thousand books of histories relating to preceding generations and kings, and works of the poets ; and she said to her father on this occasion, Why do I see thee thus changed, and oppressed with solicitude and sorrows? It has been said by one of the poets,

> Tell him who is oppressed with anxiety, that anxiety will not last:
> As happiness passeth away, so passeth away anxiety.

When the vizier heard these words from his daughter, he related to her all that had happened to him with regard to the king ; upon which she said, By Allah, O my father, give me in marriage to this king : either I shall die, and be a ransom for one of the daughters of the Mohammedans, or I shall live, and be the cause of their deliverance from him. I conjure thee, by Allah, exclaimed he, that thou expose not thyself to such peril ; but she said, It must be so. Then, said he, I fear for thee that the same will befall thee that happened in the case of the ass, and the bull, and the husbandman. And what, she asked, was that, O my father ?

Know, O my daughter, said the vizier, that there was a certain merchant, who possessed wealth and cattle, and had a wife and children ; and God, whose name be exalted, had also endowed him with the knowledge of the languages of beasts and birds. The abode of this merchant was in the country, and he had in his house an ass and a bull.

When the bull came to the place where the ass was tied, he found it swept and sprinkled; in his manger were sifted barley and sifted cut straw, and the ass was lying at his ease; his master being accustomed only to ride him occasionally, when business required, and soon to return; and it happened, one day, that the merchant overheard the bull saying to the ass, May thy food benefit thee! I am oppressed with fatigue, while thou art enjoying repose; thou eatest sifted barley, and men serve thee; and it is only occasionally that thy master rides thee and returns, while I am continually employed in plowing and turning the mill. The ass answered, When thou goest out to the field, and they place the yoke upon thy neck, lie down, and do not rise again, even if they beat thee; or if thou rise, lie down a second time; and when they take thee back and place the beans before thee, eat them not, as though thou wert sick; abstain from eating and drinking a day, or two days, or three; and so shalt thou find rest from trouble and labor.   Accordingly, when the driver came to the bull with his fodder, he ate scarcely any of it; and on the morrow, when the driver came again to take him to plow, he found him apparently quite infirm; so the merchant said, Take the ass, and make him draw the plow in his stead all the day.   The man did so, and when the ass returned at the close of the day, the bull thanked him for the favor he had conferred upon him by relieving him of his trouble on that day; but the ass returned him no answer, for he repented most grievously.   On the next day the plowman came again, and took the ass and plowed with him till evening; and the ass returned with his neck flayed by the yoke, and reduced to an extreme state of weakness, and the bull looked upon him, and thanked and praised him.   The ass exclaimed, I was living at ease, and naught but my meddling hath injured me! Then said he to the bull, Know that I am one who would give thee good advice: I heard our master say, If the bull rise not from his place, take him to the butcher, that he may kill him and make a nata[1] of his skin. I am, therefore, in fear for thee, and so I have given thee advice; and peace be on thee! When the bull heard these words of the ass, he thanked him, and said, To-morrow I will go with alacrity; so he ate the whole of his fodder, and even licked the manger. Their master, meanwhile, was listening to their conversation.

On the following morning the merchant and his wife went to the bull's crib and sat down there; and the driver came and took out the bull; and when the bull saw his master, he shook his tail, and showed his alacrity by sounds and actions, bounding about in such a manner that the merchant laughed until he fell backward. His wife, in surprise, asked him, At what dost thou laugh? He answered, At a thing that I have heard and seen; but I cannot reveal it, for if I did I should die. She said, Thou must inform me of the cause of thy laughter, even if thou die. I cannot reveal it, said he; the fear of death prevents me. Thou laughedst only at *me*, she said; and she ceased not to urge and importune him until he was quite overcome and distracted. So he called together his children, and sent for the cadi[2] and witnesses, that he might make his will, and reveal the secret to her, and die; for he

---

[1] A large piece of leather, with a running string all around the edge, which, being drawn, converts it into a bag for carrying provisions; when spread, it serves for a table.

[2] The cadi is a judge; but in small towns he often acts as a lawyer or notary.

loved her excessively, since she was the daughter of his
paternal uncle and the mother of his children, and he had
lived with her to the age of a hundred and twenty years.
Having assembled her family and his neighbors, he related
to them his story, and told them that as soon as he revealed his secret he must die; upon which every one
present said to her, We conjure thee by Allah that thou
give up this affair, and let not thy husband, and the father
of thy children, die. But she said, I will not desist until
he tell me, though he die for it. So they ceased to solicit
her; and the merchant left them and went to the stable
to perform the ablution, and then to return and tell them
the secret, and die.

Now he had a cock, with fifty hens under him, and he
had also a dog; and he heard the dog call to the cock and
reproach him, saying, Art thou happy when our master is
going to die? The cock asked, How so? and the dog
related to him the story; upon which the cock exclaimed,
By Allah, our master has little sense; *I* have *fifty* wives,
and I please this and provoke that; while *he* has but *one*
wife, and cannot manage this affair with her: why does
he not take some twigs of the mulberry-tree, and enter
her chamber, and beat her until she dies or repents? She
would never, after that, ask him a question respecting anything. When the merchant heard the words of the cock,
as he addressed the dog, he recovered his reason, and
made up his mind to beat her. Now, said the vizier to his
daughter Scheherazade, perhaps I may do to thee as the
merchant did to his wife. She asked, And what did he?
He answered, He entered her chamber, after he had cut
off some twigs of the mulberry-tree and hidden them
there; and then said to her, Come into the chamber, that

I may tell thee the secret while no one sees me, and then die; and when she had entered, he locked the chamber-door upon her, and beat her until she became almost senseless, and cried out, I repent; and she kissed his hands and his feet, and repented, and went out with him; and all the company and her own family rejoiced; and they lived together in the happiest manner until death.

When the vizier's daughter heard the words of her father, she said to him, It must be as I have requested. So he arrayed her, and went to the King Shahriar. Now she had given directions to her young sister, saying to her, When I have gone to the king, I will send to request thee to come; and when thou comest to me, and seest a convenient time, do thou say to me, O my sister, relate to me some strange story to beguile our waking hour; and I will relate to thee a story that shall, if it be the will of God, be the means of procuring deliverance.

Her father, the vizier, then took her to the king, who, when he saw him, was rejoiced, and said, Hast thou brought me what I desired? He answered, Yes. When the king, therefore, introduced himself to her, she wept; and he said to her, What aileth thee? She answered, O king, I have a young sister, and I wish to take leave of her. So the king sent to her; and she came to her sister and embraced her, and sat near the foot of the bed; and after she had waited for a proper opportunity, she said, By Allah! O my sister, relate to us a story to beguile the waking hour of our night. Most willingly, answered Scheherazade, if this virtuous king permit me. The king, hearing these words, and being restless, was pleased with the idea of listening to the story; and thus, on the first night of the thousand and one, Scheherazade commenced her recitations.

THE TRAVELLING MERCHANT.

———◦✦◦———

ONCE upon a time there was a rich merchant, wonder-
fully successful in his dealings, who had great store
of goods of all sorts, of money also, and of women, children,
and all sorts of slaves, as well as of houses, warehouses, and
lands.   And he had this wealth not only at home, but in all
the countries of the world.   He had to make journeys sometimes, so that he might see his factors and correspondents
face to face.   And once, when he was obliged to go and
collect some money, he took his scrip or travel-bag, and
packed in it some biscuit and some dates of Mecca for provision for the journey, because he would have in some
places to pass over deserts.   And so he mounted his horse
and set out upon his journey.   God gave him good success
in his travelling.   He came prosperously to the place he

sought, he finished his business prosperously, and prosperously he set out upon his return.

After he had travelled three days toward home, the fourth day was very hot. And the merchant was so much distressed by the heat that he turned aside into a garden by the wayside to rest himself under the shade of some trees he saw there. He made his resting-place under the shade of a large nut-tree, he fastened his horse so that he could not run, and then opening his scrip, he took out one or two biscuits and a few dates to make a meal. He ate the biscuits and the dates, and threw the date-stones right and left upon the ground. Then, having satisfied himself with his frugal repast, he stood up and washed himself, and then knelt down and said his prayers.

He had not finished his prayers, but was still upon his knees, when he saw before him an immense Genie, so large that while his feet were on the ground, his head was in the clouds, and so old that he was white with age. He held in his hand a long drawn sword, and before the merchant could move, the Genie cried out to him, —

"Stand up, that I may kill you with this sword, as you have killed my son!"

When the merchant heard these words of horror he was terrified by them as much as he had been at the sight of the monster; but in the midst of his terror he stammered out, "O my lord, what is my crime? why do you kill me?"

Then the Genie replied again, "I will kill you, as you have killed my son."

Then the merchant said, "Who has killed your son?"

And the Genie answered, "You."

"O my lord," said the poor merchant, "I never saw your son, and I do not know who he is."

But the Genie said, " You have killed him."

Then the merchant said, "My lord, by the living Allah, I have not killed him. How, and where, and when did I kill him?"

The Genie answered him, "Did you not lie down when you came into the garden? Did you not take dates, and did you not throw the stones about, some on the left side, and some on the right?"

"It is true, my lord," said the merchant; "I did as you say."

"Very well," said the Genie, "and so you killed my son; for my son was passing by just then, and as you threw the date-stones, one of them struck him and killed him. Does not the law say, 'Whoso killeth another shall be killed in turn'?"

"Verily, this is the law," said the merchant; "but indeed, indeed, my lord, I did not kill your son; or, if I killed him, I call upon Allah to witness, without whom is no might and no wisdom, that I did it unwittingly. Forgive me, my lord, oh, forgive me, if I have done this thing!"

"No," said the Genie; "surely you must die."

So saying, he seized the merchant and threw him upon the ground. Then he lifted his great sword into the air again, and held it ready to strike. The poor merchant thought of his home and family, of his wives and his little ones. He thought he had not a moment more to live, and he shed such floods of tears that his clothes were wet with the moisture. He cried again, "There is no power nor might but with the infinite Allah alone! and then he repeated the following verses: —

"Time knows two days:
Of one the face is bright and clear;
Of one the face is dark and drear.

" Life has two sides:
One is as warm and glad as light;
One is as cold and black as night.

" Time fooled with me:
His flattering fingers soothed with magic spell,
Just while his lying kiss was luring me to hell.

" Who sneers at me?
Are not the trees that feel the tempest's blow
The stately trees of pride that highest grow?

" Come sail with me:
See floating corpses on the topmost waves;
The precious pearls are hid in secret caves.

" See the eclipse!
A thousand stars unquenched forever blaze;
But sun and moon must hide their brighter rays.

"I looked for fruit:
On branches green and fresh no fruit I found;
I plucked the fruit from branches sere and browned.

" Night smiled on me!
Because I saw the diamonds in the sky,
Poor fool! I had forgot that death was nigh."

When the merchant had finished these verses, and had
wept to his heart's content, the Genie, who had waited
through it all, said, It is enough; now I must kill you.

What! said the merchant, will nothing change you?

Nothing, said the Genie. You must die.

Then said the merchant, Know, O Afrite, that I have
debts to pay, and I have much property, and children, and
a wife, and I have pledges, also, in my possession; let me,

therefore, go back to my house, and give to every one his due, and then I will return to thee ; I bind myself by a vow and covenant that I will return to thee, and thou shalt do what thou wilt ; and God is witness of what I say. Upon this the Genie accepted his covenant, and liberated him, granting him a respite until the expiration of the year.

The merchant, therefore, returned to his town, accomplished all that was upon his mind to do, paid every one what he owed him, and informed his wife and children of the event which had befallen him ; upon hearing which, they and all his family and women wept. He appointed a guardian over his children, and remained with his family until the end of the year, when he took his grave-clothes under his arm, bade farewell to his household and neighbors, and all his relations, and went forth in spite of himself, his family raising cries of lamentation and shrieking.

He proceeded until he arrived at the garden before mentioned ; and it was the first day of the new year ; and as he sat, weeping for the calamity which he expected soon to befall him, a sheikh,[1] advanced in years, approached him, leading a gazelle with a chain attached to its neck. This sheikh saluted the merchant, wishing him a long life, and said to him, What is the reason of thy sitting alone in this place, seeing that it is a resort of the Genii? The merchant, therefore, informed him of what had befallen him with the Afrite, and of the cause of his sitting there, at which the sheikh, the owner of the gazelle, was astonished, and said, By Allah, O my brother, thy faithfulness is great, and thy story is wonderful! if it were engraved upon the intellect, it would be a lesson to him who would be admon-

---

[1] A title of respect given only to Mohammedans — literally, "an old man."

ished! And he sat down by his side, and said, By Allah, O my brother, I will not quit this place until I see what will happen unto thee with this Afrite. So he sat down and conversed with him. And the merchant became almost senseless; fear entered him, and terror, and violent grief, and excessive anxiety. And as the owner of the gazelle sat by his side, lo! a second sheikh approached them, with two black hounds, and inquired of them, after saluting them, the reason of their sitting in that place, seeing that it was a resort of the Genii; and they told him the story from beginning to end. And he had hardly sat down when there approached them a third sheikh, with a dapple mule; and he asked them the same question, which was answered in the same manner.

Immediately after, the dust was agitated, and became an enormous revolving pillar, approaching them from the midst of the desert; and this dust subsided, and behold, the Genie, with a drawn sword in his hand, his eyes casting forth sparks of fire. He came to them, and dragged from them the merchant, and said to him, Rise, that I may kill thee, as thou killedst my son, the vital spirit of my heart. And the merchant wailed and wept; and the three sheikhs also manifested their sorrow by weeping and crying aloud, and wailing.

Here Scheherazade perceived the light of morning, and discontinued the recitation with which she had been allowed thus far to proceed. Her sister said to her, How excellent is thy story! and how pretty! and how pleasant! and how sweet! but she answered, What is this in comparison with that which I will relate to thee in the next night, if I live, and the king spare me! And the king said, By Allah, I will not kill her until I hear the remainder of her

story. Thus they pleasantly passed the night until the
morning, when the king went forth to his hall of judgment, and the vizier went thither with the grave-clothes
under his arm ; and the king gave judgment, and invested
and displaced, until the close of the day, without informing
the vizier of that which had happened ; and the minister
was greatly astonished. The court was then dissolved, and
the king returned to the privacy of his palace.

On the second night, it all happened in the very same
way. Scheherazade continued to recite, and in the morning
the king said, By Allah, I will not kill her until I hear the
remainder of her story.

But this, said Scheherazade, when she finished the story,
is not more wonderful than the story of the Fisherman.
The king asked her, And what is the story of the Fisherman? and she related it as follows :—

The Story of the Fisherman.

THERE was a certain fisherman, advanced in age, who
had a wife and three children ; and though he was in indigent circumstances, it was his custom to cast his net,
every day, no more than four times. One day he went
forth at the hour of noon to the shore of the sea, and put
down his basket, and cast his net, and waited until it
was motionless in the water, when he drew together its
strings, and found it to be heavy : he pulled, but could not
draw it up ; so he took the end of the cord, and knocked a
stake into the shore, and tied the cord to it. He then
stripped himself, and dived round the net, and continued
to pull until he drew it out ; whereupon he rejoiced, and
put on his clothes, but when he came to examine the net,

he found in it the carcass of an ass. At the sight of this he mourned, and exclaimed, There is no strength nor power but in God, the High, the Great! This is a strange piece of fortune! And he repeated the following verse:

O thou who occupiest thyself in the darkness of night, and in peril!
   Spare thy trouble; for the support of Providence is not obtained
   by toil!

He then disencumbered his net of the dead ass, and wrung it out; after which he spread it, and descended into the sea, and, exclaiming, In the name of God![1] cast it again, and waited till it had sunk and was still, when he pulled it, and found it more heavy and more difficult to raise than on the former occasion. He therefore concluded that it was full of fish ; so he tied it and stripped, and plunged and dived, and pulled until he raised it, and drew it upon the shore; when he found in it only a large jar, full of sand and mud; on seeing which, he was troubled in his heart, and repeated the following words of the poet :

O angry fate, forbear! or, if thou wilt not forbear, relent.
Neither favor from fortune do I gain, nor profit from the work of my
   hands.
I came forth to seek my sustenance, but have found it to be exhausted.
How many of the ignorant are in splendor! and how many of the wise
   in obscurity!

So saying, he threw aside the jar, and wrung out and cleansed his net ; and, begging the forgiveness of God for his impatience, returned to the sea the third time, and threw the net, and waited till it had sunk and was motionless ; he then drew it out, and found in it a quantity of broken jars and pots.

---

[1] Saying "Bismillah," the devout ejaculation which should precede every act.

Upon this, he raised his head toward heaven, and said,
O God, thou knowest that I cast not my net more than
four times; and I have now cast it three times! Then,
exclaiming, In the name of God! he cast the net again
into the sea, and waited till it was still; when he attempted
to draw it up, but could not, for it clung to the bottom.
And he exclaimed, There is no strength nor power but in
God! and stripped himself again, and dived round the net,
and pulled it until he raised it upon the shore; when he
opened it, and found in it a bottle of brass, filled with
something, and having its mouth closed with a stopper of
lead, bearing the impression of the seal of King Solomon.
At the sight of this, the fisherman was rejoiced, and said,
This I will sell in the copper-market; for it is worth ten
pieces of gold. He then shook it, and found it to be
heavy, and said, I must open it and see what is in it, and
store it in my bag; and then I will sell the bottle in the
copper-market. So he took out a knife, and picked at the
lead until he extracted it from the bottle. He then laid
the bottle on the ground, and shook it, that its contents
might pour out; but there came forth from it nothing but
smoke, which ascended toward the sky, and spread over
the face of the earth; at which he wondered excessively.
And after a little while the smoke collected together, and
was condensed, and then became agitated, and was converted into an Afrite, whose head was in the clouds, while
his feet rested upon the ground: his head was like a
dome; his hands were like winnowing forks, and his legs
like masts; his mouth resembled a cavern; his teeth were
like stones; his nostrils like trumpets, and his eyes like
lamps; and he had dishevelled and dust-colored hair.

When the fisherman beheld this Afrite, the muscles of

his sides quivered, his teeth were locked together, his spittle dried up, and he saw not his way. The Afrite, as soon as he perceived him, exclaimed, There is no deity but God : Solomon is the prophet of God. O prophet of God, slay me not ; for I will never again oppose thee in word, or rebel against thee in deed ! O Marid,[1] said the fisherman, dost thou say, Solomon is the prophet of God ? Solomon hath been dead a thousand and eight hundred years,[2] and we are now in the end of time. What is thy history, and what is thy tale, and what was the cause of thy entering this bottle ? When the Marid heard these words of the fisherman, he said, There is no deity but God ! Receive news, O fisherman ! Of what, said the fisherman, dost thou give me news ? He answered, Of thy being instantly put to a most cruel death. The fisherman exclaimed, Thou deservest, for this news, O master of the Afrites, the withdrawal of protection from thee, O thou remote ![3] Wherefore wouldst thou kill me ? and what requires thy killing me, when I have liberated thee from the bottle, and rescued thee from the bottom of the sea, and brought thee up upon the dry land ? The Afrite answered, Choose what kind of death thou wilt die, and in what manner thou shalt be killed. What is my offence, said the fisherman, that this should be my recompense from thee ? The Afrite replied, Hear my story, O fisherman. Tell it then, said the fisherman, and be short in thy words, for my soul hath sunk down to my feet.

[1] A Marid is an evil Genie of the most powerful class.

[2] Captain Burton observes that this would fix the date of the tale as in A.D. 785. " But this may be fanciful." .

[3] The word " remote " implies far from goodness, and is employed, in relating a story, as a substitute for some opprobrious expression supposed to have been actually used.

Know then, said he, that I am one of the heretical
Genii : I rebelled against Solomon, the son of David ; I
and Sacar,[1] the Genie[2] ; and he sent to me his vizier, Asaph,
the son of Barakhia, who came upon me forcibly, and took
me to him in bonds, and placed me before him ; and when
Solomon saw me, he offered up a prayer for protection
against me, and exhorted me to embrace the faith, and to
submit to his authority ; but I refused ; upon which he
called for this bottle, and confined me in it, and closed it
upon me with the leaden stopper, which he stamped with
the Most Great Name ; he then gave orders to the Genii,
who carried me away, and threw me into the midst of the
sea.   There I remained a hundred years; and I said in my
heart, Whosoever shall liberate me, I will enrich him forever ; but the hundred years passed over me, and no one
liberated me ; and I entered upon another hundred years,
and I said, Whosoever shall liberate me, I will open to him
the treasures of the earth; but no one did so; and four hundred years more passed over me, and I said, Whosoever shall
liberate me, I will perform for him three wants; but still
no one liberated me.   I then fell into a violent rage, and
said within myself, Whosoever shall liberate me now, I will
kill him, and only suffer him to choose in what manner he
will die.   And, lo! now thou hast liberated me, and I have
given thee thy choice of the manner in which thou wilt
die.

When the fisherman had heard the story of the Afrite,
he exclaimed, O Allah ! that I should not have liberated
thee but in such a time as this.   Then said he to the

[1] Sacar was a Genie of great power, who deprived Solomon of his kingdom
by treachery.
[2] The allusion is to a tale in the Hebrew Talmud.

Afrite, Pardon me, and kill me not, and so may God pardon thee ; and destroy me not, lest God give power over thee to one who will destroy thee. The Marid answered, I must positively kill thee ; therefore choose by what manner of death thou wilt die. The fisherman then felt assured of his death ; but he again implored the Afrite, saying, Pardon me, by way of gratitude for my liberating thee. Why, answered the Afrite, I am not going to kill thee but for that very reason, because thou hast liberated me. O sheikh of the Afrites, said the fisherman, do I act kindly toward thee, and dost thou recompense me with baseness ? But the proverb lieth not that saith,

We did good to them, and they returned us the reverse ; and such, by
     my life, is the conduct of the wicked.
Thus he who acteth kindly to the undeserving is recompensed in the
     same manner as the aider of Umm Amir.[1]

The Afrite, when he heard these words, answered by saying, Covet not life, for thy death is unavoidable. Then said the fisherman within himself, This is a Genie, and I am a man, and God hath given me sound reason : therefore, I will now plot his destruction with my heart and reason, like as he hath plotted with his cunning and perfidy. So he said to the Afrite, Hast thou determined to kill me? He answered, Yes. Then said he, By the Most Great Name engraved upon the seal of Solomon, I will ask thee one question ; and wilt thou answer it to me truly ? On hearing the mention of the Most Great Name, the Afrite was agitated, and trembled, and replied, Yes ; ask, and be brief. The fisherman then said, How wast thou in this bottle ? It will not contain thy hand or thy foot : how, then, can it contain thy whole body ? Dost thou not be-

---

[1] An epithet of the hyena.

lieve that I was in it? said the Afrite. The fisherman
answered, I will never believe thee until I see thee in it.
Upon this, the Afrite shook, and became converted again
into smoke, which rose to the sky, and then became condensed, and entered the bottle by little and little, until it
was all inclosed; when the fisherman hastily snatched the
sealed leaden stopper, and, having replaced it in the mouth
of the bottle, called out to the Afrite, and said, Choose in
what manner of death thou wilt die. I will assuredly
throw thee here into the sea, and build me a house on this
spot; and whosoever shall come here, I will prevent his
fishing in this place, and will say to him, Here is an Afrite,
who, to any person that liberates him, will propose various
kinds of death, and then give him his choice of one of
them. On hearing these words of the fisherman, the
Afrite endeavored to escape, but could not, finding himself
restrained by the impression of the seal of Solomon, and
thus imprisoned by the fisherman as the vilest, and filthiest,
and least of Afrites. The fisherman then took the bottle
to the brink of the sea. The Afrite exclaimed, Nay! nay!
to which the fisherman answered, Yea, without fail! yea,
without fail! The Marid then addressing him with a soft
voice and humble manner said, What dost thou intend to
do with me, O fisherman? He answered, I will throw
thee into the sea; and if thou hast been there a thousand
and eight hundred years, I will make thee to remain there
until the hour of judgment. Did I not say to thee, Spare
me, and so may God spare thee; and destroy me not, lest
God destroy thee? But thou didst reject my petition, and
wouldst nothing but treachery; therefore God hath caused
thee to fall into my hand, and I have betrayed thee. Open
to me, said the Afrite, that I may confer benefits upon

thee. The fisherman replied, Thou liest, thou accursed! I and thou art like the vizier of the Grecian king and the sage Douban. What, said the Afrite, was the case of the vizier of the Grecian king and the sage Douban, and what is their story? The fisherman answered as follows : —

The Story of the Grecian King and the Sage Douban.

KNOW, O Afrite, that there was, in former times, a monarch who was king of the Grecians, possessing great treasures and numerous forces, valiant, and having troops of every description ; but he was afflicted with leprosy, which the physicians and sages had failed to remove ; neither their potions, nor powders, nor ointments were of any benefit to him ; and none of the physicians was able to cure him. At length there arrived at the city of this king a great sage, stricken in years, who was called the sage Douban : he was acquainted with ancient Greek, Persian, modern Greek, Arabic, and Syrian books, and with medicine and astrology, both with respect to their scientific principles, and the rules of their practical applications for good and evil ; as well as the properties of plants, dried and fresh ; the injurious and the useful : he was versed in the wisdom of the philosophers, and embraced a knowledge of all medical and other sciences.

After this sage had arrived in the city, and remained in it a few days, he heard of the case of the king, of the leprosy with which God hath afflicted him, and that the physicians and men of science had failed to cure him. In consequence of this information, he passed the next night in deep study ; and when the morning came, and diffused its light, and the sun saluted the Ornament of the Good,[1] he attired himself in the richest of his apparel, and presented himself before the king. Having kissed the ground before him, and offered up a prayer for the continuance of his power and happiness, and greeted him in the best manner he was able, he informed him who he was, and said, O king, I have heard of the disease which hath attacked thy person, and that many of the physicians are unacquainted with the means of removing it; and I will cure thee without giving thee to drink any potion, or anointing thee with ointment. When the king heard his words, he wondered, and said to him, How wilt thou do this? By Allah, if thou cure me, I will enrich thee and thy children's children, and I will heap favors upon thee, and whatever thou shalt desire shall be thine, and thou be my companion and my friend. He then bestowed upon him a robe of honor and other presents, and said to him, Wilt thou cure me of this disease without potion or ointment? He answered, Yes; I will cure thee without any discomfort to thy person. And the king was extremely astonished, and said, O sage, at what time, and on what day, shall that which thou hast proposed to me be done? Hasten it, O my son. He answered, I hear and obey.

He then went out from the presence of the king, and hired a house, in which he deposited his books, and medicines, and drugs. Having done this, he selected certain of his medicines and drugs, and made a goff-stick, with a hollow handle, into which he introduced them; after which he made a ball for it, skilfully adapted; and on the following day, after he had finished these, he went again to the king, and kissed the ground before him, and directed him to

[1] A title of the Prophet Mohammed.

repair to the horse-course, and to play with ball and goff-stick.[1]   The king, attended by his emirs, and chamberlains, and viziers, went thither, and as soon as he arrived there, the sage Douban presented himself before him, and handed to him the goff-stick, saying, Take this goff-stick, and grasp it thus, and ride along the horse-course, and strike the ball with all thy force, until the palm of thy hand and thy whole body becomes moist with perspiration, when the medicine will penetrate into thy hand, and pervade thy whole body ; and when thou hast done this, and the medicine remains in thee, return to thy palace, and enter the bath, and wash thyself, and sleep: then shalt thou find thyself cured, and peace be on thee.   So the king took the goff-stick from the sage, and grasped it in his hand, and mounted his horse ; and the ball was thrown before him, and he urged his horse after it until he overtook it, when he struck it with all his force ; and when he had continued this exercise as long as was necessary, and bathed and slept, he looked upon his skin, and not a vestige of the leprosy remained ; it was clear as white silver.   Upon this he rejoiced exceedingly ; his heart was dilated, and he was full of happiness.

On the following morning he entered the council-chamber, and sat upon his throne ; and the chamberlains and great officers of his court came before him.   The sage Douban also presented himself ; and when the king saw him, he rose to him in haste, and seated him by his side. Services of food were then spread before them, and the sage ate with the king, and remained as his guest all the day ; and when the night approached, the king gave him two thousand pieces of gold, besides dresses of honor and

[1] The game is our polo; " hockey on horseback."— *Burton.*

other presents, and mounted him on his own horse, and so the sage returned to his house. And the king was astonished at his skill, saying, This man hath cured me by an external process, without anointing me with ointment : by Allah, this is consummate science ; and it is incumbent on me to bestow favors and honors upon him, and to make him my companion and familiar friend as long as I live. He passed the night happy and joyful on account of his recovery, and when he arose, he went forth again, and sat upon his throne ; the officers of his court standing before him, and the emirs and viziers sitting on his right hand and on his left ; and he called for the sage Douban, who came, and kissed the ground before him ; and the king rose, and seated him by his side, and ate with him, and greeted him with compliments : he bestowed upon him again a robe of honor and other presents, and after conversing with him till the approach of night, gave orders that five other robes of honor should be given to him, and a thousand pieces of gold ; and the sage departed, and returned to his house.

Again, when the next morning came, the king went, as usual, to his council-chamber, and the emirs, and viziers, and chamberlains surrounded him. Now there was among his viziers one of ill aspect, and of evil star ; sordid, avaricious, and of an envious and malicious disposition ; and when he saw that the king had made the sage Douban his friend, and bestowed upon him these favors, he envied him this distinction, and meditated evil against him ; agreeably with the adage which saith, There is nobody void of envy ; and another, which saith, Tyranny lurketh in the soul ; power manifesteth it, and weakness concealeth it. So he approached the king, and kissed the ground before him,

and said, O king of the age, thou art he whose goodness
extendeth to all men, and I have an important piece of
advice to give thee; if I were to conceal it from thee, I
should be a base-born wretch; therefore, if thou order me
to impart it, I will do so. The king, disturbed by these
words of the vizier, said, What is thy advice? He answered, O glorious king, it hath been said by the ancients,
He who looketh not to results, fortune will not attend him.
Now I have seen the king in a way that is not right, since
he hath bestowed favors upon his enemy, and upon him
who desireth the downfall of his dominion: he hath treated
him with kindness, and honored him with the highest
honors, and admitted him to the closest intimacy; I therefore fear for the king the consequence of this conduct.
At this the king was troubled, and his countenance
changed: and he said, Who is he whom thou regardest
as mine enemy, and to whom I show kindness? He replied, O king, if thou hast been asleep, awake! I allude
to the sage Douban.

O king, continued the vizier of the Grecian king, if thou
trust to this sage, he will kill thee in the foulest manner.
If thou continue to bestow favors upon him, and to make
him thine intimate companion, he will plot thy destruction.
Dost thou not see that he hath cured thee of the disease
by external means, by a thing that thou heldest in thy
hand? Therefore thou art not secure against his killing
thee by a thing that thou shalt hold in the same manner.
The king answered, Thou hast spoken truth; the case is
as thou hast said, O faithful vizier: it is probable that this
sage came as a spy to accomplish my death; and if he
cured me by a thing I held in my hand, he may destroy
me by a thing that I may smell: what, then, O vizier, shall

be done respecting him? The vizier answered, Send to
him immediately, and desire him to come hither; and when
he is come, strike off his head, and so shalt thou avert from
thee his evil design, and be secure from him. Betray him
before he betray thee. The king said, Thou hast spoken
right.

Immediately, therefore, he sent for the sage, who came,
full of joy, not knowing what the Compassionate had decreed against him, and addressed the king with these words
of the poet:

If I fail any day to render thee due thanks, tell me for whom I have
composed my verse and prose.
Thou hast loaded me with favors unsolicited, bestowed without delay
on thy part, or excuse.
How, then, should I abstain from praising thee as thou deservest, and
lauding thee both with my heart and voice?
Nay, I will thank thee for thy benefits conferred upon me: they are
light upon my tongue, though weighty to my back.

Knowest thou, said the king, wherefore I have summoned thee? The sage answered, None knoweth what
is secret but God, whose name be exalted! Then said the
king, I have summoned thee that I may take away thy life.
The sage, in the utmost astonishment at this announce-
ment, said, O king, wherefore wouldst thou kill me, and
what offence has been committed by me? The king
answered, It hath been told me that thou art a spy, and
that thou hast come thither to kill me; but I will prevent
thee by killing thee first: and so saying, he called out to
the executioner, Strike off the head of this traitor, and
relieve me from his wickedness. Spare me, said the sage,
and so may God spare thee; and destroy me not, lest God
destroy thee. And he repeated these words several times,

like as I did, O Afrite ; but thou wouldst not let me go, desiring to destroy me.

The Grecian king then said to the sage Douban, I shall not be secure unless I kill thee ; for thou curedst me by a thing that I held in my hand, and I have no security against thy killing me by a thing that I may smell, or by some other means. O king, said the sage, is this my recompense from thee ? Dost thou return evil for good ? The king answered, Thou must be slain without delay. When the sage, therefore, was convinced that the king intended to put him to death, and that his fate was inevitable, he said, O king, if my death is indispensable, grant me some respite, that I may return to my house and acquit myself of my duties, and give directions to my family and neighbors to bury me, and dispose of my medical books ; and among my books is one of most especial value, which I offer as a present to thee, that thou mayest treasure it in thy library. And what, said the king, is this book ? He answered, It contains things not to be enumerated ; and the smallest of the secret virtues that it possesses is this ; that, when thou hast cut off my head, if thou open this book, and count three leaves, and then read three lines on the page to the left, the head will speak to thee, and answer whatever thou shalt ask. At this the king was excessively astonished, and shook with delight, and said to him, O sage, when I have cut off thy head, will it speak ? He answered, Yes, O king ; and this is a wonderful thing.

The king then sent him in the custody of guards ; and the sage descended to his house, and settled all his affairs on that day ; and on the following day he went up to the court ; and the emirs, and viziers, and chamberlains, and deputies, and all the great officers of the state, went thither also : and the court resembled a flower-garden. And when the sage had entered, he presented himself before the king, bearing an old book, and a small pot containing a powder ; and he sat down and said, Bring me a tray. So they brought him one ; and he poured out the powder into it, and spread it. He then said, O king, take this book, and do nothing with it until thou hast cut off my head ; and when thou hast done so, place it upon this tray, and order some one to press it down upon the powder ; and when this is done, the blood will be stanched ; then open the book. As soon as the sage had said this, the king gave orders to strike off his head, and it was done. The king then opened the book, and found that its leaves were stuck together ; so he put his finger to his mouth, and moistened it with his spittle, and opened the first leaf, and the second, and the third ; but the leaves were not opened without difficulty. He opened six leaves, and looked at them ; but found upon them no writing. So he said, O sage, there is nothing written in it. The head of the sage answered, Turn over more leaves. The king did so ; and in a little while the poison penetrated into his system, for the book was poisoned ; and the king fell back and cried out, The poison hath penetrated into me ! and upon this the head of the sage Douban repeated these verses :

They made use of their power, and used it tyrannically, and soon it
  became as though it never had existed.
Had they acted equitably, they had experienced equity ; but they
  oppressed ; wherefore fortune oppressed them with calamities and
  trials.
Then did the case itself announce to them, This is the reward of your
  conduct, and fortune is blameless.

And when the head of the sage Douban had uttered these words, the king immediately fell down dead.

Continuation of the Story of the Fisherman.

Now, O Afrite, continued the fisherman, know that if the Grecian king had spared the sage Douban, God had spared him; but he refused, and desired his destruction; therefore God destroyed him; and thou, O Afrite, if thou hadst spared me, God had spared thee, and I had spared thee; but thou desiredst my death; therefore will I put thee to death imprisoned in this bottle, and will throw thee here into the sea. The Marid, upon this, cried out and said, I conjure thee by Allah, O fisherman, that thou do it not; spare me in generosity, and be not angry with me for what I did; but if I have done evil, do thou good, according to the proverb, O thou benefactor of him who hath done evil, the action that he hath done is sufficient for him: do not, therefore, as Imama did to Ateca. And what, said the fisherman, was their case? The Afrite answered, This is not a time for telling stories, when I am in this prison; but when thou liberatest me, I will relate to thee their case. The fisherman said, Thou must be thrown into the sea, and there shall be no way of escape for thee from it; for I endeavored to propitiate thee, and humbled myself before thee, yet thou wouldst nothing but my destruction, though I had committed no offence to deserve it, and had done no evil to thee whatever, but only good, delivering thee from thy confinement; and when thou didst thus unto me, I perceived that thou wast radically corrupt: and I would have thee know that my motive for throwing thee into this sea is that I may acquaint with thy story every one that shall take thee out, and caution him against thee, that he may cast thee in again; thus

shalt thou remain in this sea to the end of time, and experience varieties of torment. The Afrite then said, Liberate me, for this is an opportunity for thee to display
humanity; and I vow to thee that I will never do thee
harm; but, on the contrary, will do thee a service that
shall enrich thee forever.

Upon this the fisherman accepted his covenant that he
would not hurt him, but that he would do him good; and
when he had bound him by oaths and vows, and made him
swear by the Most Great Name of God, he opened to him;
and the smoke ascended until it had all come forth, and
then collected together, and became, as before, an Afrite
of hideous form. The Afrite then kicked the bottle into
the sea. When the fisherman saw him do this, he made
sure of destruction, and said, This is no sign of good; but
afterward he fortified his heart, and said, O Afrite, God,
whose name be exalted, hath said, Perform the covenant,
for the covenant shall be inquired into: and thou hast
covenanted with me, and sworn that thou wilt not act
treacherously toward me; therefore, if thou so act, God
will recompense thee, for He is jealous; He respiteth, but
suffereth not to escape; and remember that I said to thee
as said the sage Douban to the Grecian king, Spare me,
and so may God spare thee.

The Afrite laughed, and walking on before him, said, O
fisherman, follow me. The fisherman did so, not believing
in his escape, until they had quitted the neighborhood of
the city, and ascended a mountain, and descended into a
wide desert tract, in the midst of which was a lake of water.
Here the Afrite stopped, and ordered the fisherman to cast
his net and take some fish; and the fisherman, looking into
the lake, saw in it fish of different colors, white, and red,

and blue, and yellow ; at which he was astonished ; and he cast his net, and drew it in, and found in it four fish, each fish of a different color from the others, at the sight of which he rejoiced. The Afrite then said to him, Take them to the sultan, and present them to him, and he will give thee what will enrich thee ; and for the sake of God accept my excuse, for, at present, I know no other way of rewarding thee, having been in the sea a thousand and eight hundred years, and not seen the surface of the earth until now ; but take not fish from the lake more than once each day ; and now I commend thee to the care of God. Having thus said, he struck the earth with his feet, and it clove asunder, and swallowed him.

The fisherman then went back to the city, wondering at all that had befallen him with the Afrite, and carried the fish to his house ; and he took an earthen bowl, and, having filled it with water, put the fish into it ; and they struggled in the water ; and when he had done this, he placed the bowl upon his head, and repaired to the king's palace, as the Afrite had commanded him, and, going up unto the king, presented to him the fish ; and the king was excessively astonished at them, for he had never seen any like them in the course of his life ; and he said, Give these fish to the slave cook-maid. This maid had been sent as a present to him by the king of the Greeks, three days before ; and he had not yet tried her skill. The vizier, therefore, ordered her to fry the fish, and said to her, O maid, the king saith unto thee, I have not reserved my tear but for the time of my difficulty ; to-day, then, gratify us by a specimen of thy excellent cookery, for a person hath brought these fish as a present to the sultan. After having thus charged her, the vizier returned, and the king ordered him to give the fisherman four hundred pieces of gold; so the vizier gave them to him, and he took them in his lap, and returned to his home and his wife, joyful and happy, and bought what was needful for his family.

Such were the events that befell the fisherman : now we must relate what happened to the maid. She took the fish, and cleaned them, and arranged them in the frying-pan, and left them until one side was cooked, when she turned them upon the other side; and lo! the wall of the kitchen clove asunder, and there came forth from it a damsel of tall stature, smooth-cheeked, of perfect form, with eyes adorned with kohl,[1] beautiful in countenance, and with heavy, swelling hips, wearing a coif interwoven with blue silk, with rings in her ears, and bracelets on her wrists, and rings set with precious jewels on her fingers; and in her hand was a rod of Indian cane; and she dipped the end of the rod in the frying-pan, and said, O fish, are ye remaining faithful to your covenant? At the sight of this the cook-maid fainted. The damsel then repeated the same words a second and a third time; after which the fish raised their heads from the frying-pan, and answered, Yes, yes. Then they repeated the following verse :

If thou return, we return; and if thou come, we come; and if thou for-
    sake, we verily do the same.

And upon this the damsel overturned the frying-pan; and departed by the way she had entered, and the wall of the kitchen closed up again. The cook-maid then arose, and beheld the four fish burnt like charcoal; and she ex-

[1] A black powder applied to the edges of the eyelids as an ornament. "In England I have seen the same appearance amongst miners fresh from the colliery." — *Burton.*

claimed, In his first encounter his staff broke! and as she sat reproaching herself, she beheld the vizier standing at her head ; and he said to her, Bring the fish to the sultan ; and she wept, and informed him of what had happened.

The vizier was astonished at her words, and exclaimed, This is indeed a wonderful event ; and he sent for the fisherman, and when he was brought, he said to him, O fisherman, thou must bring to us four fish like those which thou broughtest before. The fisherman, accordingly, went forth to the lake, and threw his net, and when he had drawn it in he found in it four fish, as before ; and he took them to the vizier, who went with them to the maid, and said to her, Rise, and fry them in my presence, that I may witness this occurrence. The maid, therefore, prepared the fish, and put them in the frying-pan, and they remained but a little while, when the wall clove asunder, and the damsel appeared, clad as before, and holding the rod ; and she dipped the end of the rod in the frying-pan, and said, O fish, O fish, are ye remaining faithful to your old covenant ? Upon which they raised their heads, and answered as before ; and the damsel overturned the frying-pan with the rod, and returned by the way she had entered, and the wall closed up again.

The vizier then said, This is an event which cannot be concealed from the king : so he went to him, and informed him of what had happened in his presence ; and the king said, I must see this with my own eyes. He sent, therefore, to the fisherman, and commanded him to bring four fish like the former, granting him a delay of three days. And the fisherman repaired to the lake, and brought the fish thence to the king, who ordered again that four hundred pieces of gold should be given to him ; and then,

turning to the vizier, said to him, Cook the fish thyself
here before me. The vizier answered, I hear and obey.
He brought the frying-pan, and, after he had cleaned the
fish, threw them into it; and as soon as he had turned
them, the wall clove asunder, and there came forth from it
a negro, in size like a bull, or like one of the tribe of Ad,[1]
having in his hand a branch of a green tree; and he said,
with a clear but terrifying voice, O fish, O fish, are ye remaining faithful to your old covenant? Upon which they
raised their heads, and answered as before, Yes, yes;

If thou return, we return; and if thou come, we come; and if thou for-
    sake, we verily do the same. •

The black then approached the frying-pan, and overturned
it with the branch, and the fish became like charcoal, and
he went away as he had come.

When he had thus disappeared from before their eyes,
the king said, This is an event respecting which it is impossible to keep silence, and there must, undoubtedly, be
some strange circumstance connected with these fish. He
then ordered that the fisherman should be brought before
him, and when he had come he said to him, Whence came
these fish? The fisherman answered, From a lake between
four mountains behind this mountain which is without thy
city. The king said to him, How many days' journey distant? He answered, O our lord the sultan, a journey of
half an hour. And the sultan was astonished, and ordered
his troops to go out immediately with him and the fisherman, who began to curse the Afrite. They proceeded until
they had ascended the mountain, and descended into a wide

[1] A race of ancient Arabs, destroyed for their infidelity. They were from
60 to 100 feet high. See Koran xxvi. — *Burton.*

desert tract which they had never before seen in their whole lives ; and the sultan and all the troops wondered at the sight of this desert, which was between four mountains, and at the fish, which were of four colors, red and white and yellow and blue. The king paused in astonishment, and said to the troops, and to the other attendants who were with him, Hath any one of you before seen this lake in this place ? They all answered, No. Then said the king, By Allah, I will not enter my city, nor will I sit upon my throne, until I know the true history of this lake, and of its fish. And upon this he ordered his people to encamp around these mountains, and they did so. He then called for the vizier, who was a well-informed, sensible, prudent, and learned man ; and when he had presented himself before him, he said to him, I desire to do a thing with which I will acquaint thee ; and it is this : I have resolved to depart alone this night, to seek for information respecting this lake and its fish ; therefore sit thou at the door of my pavilion, and say to the emirs, and viziers, and chamberlains, The sultan is sick, and hath commanded me not to allow any person to go in unto him ; and acquaint no one with my intention.

The vizier was unable to oppose his design ; so the king disguised himself, and slung on his sword, and withdrew himself from the midst of his troops. He journeyed the whole of the night until the morning, and proceeded until the heat became oppressive to him ; he then paused to rest ; after which he again proceeded the remainder of the day and the second night until the morning, when there appeared before him, in the distance, something black, at the sight of which he rejoiced, and said, Perhaps I shall there find some person who will inform me of the history of the lake

and its fish.   And when he approached this black object,
he found it to be a palace built of black stones, and overlaid with iron ; and one of the leaves of its door was open,
and the other shut.   The king was glad, and he stood at
the door, and knocked gently, but heard no answer ; he
knocked a second and a third time, but again heard no
answer ; then he knocked a fourth time, and with violence,
but no one answered.   So he said, It is doubtless empty ;
and he took courage, and entered from the door into the
passage, and cried out, saying, O inhabitants of the palace,
I am a stranger and a traveller ! have ye any provision ?
And he repeated these words a second and a third time,
but heard no answer.   And upon this he fortified his heart,
and emboldened himself, and proceeded from the passage
into the midst of the palace ; but he found no one there,
and only saw that it was furnished, and that there was in
the centre of it a fountain with four lions of red gold, which
poured forth the water from their mouths, like pearls and
jewels : around this were birds ; and over the top of the
palace was extended a net which prevented their flying
out.   At the sight of these objects he was astonished, and
he was grieved that he saw no person there whom he could
ask for information respecting the lake, and the fish, and
the mountains, and the palace.   He then sat down between
the doors, reflecting upon these things ; and as he thus sat,
he heard a voice of lamentation from a sorrowful heart,
chanting these verses :

O fortune, thou pitiest me not, nor releasest me! See, my heart is
    straitened between affliction and peril!
Will not you [O my wife] have compassion on the mighty whom love
    hath abased, and the wealthy who is reduced to indigence?
We were jealous even of the zephyr which passed over you; but when
    the divine decree is issued, the eye becometh blind!

What resource hath the archer when, in the hour of conflict, he desireth
    to discharge the arrow, but findeth his bow-string broken?
And when troubles are multiplied upon the noble-minded, where shall
    he find refuge from fate and from destiny?

When the sultan heard this lamentation, he sprang upon
his feet, and, seeking the direction whence it proceeded,
found a curtain suspended before the door of a chamber ;
and he raised it, and beheld behind it a young man, sitting
on a sofa raised to the height of a cubit from the floor.
He was a handsome youth, well-shaped, and of eloquent
speech, with shining forehead, and rosy cheek, marked
with a mole resembling ambergris. The king was rejoiced
at seeing him, and saluted him ; and the young man (who
remained sitting, and was clad with a vest of silk, embroidered with gold, but who exhibited traces of grief) returned
his salutation, and said to him, O my master, excuse my
not rising. O youth ! said the king, inform me respecting
the lake, and its fish of various colors, and respecting this
palace, and the reason of thy being alone in it, and of thy
lamentation. When the young man heard these words,
tears trickled down his cheeks, and he wept bitterly. And
the king was astonished, and said to him, What causeth
thee to weep, O youth? He answered, How can I refrain
from weeping, when this is my state? and so saying, he
stretched forth his hand and lifted up the skirts of his
clothing ; and lo ! half of him, from his waist to the soles
of his feet, was stone; and from his waist to the hair of
his head he was like other men. He then said, Know,
O king, that the story of the fish is extraordinary ; if it
were engraved upon the intellect, it would be a lesson to
him who would be admonished; and he related as follows : —

The Story of the Young King of the Black Islands.

My father was lord of the Black Islands and the four mountains. When he died, I succeeded to his throne, and married my cousin. She loved me excessively, and would neither eat nor drink till she saw me again. After five years, all was changed. I found out that she had fallen into the power of an ugly black slave, whom she visited when I was asleep. Having learned this, I feigned sleep and arose and followed her to the place where the slave was. She wept and humbled herself before him, and he treated her scornfully. When she said to him, O my master, hast thou anything here that thy maid may eat? he answered, Uncover the dough pan; it contains some cooked rats' bones; eat of them and pick them. When I saw her do this, I entered, and taking the sword of the slave, I dealt him such a blow that I thought he was killed, but it appeared that he was only wounded. My cousin placed him in a tomb she caused to be built in my palace, where she visited him daily, lamenting his weakness, for more than two years. She was an enchantress, and by her power turned me, as you see, half to stone, leaving the other half in the substance of man. She also enchanted the city, its markets, fields, and inhabitants. The latter she transformed all into fish of four colors, according to the four classes of their religions — Mohammedans, Christians, Jews, and Magians.

Having said thus, the young man wept. Upon this the king proceeded to the tomb where the woman had placed the great black slave. The king slew him with one blow of his sword, and threw him into a well that was in the palace. The king then clad himself in the slave's clothes, and lay down in his place, and when the enchantress came, he feigned to speak with the voice of the slave, but in a feeble manner, reproving her for her conduct towards her husband. Had it not been for this, said the pretended slave, I had recovered my strength. Liberate him, continued the king, and give us ease.

She replied, I hear and obey; and immediately arose and went out from the tomb to the palace, and, taking a cup, filled it with water, and pronounced certain words over it, upon which it began to boil like a caldron. She then sprinkled some of it upon her cousin, saying, By virtue of what I have uttered, be changed from thy present state to that in which thou wast at first! and instantly he shook and stood upon his feet, rejoicing in his liberation, and exclaimed, I testify that there is no deity but God, and that Mohammed is God's Apostle; God favor and preserve him! She then said to him, Depart, and return not hither, or I will kill thee; and she cried out in his face: so he departed from before her, and she returned to the tomb, and said, O my master, come forth to me that I may behold thee. He replied with a weak voice, What hast thou done? Thou hast relieved me from the branch, but hast not relieved me from the root. O my beloved, she said, and what is the root? He answered, The people of this city, and of the four islands; every night, at the middle hour, the fish raise their heads, and imprecate vengeance upon me and upon thee; and this is the cause that prevents the return of vigor to my body; therefore liberate them, and come and take my hand, and raise me; for vigor hath already in part returned to me.

On hearing these words of the king, whom she imagined to be the slave, she said to him with joy, O my master, on my head and my eye! In the name of Allah! and she sprang up, full of happiness, and hastened to the lake, where, taking a little of its water, she pronounced over it some unintelligible words, whereupon the fish became agitated and raised their heads, and immediately became converted into men, as before. Thus was the enchantment removed from the inhabitants of the city, and the city became repeopled, and the market streets re-erected, and every one returned to his occupation; the mountains also became changed into islands, as they were at first. The enchantress then returned immediately to the king, whom she still imagined to be the slave, and said to him, O my beloved, stretch forth thy honored hand, that I may kiss it. Approach me, said the king in a low voice. So she drew near to him; and he, having his keen-edged sword ready in his hand, thrust it into her bosom; and the point protruded from her back: he then struck her again, and clove her in twain, and went forth.

He found the young man who had been enchanted waiting his return, and congratulated him on his safety; and the young prince kissed his hand, and thanked him. The king then said to him, Wilt thou remain in thy city, or come with me to my capital? O king of the age, said the young man, dost thou know the distance that is between thee and thy city! The king answered, Two days and a half. O king, replied the young man, if thou hast been asleep, awake: between thee and thy city is a distance of a year's journey to him who travelleth with diligence; and thou camest in two days and a half only because the city was enchanted: but, O king, I will never quit thee for the twinkling of an eye. The king rejoiced at his words, and said, Praise be to God, who hath, in his beneficence, given thee to me : thou art my son ; for during my whole life I have never been blessed with a son : and they embraced each other, and rejoiced exceedingly. They then went together into the palace, where the king, who had been enchanted, informed the officers of his court that he was about to perform the holy pilgrimage : so they prepared for him everything that he required ; and he departed with the sultan, his heart burning with reflections upon his city, because he had been deprived of the sight of it for the space of a year.

He set forth, accompanied by fifty mamlouks, and provided with presents, and they continued their journey night and day for a whole year, after which they drew near to the city of the sultan ; and the vizier and the troops, who had lost all hope of his return, came forth to meet him. The troops, approaching him, kissed the ground before him, and congratulated him on his safe return ; and he entered the city and sat upon the throne. He then acquainted the vizier with all that had happened to the young king : on hearing which, the vizier congratulated the latter, also, on his safety ; and when all things were restored to order, the sultan bestowed presents upon a number of his subjects, and said to the vizier, Bring to me the fisherman who presented to me the fish. So he sent to this fisherman, who had been the cause of the restoration of the inhabitants of the enchanted city, and brought him ; and the king invested him with a dress of honor, and inquired of him respecting his circumstances, and whether he had any children. The fisherman informed him that he had a son and two daughters ; and the king, on hearing this, took as his wife one of the daughters; and the young prince married the other. The king also conferred upon the son the office of treasurer. He then sent the vizier to the city of the young prince, the capital of the Black Islands, and invested him with its sovereignty, dispatching with him the fifty mamlouks who had accompanied him thence, with numerous robes of honor to all the emirs; and the vizier kissed his hands, and set forth on his journey; while the sultan and the young prince remained. And as to the fisherman, he became the wealthiest of the people of his age; and his daughters continued to be the wives of the kings until they died.

But this, added Scheherazade, is not more wonderful than what happened to the porter.

By this time, they had spent the second night, and the third night, and so on, in relating and listening to these stories, until they had come to the middle of the ninth night.

STORY OF THE PORTER AND THE LADIES OF BAGDAD, AND OF THE THREE ROYAL MENDICANTS, Etc.

———◦◦◦———

THERE was a man of the city of Bagdad, who was unmarried, and he was a porter; and one day, as he sat in the market, reclining against his crate, there accosted him a lady wrapped in an izar, of the manufacture of Mosul.[1] It was made of silk, embroidered with gold, with a border of gold at each end.

She raised her face-veil and, showing two black eyes fringed with jetty lashes, whose glances were soft and languishing, and whose perfect beauty was ever blandishing, she accosted the porter, and said in the suavest tones and choicest language, Take up thy crate and follow me. The porter was so dazzled that he could hardly believe he heard her aright, but he shouldered his basket in hot haste, saying to himself, O day of good luck! O day of Allah's grace! and walked after her till she stopped at the door of a house. There she rapped, and presently came out to her an old man, a Christian, to whom she gave a gold piece, receiving from him in return what she required of strained wine, clear as olive oil; and she set it safely in the hamper, saying, Lift and follow. Quoth the porter, This, by Allah, is indeed an auspicious day, a day propi-

---

[1] From this term the name of muslin is derived.

tious for the granting of all a man wisheth. He again
hoisted up the crate and followed her ; till she stopped at
a fruiterer's shop and bought of him Shami apples and
Osmani quinces and Omani peaches, and cucumbers of
Nile growth, and Egyptian limes, and Sultani oranges
and citrons; besides Aleppine jasmine, scented myrtle
berries, Damascene nenuphars, flower of privet and camo-
mile, blood-red anemones, violets and pomegranate blooms,
eglantine and narcissus, and set the whole in the porter's
crate, saying, Up with it. So he lifted, and followed
her till she stopped at a butcher's booth, and said, Cut
me off ten pounds of mutton. She paid him his price, and
he wrapped it in a banana-leaf, whereupon she laid it in
the crate, and said, Hoist, O porter. He hoisted accordingly, and followed her as she walked on till she stopped at
a grocer's, where she bought dry fruits and pistachio-kernels,
Tihamah raisins, shelled almonds, and all wanted for dessert,
and said to the porter, Lift and follow me. So he up
with his hamper and after her till she stayed at the confec-
tioner's, and she bought an earthen platter, and piled it
with all kinds of sweetmeats in his shop, open-worked tarts
and fritters scented with musk, and "soap-cakes," and lemon-
loaves and melon preserves, and " Zaynab's combs," and
" ladies' fingers," and " Kazi's tid-bits," and goodies of every
description ; and placed the platter in the porter's crate.
Thereupon quoth he (being a merry man), Thou shouldst
have told me, and I would have brought with me a pony or
a she-camel to carry all this market stuff. She smiled and
gave him a little cuff on the nape, saying, Step out, and
exceed not in words, for (Allah willing) thy wage will not
be wanting. Then she stopped at a perfumer's, and
took from him ten sorts of waters, rose scented with

musk, orange-flower, water-lily, willow-flower, violet, and five others; and she also bought two loaves of sugar, a bottle for perfume-spraying, a lump of male incense, aloe-wood, ambergris, and musk, with candles of Alexandria wax; and she put the whole in the basket, saying, Up with thy crate and after me. He did so, and followed till she stood before the green-grocer's, of whom she bought pickled safflower and olives, in brine and in oil; with tarragon and cream cheese and hard Syrian cheese; and she stowed them away in the crate, saying to the porter, Take up thy basket and follow me.[1]

He therefore took it up, and followed her until she came to a handsome house, before which was a spacious court. It was a lofty structure, with a door of two leaves, composed of ebony, overlaid with plates of red gold.

The young lady stopped at this door, and knocked gently; whereupon both its leaves were opened, and the porter, looking to see who opened it, found it to be a damsel of tall stature, high-bosomed, fair, and beautiful, and of elegant form, with a forehead like the bright new moon, eyes like those of gazelles, eyebrows like the new moon of Ramadan,[2] cheeks resembling anemones, and a mouth like the seal of Solomon: her countenance was like the full moon in its splendor, and the forms of her bosom resembled two pomegranates of equal size. When the porter beheld her, she captivated his reason; the crate

---

[1] In this elaborate description in detail, of the purchases made by the lady, the reader has a good idea of the character of the original of these stories. I have taken this passage from Captain Burton's rendering, as a good illustration of that translation and of the original. But, believing most readers would not long persevere with such detail, I have generally followed Mr. Lane's rendering, as I have explained in the preface. — E. E. H.

[2] The month of abstinence.

nearly fell from his head, and he exclaimed, Never in my
life have I seen a more fortunate day than this! The lady-
portress, standing within the door, said to the cateress and
the porter, Ye are welcome; and they entered, and proceeded to a spacious saloon, decorated with various colors,
and beautifully constructed, with carved wood-work, and
fountains, and benches of different kinds, and closets with
curtains hanging before them; there was also in it, at the
upper end, a sofa of alabaster, inlaid with large pearls and
jewels, with a mosquito curtain of red satin suspended over
it, and within this was a young lady with eyes possessing the
enchantment of Babylon,[1] and a figure like the letter Alif,[2]
with a face that put to shame the shining sun : she was like
one of the brilliant planets, or, rather, one of the most high-
born of the maidens of Arabia. This third lady, rising from
the sofa, advanced with a slow and elegant gait to the middle of the saloon, where her sisters were standing, and said
to them, Why stand ye still? Lift down the burden from
the head of this poor porter : whereupon the cateress placed
herself before him, and the portress behind him, and, the
third lady assisting them, they lifted it down from his
head. They then took out the contents of the crate, and,
having put everything in its place, gave to the porter two
pieces of gold, saying to him, Depart, O porter.

The porter, however, stood looking at the ladies, and
admiring their beauty and their agreeable dispositions; for
he had never seen any more handsome; and when he
observed that they had not a man among them, and gazed
upon the wine, and fruits, and sweet-scented flowers which
were there, he was full of astonishment, and hesitated to

---

[1] The Chaldeans were famous for magic.
[2] The form of Alif is long and slender; thus ∣.

go out; upon which one of the ladies said to him, Why dost thou not go? dost thou deem thy hire too little? Then turning to one of her sisters, she said to her, Give him another piece of gold. By Allah, O my mistress, exclaimed the porter, my hire is but two half-drachms,[1] and I thought not what ye have given me too little; but my heart and mind were occupied with reflections upon you and your state, ye being alone, with no man among you, not one to amuse you with his company; for ye know that the minaret standeth not firmly but on four walls; now ye have not a fourth, and the pleasure of women is not complete without men; ye are three only, and have need of a fourth, who should be a man, a person of sense, discreet, acute, and a concealer of secrets. We are maidens, they replied, and fear to impart our secret to him who will not keep it; for we have read, in a certain history, this verse:

Guard thy secret from another; intrust it not; for he who intrusteth a secret hath lost it.

By your existence, said the porter, I am a man of sense, and trustworthy, I have read various books, and perused histories; I make known what is fair, and conceal what is foul, and act in accordance with the sayings of the poet,

None keepeth a secret but a faithful person; with the best of mankind it remaineth concealed.

A secret is with me as in a house with a lock, whose key is lost, and whose door is sealed.

When the ladies heard the verses which he quoted, and the words with which he addressed them, they said to him, Thou knowest that we have expended here a considerable sum of money; hast thou then wherewith to requite us?

---

[1] A drachm is worth about sixpence

We will not suffer thee to remain with us, unless thou contribute a sum of money ; for thou desirest to sit with us, and to be our cup-companion, and to gaze upon our beautiful faces. If friendship is without money, said the mistress of the house, it is not equivalent to the weight of a grain ; and the portress added, If thou hast nothing, depart with nothing ; but the cateress said, O sister, let us suffer him ; for, verily, he hath not been deficient in his services for us this day ; another had not been so patient with us ; whatever, therefore, falls to his share of the expense, I will defray for him. At this the porter rejoiced, and exclaimed, By Allah, I obtained my first and only pay this day from none but thee ; and the other ladies said to him, Sit down, thou art welcome.

The cateress then arose, and having tightened her girdle, arranged the bottles, and strained the wine, and prepared the table by the pool of the fountain. She made ready all that they required, brought the wine, and sat down with her sisters ; the porter also sitting with them, thinking he was in a dream. And when they had seated themselves, the cateress took a jar of wine, and filled the first cup, and drank it ; she then filled another, and handed it to one of her sisters ; and in like manner she did to her other sister ; after which she filled again, and handed the cup to the porter, who, having taken it from her hand, repeated the verse :

I will drink the wine, and enjoy health; for, verily, this beverage is a
    remedy for disease.

The wine continued to circulate among them, and the porter, taking his part in the revels, dancing and singing with them, and enjoying the fragrant odors, began to hug and kiss them, while one slapped him, and another pulled him, and the third beat him with sweet-scented flowers, till, at length, the wine made sport with their reason ; and they threw off all restraint, indulging their merriment with as much freedom as if no man had been present.

Thus they continued until the approach of night, when they said to the porter, Depart, and show us the breadth of thy shoulders ; but he replied, Verily, the departure of my soul from my body were more easy to me than my departure from your company ; therefore suffer us to join the night to the day, and then each of us shall return to his own, or her own, affairs. The cateress, also, again interceded for him, saying, By my life I conjure you that ye suffer him to pass the night with us, that we may laugh at his drolleries, for he is a witty rogue. So they said to him, Thou shalt pass the night with us on this condition, that thou submit to our authority, and ask not an explanation of anything that thou shalt see. He replied, Good. Rise, then, said they, and read what is inscribed upon the door. Accordingly, he went to the door, and found the following inscription upon it in letters of gold : Speak not of that which doth not concern thee, lest thou hear that which will not please thee ; and he said, Bear witness to my promise that I will not speak of that which doth not concern me.

The cateress then rose, and prepared for them a repast ; and, after they had eaten a little, they lighted the candles and burned some aloes-wood. This done, they sat down again to the table ; and, while they were eating and drinking, they heard a knocking at the door, whereupon, without causing any interruption to their meal, one of them went to the door, and, on her return, said, Our pleasure this

night is now complete, for I have found at the door three
foreigners with shaven chins, and each of them is blind of
the left eye ; it is an extraordinary coincidence.   They are
strangers newly arrived, and each of them has a ridiculous
appearance ; if they come in, therefore, we shall be amused
with laughing at them.   The lady ceased not with these
words, but continued to persuade her sisters until they
consented, and said, Let them enter ; but make it a condition with them that they speak not of that which doth not
concern them, lest they hear that which will not please
them.   Upon this she rejoiced ; and, having gone again to
the door, brought in the three men blind of one eye and
with shaven chins, and they had thin and twisted mus-
taches.   Being mendicants, they saluted and drew back ;
but the ladies rose to them, and seated them ; and when
these three men looked at the porter, they saw that he
was intoxicated ; and, observing him narrowly, they thought
that he was one of their own class, and said, He is a mendicant like ourselves, and will amuse us by his conversation ; but the porter, hearing what they said, arose, and
rolled his eyes, and exclaimed to them, Sit quiet, and abstain from impertinent remarks.   Have ye not read the
inscription upon the door ?   The ladies, laughing, said to
each other, Between the mendicants and the porter we
shall find matter for amusement.   They then placed before
the former some food, and they ate, and then sat to drink.
The portress handed to them the wine, and, as the cup was
circulating among them, the porter said to them, Brothers,
have ye any tale or strange anecdote wherewith to amuse
us ?   The mendicants, heated by the wine, asked for musical instruments ; and the portress brought them a tambourine of the manufacture of Mosul, with a lute of Irak,

THE THREE ROYAL MENDICANTS.

and a Persian harp; whereupon they all arose, and one took the tambourine, another the lute, and the third the harp; and they played upon these instruments, the ladies accompanying them with loud songs; and while they were thus diverting themselves, a person knocked at the door. The portress, therefore, went to see who was there; and the cause of the knocking was this:

The Caliph Haroun Alrashid [1] had gone forth this night to see and hear what news he could collect, accompanied by Giafar his vizier, and Mesrour his executioner. It was his custom to disguise himself in the attire of a merchant, and this night, as he went through the city, he happened to pass, with his attendants, by the house of these ladies, and hearing the sounds of the musical instruments, he said to Giafar, I have a desire to enter this house, and to see who is giving this concert. They are a party who have become intoxicated, replied Giafar, and I fear that we may experience some ill usage from them; but the caliph said, We must enter, and I would that thou devise some stratagem by which we may obtain admission to the inmates. Giafar therefore answered, I hear and obey: and he advanced, and knocked at the door; and when the portress came and opened the door, he said to her, My mistress, we are merchants from Tiberias, and have been in Bagdad

---

[1] Haroun Alrashid (Aaron the Just) was born about the year 765, and died in 809. He was the most powerful monarch of the dynasty of the Abbasides. He is frequently mentioned in the Arabian Nights, — and, as in this instance, the scene of the stories is often laid in Bagdad, the seat of government of his empire. Giafar, as Galland chose to spell the name of his prime minister, elsewhere called Jafar, was one of the ancient Persian family of Barmecides. The cruel disgrace which Haroun inflicted on them was the worst blot on his reign. He was the contemporary and correspondent of Charlemagne of France.

ten days ; we have brought with us merchandise, and taken
lodgings in a khan [1]; and a merchant invited us to an entertainment this night : accordingly, we went to his house,
and he placed food before us, and we ate, and sat a while
drinking together, after which he gave us leave to depart ;
and going out in the dark, and being strangers, we missed
our way to the khan : we trust, therefore, in your generosity that you will admit us to pass the night in your house ;
by doing which you will obtain a reward in heaven.   The
portress, looking at them, and observing that they were in
the garb of merchants, and that they bore an appearance
of respectability, returned, and consulted her two companions ; and they said to her, Admit them : so she returned, and opened to them the door.   They said to her,
Shall we enter with thy permission ? She answered, Come
in.   The caliph, therefore, entered, with Giafar and Mesrour ; and when the ladies saw them, they rose to them,
and served them, saying, Welcome are our guests ; but we
have a condition to impose upon you, that ye speak not of
that which doth not concern you, lest ye hear that which
will not please you.   They answered, Good : and when they
had sat down to drink, the caliph looked at the three mendicants, and was surprised at observing that each of them
was blind of the left eye ; and he gazed upon the ladies,
and was perplexed and amazed at their fairness and beauty.
And when the others proceeded to drink and converse,
the ladies brought wine to the caliph ; but he said, I am
a pilgrim ; and drew back from them.   Whereupon the
portress spread before him an embroidered cloth, and placed
upon it a China bottle, into which she poured some willow-
flower water, adding to it a lump of ice, and sweetening it

---

[1] A sort of inn.

with sugar, while the caliph thanked her, and said within himself, To-morrow I must reward her for this kind action.

The party continued their carousal, and, when the wine took effect upon them, the mistress of the house arose and waited upon them, and afterward, taking the hand of the cateress, said, Arise, O my sister, that we may fulfil our debt. She replied, Good. The portress then rose, and, after she had cleared the middle of the saloon, placed the mendicants at the further end, beyond the doors ; after which the ladies called to the porter, saying, How slight is thy friendship! thou art not a stranger, but one of the family. So the porter arose, and girded himself, and said, What would ye? to which one of the ladies answered, Stand where thou art : and presently the cateress said to him, Assist me : and he saw two black bitches, with chains attached to their necks, and drew them to the middle of the saloon ; whereupon the mistress of the house arose from her place, and tucked up her sleeve above her wrist, and, taking a whip, said to the porter, Bring to me one of them. Accordingly, he dragged one forward by the chain. The bitch whined, and shook her head at the lady ; but the latter fell to beating her upon the head, notwithstanding her howling, until her arms were tired, when she threw the whip from her hand, and pressed the bitch to her bosom, and wiped away her tears, and kissed her head ; after which she said to the porter, Take her back, and bring the other ; and he brought her, and she did to her as she had done to the first. At the sight of this, the mind of the caliph was troubled, and his heart was contracted, and he winked to Giafar that he should ask her the reason ; but he replied by a sign, Speak not.

The mistress of the house then looked toward the por-

tress, and said to her, Arise to perform what thou hast to
do.   She replied, Good: and the mistress of the house
seated herself upon a sofa of alabaster, overlaid with gold
and silver, and said to the portress and the cateress, Now
perform your parts.   The portress then seated herself upon
a sofa by her, and the cateress, having entered a closet,
brought out from it a bag of satin with green fringes, and,
placing herself before the lady of the house, shook it, and
took out from it a lute, and she tuned its strings, and sang
to it these verses :

Restore to my eyelids the sleep which hath been ravished; and inform
    me of my reason, whither it hath fled.
I discovered, when I took up my abode with love, that slumber had
    become an enemy to my eyes.
They said, We saw thee to be one of the upright; what, then, hath
    seduced thee?   I answered, Seek the cause from his glance.
Verily, I excuse him for the shedding of my blood, admitting that I
    urged him to the deed by vexation.
He cast his sun-like image upon the mirror of my mind, and its reflec-
    tion kindled a flame in my vitals.

When the portress had heard this song, she exclaimed,
Allah, approve thee! and she rent her clothes, and fell
upon the floor in a swoon ; and when her bosom was thus
uncovered, the caliph saw upon her the marks of beating,
as if from sticks and whips ; at which he was greatly surprised.   The cateress immediately arose, sprinkled water
upon her face, and brought her another dress, which she
put on.   The caliph then said to Giafar, Seest thou not
this woman, and the marks of beating upon her ?   I cannot keep silence respecting this affair, nor be at rest until
I know the truth of the history of this damsel, and that of
these two bitches.   But Giafar replied, O our lord, they

have made a covenant with us that we shall not speak excepting of that which concerneth us, lest we hear that which will not please us. The cateress then took the lute again, and, placing it against her bosom, touched the chords with the ends of her fingers, and thus sang to it :

If of love we complain, what shall we say?   Or consuming through
    desire, how can we escape?

On hearing these verses of the cateress, the portress again rent her clothes and cried out, and fell upon the floor in a swoon ; and the cateress, as before, put on her another dress, after she had sprinkled some water upon her face.

The mendicants, when they witnessed this scene, said, Would that we had never entered this house, but rather had passed the night upon the mounds[1] ; for our night hath been rendered foul by an event that breaketh the back! The caliph, looking toward them, then said, Wherefore is it so with you ? They answered, Our hearts are troubled by this occurrence. Are ye not, he asked, of this house ? No, they answered ; nor did we imagine that this house belonged to any but the man who is sitting with you : upon which the porter said, Verily, I have never seen this place before this night ; and I would that I had passed the night upon the mounds rather than here. They then observed one to another, We are seven men, and they are but three women ; we will, therefore, ask them of their history, and if they answer us not willingly, they shall do it in spite of themselves : and they all agreed to this, excepting Giafar, who said, This is not a right determination ; leave them to themselves, for we are their guests, and they

---

[1] Eastern cities are often surrounded by mounds of ruins and rubbish.

made a covenant with us which we should fulfil : there
remaineth but little of the night, and each of us shall soon
go his way.   Then, winking to the caliph, he said, There
remaineth but an hour ; and to-morrow we will bring them
before thee, and thou shalt ask them their story.   But the
caliph refused to do so, and said, I have not patience to
wait so long for their history.   Words followed words, and
at last they said, Who shall put the question to them ? and
one answered, The porter.

The ladies then said to them, O people, of what are ye
talking ? whereupon the porter approached the mistress of
the house and said to her, O my mistress, I ask thee, and
conjure thee by Allah, to tell us the story of the two
bitches, and for what reason you beat them, and then
wept, and kissed them, and that thou acquaint us with the
cause of thy sister's having been beaten with sticks ! this
is our question, and peace be on you.   Is this true that he
saith of you ? inquired the lady of the other men ; and
they all answered, Yes, excepting Giafar, who was silent.
When the lady heard their answer, she said, Verily, O our
guests, ye have wronged us excessively ; for we made a
covenant with you beforehand, that he who should speak
of that which concerned him not should hear that which
would not please him.   Is it not enough that we have
admitted you into our house, and fed you with our provisions ?   But it is not so much your fault as the fault of her
who introduced you to us.   She then tucked up her sleeve
above her wrist, and struck the floor three times, saying,
Come ye quickly ! and immediately the door of a closet
opened, and there came forth from it seven black slaves,
each having in his hand a drawn sword.   The lady said to
them, Tie behind them the hands of these men of many

words, and bind each of them to another : and they did so, and said, O virtuous lady, dost thou permit us to strike off their heads ? She answered, Give them a short respite, until I shall have inquired of them their histories, before ye behead them. By Allah, O my mistress, exclaimed the porter, kill me not for the offence of others ; for they have all transgressed and committed an offence excepting me. Verily, our night had been pleasant if we had been preserved from these mendicants, whose presence is enough to convert a well-peopled city into a heap of ruins ! He then repeated this couplet :

How good is it to pardon one able to resist ! and how much more so
    one who is helpless ;
For the sake of the friendship that subsisted between us, destroy not
    one for the crime of another.

On hearing these words of the porter, the lady laughed after her anger. Then approaching the men, she said, Acquaint me with your histories, for there remaineth of your lives no more than an hour. Were ye not persons of honorable and high condition, or governors, I would hasten your recompense. The caliph said to Giafar, Woe to thee, O Giafar ! make known to her who we are ; otherwise she will kill us. It were what we deserve, replied he. Jesting, said the caliph, is not befitting in a time for seriousness ; each has its proper occasion. The lady then approached the mendicants, and said to them, Are ye brothers ? They answered, No, indeed ; we are only poor foreigners. She said then to one of them, Wast thou born blind of one eye ? No, verily, he answered ; but a wonderful event happened to me when my eye was destroyed, and the story of it, if engraved on the understanding, would serve as a lesson to him who would be admonished. She asked the second and the third also ; and they answered her as the first ; adding, Each of us is from a different country, and our history is wonderful and extraordinary. The lady then looked toward them and said, Each of you shall relate his story, and the cause of his coming to our abode, and then stroke his head and go his way.

The first who advanced was the porter, who said, O my mistress, I am a porter ; and this cateress loaded me and brought me hither, and what hath happened to me here in your company ye know. This is my story, and peace be on you. Stroke thy head, then, said she, and go. But he replied, By Allah, I will not go until I shall have heard the story of my companions. The first mendicant then advanced, and related as follows : [1] —

The Story of the First Royal Mendicant.

KNOW, O my mistress, that the cause of my having shaved my beard, and of the loss of my eye, was this : My father was a king, and he had a brother who was also a king, and who resided in another capital. It happened that my mother gave birth to me on the same day on which the son of my uncle was born ; and years and days passed away until we attained to manhood. Now it was my custom, some years, to visit my uncle, and to remain with him several months ; and on one of these occasions my cousin paid me great honor ; he slaughtered sheep for me, and strained the wine for me, and we sat down to drink ; and when the wine had affected us, he said to me,

[1] The Royal Mendicants of Lane's version, which we follow here, are the Kalendars of Burton's version, and others. The word was not known to Dr. Johnson.

O son of my uncle, I have need of thine assistance in an affair of interest to me, and I beg that thou wilt not oppose me in that which I desire to do.   I replied, I am altogether at thy service : and he made me swear to him by great oaths, and, rising immediately, absented himself for a little while, and then returned, followed by a woman decked with ornaments, and perfumed, and wearing a dress of extraordinary value.   He looked toward me, while the woman stood behind him, and said, Take this woman, and go before me to the burial-ground which is in such a place : and he described it to me, and I knew it.   He then added, Enter the burial-ground, and there wait for me.

I could not oppose him, nor refuse to comply with his request, on account of the oaths which I had sworn to him ; so I took the woman, and went with her to the burial-ground ; and when we had sat there a short time, my cousin came, bearing a basin of water, and a bag containing some plaster, and a small adze.   Going to a tomb in the midst of the burial-ground, he took the adze and disunited the stones, which he placed on one side ; he then dug up the earth with the adze, and uncovered a flat stone, of the size of a small door, under which there appeared a vaulted staircase.   Having done this, he made a sign to the woman, and said to her, Do according to thy choice : whereupon she descended the stairs.   He then looked toward me, and said, O son of my uncle, complete thy kindness when I have descended into this place, by replacing the trap-door and the earth above it as they were before : then, this plaster which is in the bag, and this water which is in the basin, do thou knead together, and plaster the stones of the tomb as they were, so that no man may know it, and say, This hath been lately opened,

but its interior is old ; for during the space of a whole
year I have been preparing this, and no one knew it but
God: this is what I would have thee do. He then said
to me, May God never deprive thy friends of thy presence,
O son of my uncle! and, having uttered these words, he
descended the stairs.

When he had disappeared from before my eyes, I replaced the trap-door, and busied myself with doing as he
had ordered me, until the tomb was restored to the state
in which it was at first ; after which I returned to the
palace of my uncle, who was then absent on a hunting
excursion. I slept that night, and when the morning
came, I reflected upon what had occurred between me and
my cousin, and repented of what I had done for him,
when repentance was of no avail. I then went out to the
burial-ground and searched for the tomb, but could not
discover it. I ceased not in my search until the approach
of night ; and not finding the way to it, returned again to
the palace ; and I neither ate nor drank: my heart was
troubled respecting my cousin, since I knew not what had
become of him, and I fell into excessive grief. I passed
the night sorrowful until the morning, and went again to
the burial-ground, reflecting upon the action of my cousin,
and repenting of my compliance with his request ; and I
searched among all the tombs, but discovered not that for
which I looked. Thus I persevered in my search seven
days without success.

My trouble continued and increased, until I was almost
mad ; and I found no relief but in departing, and returning
to my father ; but on my arrival at his capital, a party at
the city-gate sprang upon me and bound me. I was struck
with the utmost astonishment, considering that I was the

son of the sultan of the city, and that these were the servants of my father and myself: excessive fear of them
overcame me, and I said within myself, What hath happened to my father? I asked of those who had bound me
the cause of this conduct; but they returned me no
answer, till after a while, when one of them, who had been
my servant, said to me, Fortune hath betrayed thy father;
the troops have been false to him, and the vizier hath
killed him; and we were lying in wait to take thee. They
took me, and I was as one dead, by reason of this news
which I had heard respecting my father; and I stood
before the vizier who had killed my father.

Now there was an old enmity subsisting between me
and him; and the cause of it was this: I was fond of
shooting with the cross-bow; and it happened one day that,
as I was standing on the roof of my palace, a bird alighted
on the roof of the palace of the vizier, who was standing
there at the time, and I aimed at the bird; but the bolt
missed it, and struck the eye of the vizier, and knocked it
out, in accordance with the appointment of fate and
destiny, as the poet hath said :

We trod the steps appointed for us; and the man whose steps are
  appointed must tread them.
He whose death is decreed to take place in one land will not die in any
  land but that.

When I had thus put out the eye of the vizier, he could say
nothing, because my father was king of the city. This
was the cause of the enmity between him and me: and
when I stood before him, with my hands bound behind
me, he gave the order to strike off my head. I said to
him, Wouldst thou kill me for no offence? What offence,

he exclaimed, could be greater than this? and he pointed to the place of the eye which was put out. I did that, said I, unintentionally. He replied, If thou didst it unintentionally, I will do the same to thee purposely; and immediately he said, Bring him forward to me: and when they had done so, he thrust his finger into my left eye, and pulled it out. Thus I became deprived of one eye, as ye see me. He then bound me firmly, and placed me in a chest, and said to the executioner, Take this fellow, and draw thy sword, and convey him without the city; then put him to death, and let the wild beasts devour him.

Accordingly, he went forth with me from the city, and having taken me out from the chest, bound hand and foot, was about to bandage my eye, and kill me; whereupon I wept, and exclaimed,

How many brothers have I taken as armor! and such they were; but
     to guard my enemies.
I thought they would be as piercing arrows; and such they were; but
     to enter my heart!

The executioner, who had served my father in the same capacity, and to whom I had shown kindness, said, on hearing these verses, O my master, what can I do, being a slave under command? but presently he added, Depart with thy life, and return not to this country, lest thou perish, and cause me to perish with thee. The poet saith,

Flee with thy life if thou fearest oppression, and leave the house to tell
     its builder's fate.
Thou wilt find, for the land thou quittest, another: but no soul wilt
     thou find to replace thine own.

As soon as he had thus said, I kissed his hands, and believed not in my safety until I had fled from his presence.

The loss of my eye appeared light to me when I considered my escape from death; and I journeyed to my uncle's capital, and, presenting myself before him, informed him of what had befallen my father, and of the manner in which I had lost my eye: upon which he wept bitterly, and said, Thou hast added to my trouble and my grief; for thy cousin hath been lost for some days, and I know not what hath happened to him, nor can any one give me information respecting him. Then he wept again, until he became insensible; and when he recovered, he said, O my son, the loss of thine eye is better than the loss of thy life.

Upon this I could no longer keep silence respecting his son, my cousin; so I informed him of all that happened to him; and, on hearing this news, he rejoiced exceedingly, and said, Show me the tomb. By Allah, O my uncle, I replied, I know not where it is; for I went afterward several times to search for it, and could not recognize its place. We, however, went together to the burial-ground, and, looking to the right and left, I discovered it; and both I and my uncle rejoiced. I then entered the tomb with him, and when we had removed the earth, and lifted up the trap-door, we descended fifty steps, and, arriving at the bottom of the stairs, there issued forth upon us a smoke which blinded our eyes; whereupon my uncle pronounced those words which relieve from fear him who uttereth them, There is no strength nor power but in God, the High, the Great! After this, we proceeded, and found ourselves in a saloon, filled with flour and grain, and various eatables; and we saw there a curtain suspended over a couch, upon which my uncle looked, and found there his son and the woman who had descended with him, lying side by side, and converted into black charcoal, as if they had been thrown into a pit of fire. And when he beheld this spectacle, he spat in his son's face, and exclaimed, This is what thou deservest, O thou wretch! This is the punishment of the present world, and there remaineth the punishment of the other world, which will be more severe and lasting! and he struck him with his shoes. Astonished at this action, and grieved for my cousin, seeing him and the damsel thus converted into charcoal, I said, By Allah, O my uncle, moderate the trouble of thy heart, for my mind is perplexed by that which hath happened to thy son, and by thinking how it hath come to pass that he and the damsel are converted into black charcoal. Dost thou not deem it enough for him to be in this state, that thou beatest him with thy shoes?[1]

O son of my brother, he replied, this my son was, from his early years, inflamed with love for his foster-sister, and I used to forbid him from entertaining this passion for her, and to say within myself, They are now children, but when they grow older a base act will be committed by them; and, indeed, I heard that such had been the case, but I believed it not. I, however, reprimanded him severely, and said to him, Beware of so foul an action, which none before thee hath committed, nor will any commit after thee; otherwise we shall suffer disgrace and disparagement among the kings until we die, and our history will spread abroad with the caravans: have a care for thyself that such an action proceed not from thee; for I should be incensed against thee, and kill thee. I then separated him from her, and her from him: but the vile woman loved him excessively; the devil got possession of them both; and when my son saw that I had separated him, he secretly made this place

---

[1] To strike with the shoe is a special sign of contempt.

beneath the earth, and, having conveyed hither the provisions which thou seest, took advantage of my inadvertence when I had gone out to hunt, and came hither; but the Truth [1] (whose perfection be extolled and whose name be exalted!) was jealously vigilant over them, and consumed them by fire: and the punishment of the world to come will be more severe and lasting. He then wept, and I wept with him; and he said to me, Thou art my son in his stead. I remained a while reflecting upon the world and its vicissitudes, upon the murder of my father by the vizier, and his usurping his throne, and the loss of my eye, and the strange events which had happened to my cousin, and I wept again.

We then ascended, and, having replaced the trap-door and the earth above it, and restored the tomb to its former state, returned to our abode; but scarcely had we seated ourselves when we heard the sounds of drums and trumpets, warriors galloped about, and the air was filled with dust raised by the horses' hoofs. Our minds were perplexed, not knowing what had happened, and the king, asking the news, was answered, The vizier of thy brother hath slain him, and his soldiers and guards, and come with his army to assault the city unawares, and the inhabitants, being unable to withstand, have submitted to him: whereupon I said within myself, If I fall into his hand, he will slay me. Griefs overwhelmed me, and I thought of the calamities which had befallen my father and my mother, and knew not what to do; for if I appeared, the people of the city would know me, and the troops of my father would hasten to kill and destroy me. I knew no way of escape but to shave off my beard: so I shaved it, and,

[1] One of the names of God.

having changed my clothes, departed from the city, and
came hither, to this abode of peace, in the hope that some
person would introduce me to the Prince of the Faithful,[1]
the caliph of the lord of all creatures, that I might relate
to him my story, and all that had befallen me. I arrived
in this city this night ; and as I stood perplexed, not knowing whither to direct my steps, I saw this mendicant, and
saluted him, and said, I am a stranger. He replied, And
I, too, am a stranger : and while we were thus addressing
each other, our companion, this third person, came up to
us, and, saluting us, said, I am a stranger. We replied,
And we, also, are strangers. So we walked on together,
and darkness overtook us, and destiny directed us unto
your abode. This was the cause of the shaving of my
beard, and of the loss of my eye.

The lady then said to him, Stroke thy head, and depart ;
but he replied, I will not depart until I have heard the
stories of the others. And they wondered at his tale ; and
the caliph said to Giafar, Verily, I have never known the
like of that which hath happened to this mendicant.

The second mendicant then advanced, and, having kissed
the ground, said : —

The Story of the Second Royal Mendicant.

O MY mistress, I was not born with only one eye ; but
my story is wonderful, and, if written, would serve as a
lesson to him who would be admonished. I am a king,
and son of a king : I read the Koran according to the seven

---

[1] This title often occurs. It was assumed by Omar to avoid the inconven-
ience of the word " khalifah," our " caliph." For " khalifah " means properly
a successor, and to say successor to the successor was of course inconvenient.

traditions, and perused various works under the tuition of
different learned professors of their subjects : I studied
the science of the stars, and the writings of the poets, and
made myself a proficient in all the sciences ; so that I surpassed the people of my age. My handwriting was extolled among all the scribes, my fame spread among all
countries, and my history among all kings ; and the King
of India, hearing of me, requested my father to allow me
to visit him, sending him various gifts and curious presents, such as were suitable to kings. My father, therefore,
prepared for me six ships, and we proceeded by sea for the
space of a whole month, after which we came to land, and,
having disembarked some horses which we had with us in
the ship, we loaded ten camels with presents, and commenced our journey ; but soon there appeared a cloud of
dust, which rose and spread until it filled the air before us,
and, after a while, cleared a little, and discovered to us in
the midst of it sixty horsemen like fierce lions, whom we
perceived to be Arab highwaymen ; and when they saw us,
that we were a small company, with ten loads of presents
for the King of India, they galloped toward us, pointing
their spears at us. We made signs to them with our
fingers, and said, We are embassadors to the honored King
of India ; therefore do us no injury : but they replied, We
are not in his territories, nor under his government. They
slew certain of the young men, and the rest fled. I also
fled, after I had received a severe wound ; the Arabs being
employed, without further regard to us, in taking possession of the treasure and presents which we had with us.

I proceeded without knowing whither to direct my course,
reduced from a mighty to an abject state, and journeyed
till I arrived at the summit of a mountain, where I took

shelter in a cavern until the next morning. I then resumed
my journey, and arrived at a flourishing city ; the winter,
with its cold, had passed away, and the spring had come,
with its flowers ; and I rejoiced at my arrival there, being
wearied with my journey, anxious and pallid. My condition being thus changed, I knew not whither to bend my
steps, and, turning to a tailor sitting in his shop, I saluted
him, and he returned my salutation, and welcomed me, and
wished me joy, asking me the reason of my having come
thither. I acquainted him, therefore, with what had befallen me from first to last, and he was grieved for me, and
said, O young man, reveal not thy case, for I fear what the
king of this city might do to thee, since he is the greatest
of thy father's enemies, and hath a debt of blood [1] against
him. He then placed some food and drink before me, and
we ate together, and I conversed with him till night, when
he lodged me in a place by his shop, and brought me a bed
and coverlet ; and, after I had remained with him three
days, he said to me, Dost thou not know any trade by which
to make gain ? I answered, I am acquainted with the law,
a student of sciences, a writer, and an arithmetician. Thy
occupation, he said, is profitless in our country : there is no
one in our city acquainted with science or writing, but only
with getting money. Verily, I replied, I know nothing but
what I have told thee. Gird thyself, then, said he, and
take an axe and a rope, and cut fire-wood in the desert, and
so obtain thy subsistence until God dispel thy affliction ;
but acquaint no one with thy history, else they will kill thee.
He then bought for me an axe and a rope, and sent me with
a party of wood-cutters, giving them a charge respecting

---

[1] Like the Italian *vendetta*, or similar retaliatory customs in other countries.

me. Accordingly, I went forth with them, and cut some wood, and brought back a load upon my head, and sold it for half a piece of gold, part of which I expended in food, laying by the remainder.

Thus I continued for the space of a year, after which I went one day into the desert, according to my custom, to cut fire-wood, and, finding there a tract[1] with abundance of wood, I entered it, and came to a tree, around which I dug; and as I was removing the earth from its roots, the axe struck against a ring of brass; and I cleared away the earth from it, and found that it was affixed to a trap-door of wood, which I immediately removed. Beneath it appeared a staircase, which I descended; and at the bottom of this I entered a door, and beheld a palace, strongly constructed, where I found a lady, like a pearl of great price, whose aspect banished from the heart all anxiety, and grief, and affliction. At the sight of her I prostrated myself in adoration of her Creator for the fairness and beauty which He had displayed in her person; and she, looking toward me, said, Art thou a man or a Genie? I answered her, I am a man. And who, she asked, hath brought thee to this place, in which I have lived five-and-twenty years without ever seeing a human being? Her words sounded sweetly to me, and I answered her, O my mistress, God hath brought me to thy abode, and, I hope, will put an end to my anxiety and grief: and I related to her my story from beginning to end. She was grieved at my case, and wept, and said, I also will acquaint thee with my story. Know that I am the daughter of the king of the further parts of India, the lord of the Ebony Island. My father had married me to the son of my uncle; but on the night of my

---

[1] A "hollow," or thickly grown lowland with abundance of water.

bridal festivities, an Afrite, named Jarjaris, the son of
Rejmoos, the son of Eblis, carried me off, and, soaring
with me through the air, alighted in this place, to which he
conveyed all things necessary for me, such as ornaments,
and garments, and linen, and furniture, and food, and drink ;
and once in every ten days he cometh to me ; and he hath
appointed with me, that, in case of my wanting anything
by night or day, I should touch with my hand these two
lines which are inscribed upon the arched door, and as soon
as I remove my hand I see him before me.   Four days have
now passed since he was last with me, and there remain,
therefore, six days before he will come again ; wilt thou,
then, remain with me five days, and depart one day before
his visit ?   I answered, Yes ; rejoicing at the proposal ; and
she arose, and taking me by the hand, conducted me
through the arched door to a small and elegant bath, where
I took off my clothes, while she seated herself upon a mattress.   After this, she seated me by her side, and brought
me some sherbet of sugar infused with musk, and handed
it to me to drink : she then placed some food before me,
and after we had eaten and conversed together, she said to
me, Sleep, and rest thyself ; for thou art fatigued.

I slept, O my mistress, and forgot all that had befallen
me ; and when I awoke, I found her rubbing my feet ;
upon which I called to her, and we sat down again and
conversed a while ; and she said to me, By Allah, I was
straitened in my heart, living here alone, without any person to talk with me, five-and-twenty years.   Praise be to
God, who hath sent thee to me.   I thanked her for her
kind expressions ; and love of her took possession of my
heart, and my anxiety and grief fled away.   We then sat
down to drink together ; and I delighted with her com-

pany, for I had never seen her like in my whole life ; and when we were both full of joy, I said to her, Shall I take thee up from this subterranean place, and release thee from the Genie ? But she laughed and replied, Be content, and hold thy peace ; for of every ten days one day shall be for the Afrite, and nine for thee. I persisted, however, and said, I will this instant demolish this arch upon which the inscription is engraved, and let the Afrite come, that I may slay him : for I am predestined to kill Afrites. She entreated me to refrain ; but, paying no attention to her words, I kicked the door with violence ; upon which she exclaimed, The Afrite hath arrived ! Did I not caution thee against this ? Verily, thou hast brought a calamity upon me ; but save thyself, and ascend by the way that thou camest.

In the excess of my fear I forgot my sandals and my axe, and when I had ascended two steps, turning round to look for them, I saw that the ground had opened, and there arose from it an Afrite of hideous aspect, who said, Wherefore is this disturbance with which thou hast alarmed me, and what misfortune hath befallen thee ? She answered, No misfortune hath happened to me, excepting that my heart was contracted, and I desired to drink some wine to dilate it, and, rising to perform my purpose, I fell against the door. Thou liest, vile woman, he exclaimed ; and, looking about the palace to the right and left, he saw the sandals and axe ; and said to her, These are the property of none but a man. Who hath visited thee ? I have not seen them, she answered, until this instant ; probably they caught to thee. This language, said he, is absurd, and will have no effect upon me, thou shameless woman ! and, so saying, he stripped her of her clothing, and tied her down, with her arms and legs extended, to four stakes, like one crucified,[1] and began to beat her, urging her to confess what had happened.

For myself, being unable to endure her cries, I ascended the stairs overpowered by fear, and, arriving at the top, replaced the trap-door as it was at first, and covered it over with earth. I repented bitterly of what I had done, and reflecting upon the lady and her beauty, and how this wretch was torturing her after she had lived with him five-and-twenty years, and that he tortured her only on my account; and reflecting also upon my father and his kingdom, and how I had been reduced to the condition of a wood-cutter, I repeated this verse:

When fortune bringeth thee affliction, console thyself by remembering that one day thou must see prosperity, and another day difficulty.

Returning to my companion, the tailor, I found him awaiting my return as if he were placed in a pan upon burning coals. I passed last night, said he, with anxious heart on thy account, fearing for thee from some wild beast or other calamity. Praise be to God for thy safe return. I thanked him for his tender concern for me, and entered my apartment; and as I sat meditating upon that which had befallen me, and blaming myself for having kicked the kubbeh, my friend the tailor came in to me, and said, In the shop is a foreigner, who asks for thee, and he has thy axe and sandals; he came with them to the wood-cutters, and said to them, I went out at the time of the call of the Mueddin, to morning prayer, and stumbled upon these, and know not to whom they belong: can ye guide me to their owner?

[1] The Koran alludes to crucifixion. Pharaoh threatens the magicians with crucifixion, chap. xx.

The wood-cutters, therefore, directed him to thee : he is sitting in my shop ; so go out to him and thank him, and take thy axe and thy sandals. On hearing these words, my countenance turned pale, and my whole state became changed ; and while I was in this condition, the floor of my chamber clove asunder, and there arose from it the stranger, and lo, he was the Afrite ; he had tortured the lady with the utmost cruelty ; but she would confess nothing : so he took the axe and the sandals, and said to her, If I am Jarjaris, of the descendants of Eblis, I will bring the owner of this axe and these sandals. Accordingly he came, with the pretence before mentioned, to the wood-cutters, and, having entered my chamber, without granting me any delay, seized me, and soared with me through the air : he then descended, and dived into the earth, and brought me up into the palace where I was before.

Here I beheld the lady stripped of her clothing, and with blood flowing from her sides ; and tears trickled from my eyes. The Afrite then took hold of her, and said, Vile woman, this is thy lover : whereupon she looked at me, and replied, I know him not, nor have I ever seen him until this instant. The Afrite said to her, With all this torture wilt thou not confess ? She answered, Never in my life have I seen him before, and it is not lawful in the sight of God that I should speak falsely against him. Then, said he, if thou know him not, take this sword and strike off his head. She took the sword, and came to me, and stood over my head ; but I made a sign to her with my eyebrow, while tears ran down my cheeks. She replied in a similar manner, Thou art he who hath done all this to me . I made a sign to her, however, that this was a time for pardon, conveying my meaning in the manner thus described by the poet :

Our signal in love is the glance of our eyes ; and every intelligent person
understands the sign.

Our eyebrows carry on an intercourse between us ; we are silent ; but
love speaketh.

And when she understood me, she threw the sword from
her hand, O my mistress, and the Afrite handed it to me,
saying, Strike off her head, and I will liberate thee, and do
thee no harm. I replied, Good : and quickly approaching
her, raised my hand; but she made a sign as though she
would say, I did no injury to thee ; whereupon my eyes
poured with tears, and, throwing down the sword, I said,
O mighty Afrite, and valiant hero, if a woman, deficient in
sense and religion, seeth it not lawful to strike off my head,
how is it lawful for me to do so to her, and especially when
I have never seen her before in my life ? I will never do it,
though I should drink the cup of death and destruction.
There is affection between you, said the Afrite, and, taking
the sword, he struck off one of the hands of the lady ; then
the other ; after this, her right foot ; and then her left foot :
thus with four blows he cut off her four extremities, while
I looked on, expecting my own death. She then made a
sign to me with her eye ; and the Afrite, observing her,
exclaimed, Now thou hast been guilty of incontinence with
thine eye ; and with a blow of his sword struck off her
head ; after which, he turned toward me, and said, O man,
it is allowed us by our law, to put a wife to death. This
woman I carried off on her wedding-night, when she was
twelve years of age, and I killed her ; but as for thee,
choose, therefore, what injury I shall do to thee.

Upon this, O my mistress, I rejoiced exceedingly, and,
eager to obtain his pardon, I said to him, What shall I
choose from thy hands ? Choose, he answered, into what

form I shall change thee ; either the form of a dog, or that of an ass, or that of an ape. I replied, in my desire of for-giveness, Verily, if thou wilt pardon me, God will pardon thee in recompense for thy showing mercy to a Mohamme-dan who hath done thee no injury. The Afrite replied, Lengthen not thy words to me : as to my killing thee, fear it not ; and as to my pardoning thee, covet it not ; but as to my enchanting thee, there is no escape from it ; and, so saying, he clove the earth asunder, and soared with me through the sky to such a height that I beheld the world be-neath me as though it were a bowl of water ;[1] then alighting upon a mountain, he took up a little dust, and, having mut-tered and pronounced certain words over it, sprinkled me with it, saying, Quit this form, and take the form of an ape ! whereupon I became like an ape of a hundred years of age.

When I saw myself changed into this ugly form I wept for myself, but determined to be patient under the tyranny of fortune, knowing it to be constant to no one. I de-scended from the summit of the mountain, and, after having journeyed for the space of a month, arrived at the seashore ; and when I had stood there a short time, I saw a vessel in the midst of the sea, with a favorable wind ap-proaching the land ; I therefore hid myself behind a rock on the beach, and when the ship came close up I sprang into the midst of it. But as soon as the persons on board saw me, one of them cried, Turn out this unlucky brute from the ship : another said, Let us kill him : and a third exclaimed, I will kill him with this sword. I, however, caught hold of the end of the sword, and tears flowed from my eyes ; at the sight of which the captain took compas-

---

[1] Burton reads " as if it were a saucer," and observes that this is the descrip-tion given by those who ascend above it, now,

sion on me, and said to the passengers, O merchants, this ape hath sought my aid, and I give it him ; he is under my protection ; let no one, therefore, oppose or trouble him. He then treated me with kindness, and whatever he said to me I understood, and all that he required to be done I performed as his servant.

We continued our voyage for fifty days with a fair wind, and cast anchor under a large city containing a population which no one but God, whose name be exalted, could reckon ; and when we had moored our vessel, there came to us some mamlouks [1] from the king of the city ; who came on board the ship, and complimented the merchants on their safe arrival, saying, Our king greeteth you, rejoicing in your safety, and hath sent to you this roll of paper, desiring that each of you shall write a line upon it ; for the king had a vizier who was an eminent caligraphist, and he is dead, and the king hath sworn that he will not appoint any person to his office who cannot write équally well. Though in the form of an ape, I arose and snatched the paper from their hands ; upon which, fearing that I would tear it and throw in into the sea, they cried out against me, and would have killed me ; but I made signs to them that I would write, and the captain said to them, Suffer him to write, and if he scribble we will turn him away ; but if he write well I will adopt him as my son ; for I have never seen a more intelligent ape. So I took the pen, and demanded the ink, and wrote in an epistolary hand this couplet :

Fame hath recorded the virtues of the noble; but no one hath been able to reckon thine.

May God not deprive mankind of such a father ; for thou art the parent of every excellence.

[1] Privileged servants.

Then in a more formal large hand, I wrote the following verses :

There is no writer that shall not perish; but what his hand hath written shall endure.
Write, therefore, nothing but what will please thee when thou shalt see it on the day of resurrection.

Two other specimens I wrote, in two different and smaller hands, and returned the paper to the mamlouks, who took it back to the king; and when he saw what was written upon it, the hand of no one pleased him excepting mine; and he said to his attendants, Go to the author of this handwriting, put upon him this dress, and mount him upon a mule, and conduct him, with a band of music before him, to my presence. On hearing this order they smiled; and the king was angry with them, and said, How is it that I give you an order, and ye laugh at me? They answered, O king, we laugh not at thy words, but because he who wrote this is an ape, and not a son of Adam : he is with the captain of the ship newly arrived.

The king was astonished at their words; he shook with delight, and said, I would purchase this ape. He then sent some messengers to the ship, with the mule and the dress of honor, saying to them, Ye must clothe him with this dress, and mount him upon the mule, and bring him hither. So they came to the ship, and, taking me from the captain, clad me with the dress; and the people were astonished, and flocked to amuse themselves with the sight of me. And when they brought me to the king, and I beheld him, I kissed the ground before him three times, and he ordered me to sit down : so I sat down upon my knees; and the persons present were surprised at my polite manners, and especially the king, who presently ordered his people to

retire. They therefore did so; none remaining but the
king, and a eunuch, and a young mamlouk, and myself.
The king then commanded that a repast should be brought;
and they placed before him a service of viands such as
gratified the appetite and delighted the eye; and the king
made a sign to me that I should eat; whereupon I arose,
and, having kissed the ground before him seven times, sat
down to eat with him; and when the table was removed,
I washed my hands, and, taking the ink-case, and pen and
paper, I wrote these two verses:

Great is my appetite for thee, O Kunafeh![1] I cannot be happy nor
    endure without thee.
Be thou every day and night my food; and may drops of honey not be
    wanting to moisten thee.

Having done this, I arose, and seated myself at a distance;
and the king, looking at what I had written, read it with
astonishment, and exclaimed, Can an ape possess such
fluency and such skill in caligraphy?   This is, indeed, a
wonder of wonders!   Afterward, a chess-table was brought
to the king, and he said to me, Wilt thou play? By a motion of my head I answered, Yes; and I advanced, and
arranged the pieces.   I played with him twice, and beat
him; and the king was perplexed, and said, Were this a
man, he would surpass all the people of his age.

He then said to his eunuch,[2] Go to thy mistress, and say
to her, Answer the summons of the king: that she may
come and gratify her curiosity by the sight of this wonderful ape.   The eunuch therefore went, and returned
with his mistress, the king's daughter, who, as soon as she
saw me, veiled her face, and said, O my father, how is it

---

[1] A sort of vermicelli.
[2] Attending in the harem, or women's palace.

that thou art pleased to send for me, and suffer strange men to see me? O my daughter, answered the king, there is no one here but the young mamlouk, and the eunuch who brought thee up, and this ape, with myself, thy father: from whom, then, dost thou veil thy face? This ape, said she, is the son of a king, and the name of his father is Eymar: he is enchanted, and it was the Afrite Jarjaris, a descendant of Eblis, who transformed him, after having slain his own wife, the daughter of King Aknamus. This, whom thou supposest to be an ape, is a learned and wise man. The king was amazed at his daughter's words, and, looking toward me, said, Is it true that she saith of thee? I answered, by a motion of my head, Yes; and wept. The king then said to his daughter, By what means didst thou discover that he was enchanted? O my father, she answered, I had with me in my younger years an old woman who was a cunning enchantress, and she taught me the art of enchantment: I have committed its rules to memory, and know it thoroughly, being acquainted with a hundred and seventy modes of performing it, by the least of which I could transport the stones of thy city beyond Mount Caucasus, and make its site to be an abyss of the sea, and convert its inhabitants into fish in the midst of it. I conjure thee, then, by the name of Allah, said her father, to restore this young man, that I may make him my vizier. Is it possible that thou possessedst this excellence, and I knew it not? Restore him, that I may make him my vizier, for he is a polite and intelligent youth.

She replied, With pleasure: and, taking a knife upon which were engraved some Hebrew names, marked with it a circle in the midst of the palace. Within this she wrote certain names and talismans, and then she pronounced invocations, and uttered unintelligible words ; and soon the palace around us became immersed in gloom, to such a degree that we thought the whole world was overspread ; and lo! the Afrite appeared before us in a most hideous shape, with hands like winnowing-forks, and legs like masts, and eyes like burning torches ; so that we were terrified at him. The king's daughter exclaimed, No welcome to thee! to which the Afrite, assuming the form of a lion, replied, Thou traitress, how is it that thou hast broken thine oath? Did we not swear that we would not oppose one another? Thou wretch, said she, when didst thou receive an oath? The Afrite, still in the form of the lion, then exclaimed, Take what awaiteth thee! and, opening his mouth, rushed upon the lady : but she instantly plucked a hair from her head and muttered with her lips, whereupon the hair became converted into a piercing sword, with which she struck the lion, and he was cleft in twain by the blow ; but his head became changed into a scorpion. The lady immediately transformed herself into an enormous serpent, and crept after the execrable wretch in the shape of a scorpion, and a sharp contest ensued between them ; after which, the scorpion became an eagle, and the serpent, changing to a vulture, pursued the eagle for a length of time. The latter then transformed himself into a black cat, and the king's daughter became a wolf, and they fought together long and fiercely, till the cat, seeing himself overcome, changed himself into a large red pomegranate [1] which fell into a pool ; but the wolf pursuing it, it ascended into the air, and then fell upon the

---

[1] Each pomegranate is supposed to contain one seed from the Garden of Eden.

pavement of the palace, and broke in pieces, its grains became scattered, each apart from the others, and all spread about the whole space of ground inclosed by the palace. The wolf, upon this, transformed itself into a cock, in order to pick up the grains, and not leave one of them; but, according to the decree of fate, one. grain remained hidden by the side of the pool of the fountain. The cock began to cry, and flapped its wings, and made a sign to us with its beak; but we understood not what it would say. It then uttered at us such a cry that we thought the palace had fallen down upon us; and it ran about the whole of the ground, until it saw the grain that had lain hid by the side of the pool, when it pounced upon it to pick it up; but it fell into the midst of the water, and became transformed into a fish, and sank into the water; upon which the cock became a fish of a larger size, and plunged in after the other. For a while it was absent from our sight; but at length we heard a loud cry, and trembled at the sound; after which, the Afrite arose as a flame of fire, casting fire from his mouth, and fire and smoke from his eyes and nostrils; the king's daughter also became as a vast body of fire; and we would have plunged into the water from fear of our being burned and destroyed; but suddenly the Afrite cried out from within the fire, and came toward us upon the raised floor, blowing fire at our faces. The lady, however, overtook him, and blew fire in like manner in his face; and some sparks struck us both from her and from him; her sparks did us no harm; but one from him struck me in my eye, and destroyed it, I being still in the form of an ape; and a spark from him reached the face of the king, and burned the lower half, with his beard and mouth, and struck out

his lower teeth ; another spark also fell upon the breast of
the eunuch, who was burned, and died immediately. We
expected destruction, and gave up all hope of preserving
our lives ; but while we were in this state, a voice exclaimed, God is most great ! God is most great ! He hath
conquered and aided, and abandoned the denier of the
faith of Mohammed, the chief of mankind ! The person
from whom this voice proceeded was the king's daughter ;
she had burned the Afrite ; and when we looked toward
him, we perceived that he had become a heap of ashes.

The lady then came to us, and said, Bring me a cup of
water ; and when it was brought to her, she pronounced
over it some words which we understood not, and, sprink-
ling me with it, said, Be restored, by virtue of the name of
the Truth, and by virtue of the most great name of God,
to thy original form ! whereupon I became a man as I was
at first, excepting that my eye was destroyed. After this,
she cried out, The fire ! the fire ! O my father, I shall no
longer live, for I am predestined to be killed. Had he
been a human being, I had killed him at the first of the
encounter. I experienced no difficulty till the scattering
of the grains of the pomegranate, when I picked them up,
excepting the one in which was the life of the Genie ; had
I picked up that, he had instantly died ; but I saw it not, as
fate and destiny had appointed ; and suddenly he came
upon me, and a fierce contest ensued between us under
the earth, and in the air, and in the water ; and every time
that he tried against me a new mode, I employed against
him one more potent, until he tried against me the mode
of fire ; and rarely does one escape against whom the mode
of fire is employed. Destiny, however, aided me, so that I
burned him first ; but I exhorted him previously to embrace

STORY OF THE PORTER, ETC.

the Mohammedan faith. Now I die; and may God supply
my place to you. Having thus said, she ceased not to
pray for relief from the fire; and lo! a spark ascended to
her breast, and thence to her face; and when it reached
her face, she wept, and exclaimed, I testify that there is
no deity but God, and I testify that Mohammed is God's
apostle! We then looked toward her, and saw that she
had become a heap of ashes by the side of the ashes of the
Afrite.

We were plunged into grief on her account, and I wished
that I had been in her place rather than have seen that
sweet-faced creature who had done me this kindness reduced to a heap of ashes; but the decree of God cannot
be averted. The king, on beholding his daughter in this
state, plucked out what remained of his beard, and slapped
his face, and rent his clothes; and I also did the same,
while we both wept for her. Then came the chamberlains·
and other great officers of the court, who, finding the king
in a state of insensibility, with two heaps of ashes before
him, were astonished, and remained encompassing him
until he recovered from his fit, when he informed them of
what had befallen his daughter with the Afrite; and great
was their affliction. The women shrieked, with the female
slaves, and continued their mourning seven days. After
this, the king gave orders to build over the ashes of his
daughter a great tomb with a dome, and illuminated it
with candles and lamps; but the ashes of the Afrite they
scattered in the wind, exposing them to the curse of God.
The king then fell sick, and was near unto death; his illness lasted a month; but after this he recovered his health,
and, summoning me to his presence, said to me, O young
man, we passed our days in the enjoyment of the utmost

happiness, secure from the vicissitudes of fortune, until thou camest to us, when troubles overcame us. Would that we had never seen thee, nor thy ugly form, on account of which we have been reduced to this state of privation; for, in the first place, I have lost my daughter, who was worth a hundred men; and, secondly, I have suffered this burning, and lost my teeth; my eunuch also is dead; but it was not in thy power to prevent these afflictions; the decree of God hath been fulfilled on us and on thee; and praise be to God that my daughter restored thee, though she destroyed herself. Now, however, depart, O my son, from my city. It is enough that hath happened on thy account; but as it was decreed against us and thee, depart in peace.

So I departed, O my mistress, from his presence; but before I quitted the city I entered a public bath and shaved my beard. I traversed various regions, and passed through great cities, and bent my course to the Abode of Peace,[1] Bagdad, in the hope of obtaining an interview with the Prince of the Faithful, that I might relate to him all that had befallen me.

The third mendicant then advanced, and thus related his story:—

The Story of the Third Royal Mendicant.

O ILLUSTRIOUS lady, my story is not like those of my two companions, but more wonderful: the course of fate and destiny brought upon them events against which they

[1] Bagdad received this name either on account of its superior police, or simply because it was the capital of the Caliphate. The river Tigris was known as the River of Peace.

could not guard ; but as to myself, the shaving of my beard
and the loss of my eye were occasioned by my provoking
fate and misfortune ; and the cause was this :

I was a king, and the son of a king; and when my father
died, I succeeded to his throne, and governed my subjects
with justice and beneficence. I took pleasure in sea-
voyages; and my capital was on the shore of an extensive
sea, interspersed with fortified and garrisoned islands,
which I desired, for my amusement, to visit ; I therefore
embarked with a fleet of ten ships, and took with me provisions sufficient for a whole month. I proceeded twenty
days, after which there arose against us a contrary wind ;
but at daybreak it ceased, and the sea became calm, and
we arrived at an island, where we landed, and cooked some
provisions, and ate ; after which we remained there two
days. We then continued our voyage; and when twenty
days more had passed, we found ourselves in strange
waters, unknown to the captain, and he desired the watch
to look out from the mast-head : so he went aloft, and when
he had come down he said to the captain, I saw, on my
right hand, fish floating upon the surface of the water; and
looking toward the midst of the sea, I perceived something
looming in the distance, sometimes black, and sometimes
white.

When the captain heard this report of the watch, he
threw his turban on the deck, and plucked his beard, and
said to those who were with him, Receive warning of our
destruction, which will befall all of us : not one will escape !
So saying, he began to weep; and all of us in like manner
bewailed our lot. I desired him to inform us of that which
the watch had seen. O my lord, he replied, know that we
have wandered from our course since the commencement

of the contrary wind that was followed in the morning by
a calm, in consequence of which we remained stationary
two days; from that period we have deviated from our
course for twenty-one days, and we have no wind to carry
us back from the fate which awaits us after this day : to-
morrow we shall arrive at a mountain of black stone, called
loadstone : the current is now bearing us violently toward
it, and the ships will fall in pieces, and every nail in them
will fly to the mountain, and adhere to it ; for God hath
given to the loadstone a secret property by virtue of which
everything of iron is attracted toward it. On that mountain is such a quantity of iron as no one knoweth but God,
whose name be exalted ; for from times of old great numbers of ships have been destroyed by the influence of that
mountain. There is, upon the summit of the mountain, a
cupola of brass supported by ten columns, and upon the
top of this cupola is a horseman upon a horse of brass [1]
having in his hand a brazen spear, and upon his breast
suspended a tablet of lead, upon which are engraved mys-
terious names and talismans ; and as long, O king, as this
horseman remains upon the horse, so long will every ship
that approaches be destroyed, with every person on board,
and all the iron contained in it will cleave to the mountain :
no one will be safe until the horseman shall have fallen from
the horse. The captain then wept bitterly ; and we felt
assured that our destruction was inevitable, and every one
of us bade adieu to his friend.

On the following morning we drew near to the mountain ;
the current carried us toward it with violence, and when the
ships were almost close to it, they fell asunder, and all the

[1] Such a horseman was described by Western writers as pointing westward
from the Fortunate Islands, and afterwards, from the Azores.

nails, and everything else that was of iron, flew from them toward the loadstone.[1] It was near the close of day when the ships fell in pieces. Some of us were drowned, and some escaped ; but the greater number were drowned, and of those who saved their lives none knew what became of the others, so stupefied were they by the waves and the boisterous wind. As for myself, O my mistress, God, whose name be exalted, spared me on account of the trouble, and torment, and affliction that He had predestined to befall me. I placed myself upon a plank, and the wind and waves cast it upon the mountain ; and when I had landed, I found a practicable way to the summit, resembling steps cut in the rock ; so I exclaimed, In the name of God! and offered up a prayer, and attempted the ascent, holding fast by the notches ; and presently God stilled the wind and assisted me in my endeavors, so that I arrived in safety at the summit. Rejoicing greatly in my escape, I immediately entered the cupola, and performed the prayers of two rekahs[2] in gratitude to God for my preservation ; after which I slept beneath the cupola, and heard a voice saying to me, O son of Cassib, when thou awakest from thy sleep, dig beneath thy feet, and thou wilt find a bow of brass, and three arrows of lead, whereon are engraved talismans: then take the bow and arrows, and shoot at the horseman that is upon the top of the cupola, and relieve mankind from this great affliction ; for when thou hast shot at the horseman he will fall into the sea ; the bow will also fall, and do thou bury it in its place ; and as soon as thou

---

[1] The story of an iron mountain so magnetic that it drew the nails from ships is as old as Ptolemy. See book vii. 2; and the story is repeated, perhaps from the Arabian Nights, in Peter Wilkins.

[2] Repetitions of set forms of words, chiefly from the Koran.

hast done this, the sea will swell and rise until it has attained the summit of the mountain ; and there will appear upon it a boat bearing a man, different from him whom thou shalt have cast down, and he will come to thee, having an oar in his hand : then do thou embark with him ; but utter not the name of God ; and he will convey thee in ten days to a safe sea, where, on thy arrival, thou wilt find one who will take thee to thy city. All this shall be done if thou utter not the name of God.

Awaking from my sleep, I sprang up, and did as the voice had directed. I shot at the horseman, and he fell into the sea ; and the bow having fallen from my hand, I buried it : the sea then became troubled, and rose to the summit of the mountain ; and when I had stood waiting there a little while, I beheld a boat in the midst of the sea, approaching me. I praised God, whose name be exalted, and when the boat came to me I found in it a man of brass, with a tablet of lead upon his breast, engraven with names and talismans. Without uttering a word, I embarked in the boat, and the man rowed me ten successive days, after which I beheld the islands of security, whereupon, in the excess of my joy, I exclaimed, In the name of God ! There is no deity but God ! God is most great ! and as soon as I had done this, he cast me out of the boat, and sank in the sea.

Being able to swim, I swam until night, when my arms and shoulders were tired, and, in this perilous situation, I repeated the profession of the faith, and gave myself up as lost ; but the sea rose with the violence of the wind, and a wave like a vast castle threw me upon the land, in order to the accomplishment of the purpose of God. I ascended the shore, and after I had wrung out my clothes, and spread them upon the ground to dry, I slept ; and in the morning I put on my clothes again, and, looking about to see which way I should go, I found a tract covered with trees, to which I advanced ; and when I had walked round it, I found that I was upon a small island in the midst of the sea ; upon which I said within myself, Every time that I˙ escape from one calamity I fall into another that is worse : but while I was reflecting upon my unfortunate case, and wishing for death, I beheld a vessel bearing a number of men. I arose immediately, and climbed into a tree ; and lo, the vessel came to the shore, and there landed from it ten black slaves bearing axes. They proceeded to the middle of the island, and, digging up the earth, uncovered and lifted a trap-door, after which they returned to the vessel, and brought from it bread and flour, and clarified butter[1] and honey, and sheep, and everything that the wants of an inhabitant would require, continuing to pass backward and forward between the vessel and the trap-door, bringing loads from the former, and entering the latter, until they had removed all the stores from the ship. They then came out of the vessel with various clothes of the most beautiful description, and in the midst of them was an old sheikh, enfeebled and wasted by extreme age, leading by the hand a young man cast in the mould of graceful symmetry, and invested with such perfect beauty as deserved to be a subject for proverbs. He was like a fresh and slender twig, enchanting and captivating every heart by his elegant form. The party

---

[1] This is the *samn* of Arabia, the *raughan* of Persia, the *ghi* of Hindostan, the butter of the Old Testament. Fresh butter is melted over the fire, and skimmed to make it. It will then keep, in leather bottles, for a hundred years.

proceeded to the trap-door, and, entering it, became concealed from my eyes.

They remained beneath about two hours, or more; after which, the sheikh and the slaves came out: but the youth came not with them; and they replaced the earth, and embarked and set sail. Soon after, I descended from the tree and went to the excavation. I removed the earth, and, entering the aperture, saw a flight of wooden steps, which I descended; and at the bottom I beheld a handsome dwelling-place, furnished with a variety of silken carpets; and there was the youth, sitting upon a high mattress, with sweet-smelling flowers and fruits placed before him. On seeing me, his countenance became pale; but I saluted him, and said, Let thy mind be composed, O my master: thou hast nothing to fear, O delight of my eye; for I am a man, and the son of a king like thyself: fate hath impelled me to thee, that I may cheer thee in thy solitude. The youth, when he heard me thus address him, and was convinced that I was one of his own species, rejoiced exceedingly at my arrival, his color returned, and, desiring me to approach him, he said, O my brother, my story is wonderful: my father is a jeweller: he had slaves who made voyages by his orders, for the purposes of commerce, and he had dealings with kings; but he had never been blessed with a son; and he dreamed that he was soon to have a son, but one whose life would be short; and he awoke sorrowful. Shortly after, in accordance with the decrees of God, my mother conceived me, and when her time was complete, she gave birth to me; and my father was greatly rejoiced: the astrologers,[1] however, came to

---

[1] Mohammed condemned astrologers as liars; but the Arabian Nights, as in this passage, often refers to their skill and success.

him, and said, Thy son will live fifteen years; his fate is intimated by the fact that there is in the sea a mountain, called the Mountain of Loadstone, whereon is a horseman, on a horse of brass, on the former of which is a tablet of lead suspended to his neck; and when the horseman shall be thrown down from his horse, thy son will be slain; the person who is to slay him is he who will throw down the horseman, and his name is King Ajib, the son of King Cassib. My father was greatly afflicted at this announce-ment: and when he had reared me until I had nearly attained the age of fifteen years, the astrologers came again, and informed him that the horseman had fallen into the sea, and that it had been thrown down by King Ajib, the son of King Cassib: on hearing which, he prepared for me this dwelling, and here left me to remain until the completion of the term, of which there now remain ten days. All this he did from fear lest King Ajib should kill me.

When I heard this I was filled with wonder, and said within myself, I am King Ajib, the son of King Cassib, and it was I who threw down the horseman; but, by Allah, I will neither kill him nor do him any injury. Then said I to the youth, Far from thee be both destruction and harm, if it be the will of God, whose name be exalted: thou hast nothing to fear: I will remain with thee to serve thee, and will go forth with thee to thy father, and beg of him to send me back to my country, for the which he will obtain a reward. The youth rejoiced at my words, and I sat and conversed with him until night, when I spread his bed for him, and covered him, and slept near to his side.

Next morning I arose and warmed a little water, then lifted him gently, so as to awake him, and brought him the warm water wherewith he washed his face. And he said to me, Heaven requite thee for me with every blessing. O youth! by Allah, if I get rid of this danger, I will make my father reward thee and send thee home healthy and wealthy; and if I die, my blessing be upon thee. I answered, May the day never dawn when evil shall betide thee, and may Allah make my last day before thy last day. Then I set before him somewhat of food and water; and I got ready perfumes for fumigating the hall; and he was pleased. Moreover, I made him a Mankalah cloth,[1] and we played and ate sweetmeats, and we played again, and took our pleasure till nightfall, when I rose, and lighted the lamps and set before him somewhat to eat, and sat telling him stories till the hours of darkness were far spent. Then he lay down to rest, and I covered him up and rested also.

I continued to serve him for nine days; and on the tenth day the youth rejoiced at finding himself in safety, and said to me, O my brother, I wish that thou wouldst, in thy kindness, warm for me some water, that I may wash myself and change my clothes; for I have smelt the odor of escape from death, in consequence of thy assistance. With pleasure, I replied; and I arose and warmed the water; after which he entered a place concealed from my view, and, having washed himself and changed his clothes, laid himself upon the mattress to rest after his bath. He then said to me, Cut up for me, O my brother, a watermelon, and mix its juice with some sugar: so I arose, and taking a melon, brought it upon a plate, and said to him, Knowest thou, O my master, where is the knife? See, here it is, he answered, upon the shelf over my

---

[1] A game played on a checked cloth, not on a board like our draughts.

head. I sprang up hastily and took it from its sheath, and as I was drawing back, my foot slipped, as God had decreed, and I fell upon the youth, grasping in my hand the knife, which entered his body, and he died instantly. When I perceived that he was dead, and that I had killed him, I uttered a loud shriek, and beat my face, and rent my clothes, saying, This is, indeed, a calamity! O what a calamity! O my Lord, I implore thy pardon, and declare to Thee my innocence of his death! Would that I had died before him! How long shall I devour trouble after trouble!

With these reflections I ascended the steps, and, having replaced the trap-door, returned to my first station, and looked over the sea, where I saw the vessel that had come before, approaching, and cleaving the waves in its rapid course. Upon this I said within myself, Now will the men come forth from the vessel, and find the youth slain, and they will slay me also: so I climbed into a tree, and, concealing myself among its leaves, sat there till the vessel arrived and cast anchor, when the slaves landed with the old sheikh, the father of the youth, and went to the place, and removed the earth. They were surprised at finding it moist, and, when they had descended the steps, discovered the youth lying on his back, exhibiting a face beaming with beauty, though dead, and clad in white and clean clothing, with the knife remaining in his body. They all wept at the sight, and the father fell down in a swoon, which lasted so long that the slaves thought he was dead. At length, however, he recovered, and came out with the slaves, who had wrapped the body of the youth in his clothes. They then took back all that was in the subterranean dwelling to the vessel, and departed.

I remained, O my mistress, by day hiding myself in a tree, and at night walking about the open part of the island. Thus I continued for the space of two months; and I perceived that, on the western side of the island, the water of the sea every day retired, until, after three months, the land that had been beneath it became dry. Rejoicing at this, and feeling confident now in my escape, I traversed this dry tract, and arrived at an expanse of sand; whereupon I emboldened myself and crossed it. I then saw in the distance an appearance of fire, and advancing toward it, found it to be a palace, overlaid with plates of copper, which, reflecting the rays of the sun, seemed from a distance to be fire : and when I drew near to it, reflecting upon this sight, there approached me an old sheikh, accompanied by ten young men who were all blind of one eye, at which I was extremely surprised. As soon as they saw me, they saluted me, and asked me my story, which I related to them from first to last; and they were filled with wonder. They then conducted me into the palace, where I saw ten benches, upon each of which was a mattress covered with a blue stuff; [1] and each of the young men seated himself upon one of these benches, while the sheikh took his place upon a smaller one; after which they said to me, Sit down, O young man, and ask no question respecting our condition, nor respecting our being blind of one eye. Then the sheikh arose and brought to each of them some food, and the same to me also; and next he brought to each of us some wine : and after we had eaten, we sat drinking together until the time for sleep, when the young men said to the sheikh, Bring to us our accustomed supply :

[1] Dark blue is the color of mourning in the East, as it was in the Roman Republic.

upon which the sheikh arose and entered a closet, from
which he brought upon his head ten covered trays. Placing these upon the floor, he lighted ten candles, and stuck
one of them upon each tray; and, having done this, he
removed the covers, and there appeared beneath them
ashes mixed with pounded charcoal. The young men then
tucked up their sleeves above the elbow, and blackened
their faces, and slapped their cheeks, exclaiming, We were
reposing at our ease, and our impertinent curiosity suffered
us not to remain so! Thus they did until the morning,
when the sheikh brought them some hot water, and they
washed their faces, and put on other clothes.

On witnessing this conduct, my reason was confounded,
my heart was so troubled that I forgot my own misfortunes,
and I asked them the cause of their strange behavior;
upon which they looked toward me, and said, O young
man, ask not respecting that which doth not concern thee,
but be silent; for in silence is security from error. I
remained with them a whole month, during which every
night they did the same; and at length I said to them, I
conjure you by Allah to remove this disquiet from my mind,
and to inform me of the cause of your acting in this manner,
and of your exclaiming, We were reposing at our ease, and
our impertinent curiosity suffered us not to remain so! if
ye inform me not, I will leave you, and go my way; for the
proverb saith, When the eye seeth not, the heart doth not
grieve. On hearing these words, they replied, We have
not concealed this affair from thee but in our concern for
thy welfare, lest thou shouldst become like us, and the
same affliction that hath befallen us happen also to thee.
I said, however, Ye must positively inform me of this matter. We give thee good advice, said they, and do thou

receive it, and ask us not respecting our case; otherwise
thou wilt become blind of one eye, like us : but I still persisted in my request ; whereupon they said, O young man,
if this befall thee, know that thou wilt be banished from
our company. They then all arose, and, taking a ram,
slaughtered and skinned it, and said to me, Take this knife
with thee, and introduce thyself into the skin of the ram,
and we will sew thee up in it, and go away ; whereupon a
bird called the roc[1] will come to thee, and taking thee up
by its talons, will fly away with thee, and set thee down
upon a mountain : then cut open the skin with this knife,
and get out, and the bird will fly away. Thou must arise,
as soon as it hath gone, and journey for half a day, and
thou wilt see before thee a lofty palace, encased with red
gold, set with various precious stones, such as emeralds
and rubies, &c. ; and if thou enter it thy case will be as
ours ; for our entrance into that palace was the cause of
our being blind of one eye ; and if one of us would relate
to thee all that hath befallen him, his story would be too
long for thee to hear.

Then they sewed me up in the skin and entered their
palace ; and soon after, there came an enormous white bird,
which seized me, and flew away with me, and set me down
upon the mountain ; whereupon I cut open the skin and
got out ; and the bird, as soon as it saw me, flew away. I
rose up quickly, and proceeded toward the palace, which
I found to be as they had described it to me ; and when I
had entered it, I beheld, at the upper end of a saloon, forty
young damsels, beautiful as so many moons, and magnifi-

---

[1] This spelling, introduced by Galland, is familiar to all Western readers.
This gigantic bird, the *rukh*, appears in Sindbad's stories, and his egg in
Aladdin.

cently attired, who, as soon as they saw me, exclaimed,
Welcome! welcome! O our master and our lord! We
have been for a month expecting thee. Praise be to God,
who hath blessed us with one who is worthy of us, and one
of whom we are worthy! After having thus greeted me,
they seated me upon a mattress, and said, Thou art from
this day our master and prince, and we are thy handmaids,
and entirely under thy authority. They then brought to
me some refreshments, and, when I had eaten and drunk,
they sat and conversed with me, full of joy and happiness.
So lovely were these ladies, that even a devotee, if he saw
them, would gladly consent to be their servant, and to
comply with all that they would desire. At the approach
of night they all assembled around me, and placed before
me a table of fresh and dried fruits, with other delicacies
that the tongue cannot describe, and wine; and one began
to sing, while another played upon the lute. The wine-
cups circulated among us, and joy overcame me to such a
degree as to obliterate from my mind every earthly care,
and make me exclaim, This is indeed a delightful life!

In this manner I lived with them a whole year; but on
the first day of the new year they seated themselves around
me, and began to weep, and bade me adieu, clinging to my
skirts. What calamity hath befallen you? said I. Ye
have broken my heart. They answered, Would that we
had never known thee; for we have associated with many
men, but have seen none like thee. May God, therefore,
not deprive us of thy company. And they wept afresh.
I said to them, I wish that you would acquaint me with
the cause of this weeping. Thou, they replied, art the
cause; yet now, if thou wilt attend to what we tell thee,
we shall never be parted; but if thou act contrary to it, we

are separated from this time; and our hearts whisper to us that thou wilt not regard our warning. Inform me, said I, and I will attend to your directions; and they replied, If, then, thou wouldst inquire respecting our history, know that we are the daughters of kings : for many years it hath been our custom to assemble here, and every year we absent ourselves during a period of forty days ; then returning, we indulge ourselves for a year in feasting and drinking. This is our usual practice ; and now we fear that thou wilt disregard our directions when we are absent from thee. We deliver to thee the keys of the palace, which are a hundred in number, belonging to a hundred closets. Open each of these, and amuse thyself, and eat and drink, and refresh thyself, excepting the closet that hath a door of red gold ; for if thou open this, the consequence will be a separation between us and thee. We conjure thee, therefore, to observe our direction, and to be patient during this period. Upon hearing this, I swore to them that I would never open the closet to which they alluded; and they departed, urging me to be faithful to my promise.

I remained alone in the palace, and at the approach of evening I opened the first closet, and, entering it, found a mansion like paradise, with a garden containing green trees loaded with ripe fruits, and abounding with singing birds, and watered by copious streams. My heart was soothed by the sight, and I wandered among the trees, scenting the fragrance of the flowers and listening to the warbling of the birds as they sang the praises of the One, the Almighty. After admiring the mingled colors of the apple resembling the hue upon the cheek of a beloved mistress and the sallow countenance of the perplexed and timid lover, the sweet-smelling quince diffusing an odor

like musk and ambergris, and plum shining as the ruby,
I retired from this place, and having locked the door,
opened that of the next closet, within which I beheld a
spacious tract planted with numerous palm-trees, and
watered by a river flowing among rose-trees, and jasmine,
and marjoram, and eglantine, and narcissus, and gilliflower,
the odors of which, diffused in every direction by the wind,
inspired me with the utmost delight.   I locked again the
door of the second closet, and opened that of the third.
Within this I found a large saloon, paved with marbles of
various colors, and with costly minerals and precious gems,
and containing cages constructed of sandal and aloes wood,
with singing birds within them, and others upon the
branches of trees which were planted there.   My heart
was charmed, my trouble was dissipated, and I slept there
until the morning.   I then opened the door of the fourth
closet, and within this door I found a great building, in
which were forty closets with open doors ; and, entering
these, I beheld pearls, and rubies, and chrysolites, and
emeralds, and other precious jewels such as the tongue cannot describe.   I was astonished at the sight, and said,
Such things as these, I imagine, are not found in the
treasury of any king.   I am now the king of my age, and
all these treasures, through the goodness of God, are mine,
together with forty damsels under my authority who have
no man to share them with me.

Thus I continued to amuse myself, passing from one
place to another, until thirty-nine days had elapsed, and I
had opened the doors of all the closets excepting that which
they had forbidden me to open.   My heart was then disturbed by curiosity respecting this hundredth closet, and
the devil, in order to plunge me into misery, induced me

to open it. I had not patience to abstain, though there remained of the appointed period only one day; so I approached the closet and opened the door; and when I had entered, I perceived a fragrant odor, such as I had never before smelled, which intoxicated me so that I fell down insensible, and remained some time in this state; but at length recovering, I fortified my heart, and proceeded. I found the floor overspread with saffron, and the place illuminated by golden lamps and by candles, which diffused the odors of musk and ambergris; and two large perfuming vessels filled with aloes-wood and ambergris, and a perfume compounded with honey, spread fragrance through the whole place. I saw also a black horse, of the hue of the darkest night, before which was a manger of white crystal filled with cleansed sesame, and another similar to it, containing rose-water infused with musk : he was saddled and bridled, and his saddle was of red gold. Wondering at the sight of him, I said within myself, This must be an animal of extraordinary qualities; and, seduced by the devil, I led him out, and mounted him ; but he moved not from his place : I kicked him with my heel, but still he moved not : so I took a stick and struck him with it : and as soon as he felt the blow he uttered a sound like thunder, and, expanding a pair of wings [1] soared with me to an immense height through the air, and then alighted upon the roof of another palace, where he threw me from his back, and, by a violent blow with his tail upon my face, as I sat on the roof, struck out my eye, and left me.

[1] "The Flying Horse is Pegasus," says Captain Burton, "which is a Greek travesty of an Egyptian myth developed in India." But the idea of a winged horse is so simple, that we need not trace it from nation to nation. Winged dragons are to be found fossilized and are probably in all folk-lore, — as winged fishes are in all warm seas.

In this state I descended from the roof, and below I found the one-eyed young men before mentioned, who, as soon as they beheld me, exclaimed, No welcome to thee! Receive me, said I, into your company; but they replied, By Allah, thou shalt not remain with us: so I departed from them, with mournful heart and weeping eye, and, God having decreed me a safe journey hither, I arrived at Bagdad, after I had shaved my beard, and become a mendicant.

THE mistress of the house then looked toward the caliph and Giafar and Mesrour, and said to them, Acquaint me with your histories: upon which Giafar advanced toward her, and related to her the same story that he had told to the portress before they entered: and when she had heard it, she liberated them all. They accordingly departed, and when they had gone out into the street, the caliph inquired of the mendicants whither they were going. They answered that they knew not whither to go: whereupon he desired them to accompany his party; and then said to Giafar, Take them home with thee, and bring them before me to-morrow, and we will see the result. Giafar, therefore, did as he was commanded, and the caliph returned to his palace; but he was unable to sleep during the remainder of the night.

On the following morning he sat upon his throne, and when his courtiers had presented themselves before him, and departed, excepting Giafar, he said to him, Bring before me the three ladies, and the two bitches, and the mendicants. So Giafar arose, and brought them, and, placing the ladies behind the curtains, said to them, We have forgiven you on account of your previous kindness to

us, and because you knew us not ; and now I acquaint you
that ye are in the presence of the fifth of the sons of Abbas,
Haroun Alrashid; therefore relate to him nothing but the
truth.   And when the ladies heard the words which Giafar
addressed to them on the part of the caliph, the eldest of
them advanced, and thus related her story : —

The Story of the First of the Three Ladies of Bagdad.

O PRINCE of the Faithful, my story is wonderful ; for
these two bitches are my sisters, born to my father, but of
another mother ;   and I am the youngest of the three.
After the death of our father, who left us five thousand
pieces of gold, these my two sisters married ; and when
they had resided some time with their husbands, each of
the latter prepared a stock of merchandise, and received
from his wife a thousand pieces of gold, and they all set
forth on a journey together, leaving me here ; but after
they had been absent four years, my sisters' husbands lost
all their property, and abandoned them in a strange land,
and they returned to me in the garb of beggars.   When I
first saw them in this state, I knew them not ; and, as
soon as I recognized them, I exclaimed, How is it that ye
are in this condition ?   O our sister, they answered, thy
inquiry now is of no use ; the pen hath written what God
hath decreed.   I sent them, therefore, to the bath, and
having clad them in new apparel, said to them, O my sisters, ye are my elders, and I am young ; so ye shall be to
me in the places of my father and mother.   The inheri-
tance which I shared with you God hath blessed : partake,

then, of its increase, for my affairs are prosperous ; and I
and ye shall fare alike. I treated them with the utmost
kindness, and during a whole year they remained with me,
and enriched themselves by the money that I had given
them ; but after this period they said to me, It will be
more agreeable to us to marry again, for we can no longer
abstain from doing so. O my sisters, I replied, ye have
seen no happiness in marriage : a good husband in this age
is rarely found ; and ye have already had experience of the
marriage state. They, however, heeded not my words, but
married against my consent : yet I gave them dowries from
my own property, and continued to them my protection.
They went to their husbands, and the latter, after they had
resided with them a short time, defrauded them of all that
they possessed, and, setting forth on a journey, left them
destitute : so again they returned to me, and, in a state of
nudity, implored my forgiveness, saying, Be not angry
with us ; for, though thou art younger than we, thou hast
more mature sense ; and we promise thee that we will never
again mention the subject of marriage. I replied, Ye are
welcome, O my sisters ; for I have no one dearer to me
than yourselves : and I received them and treated them
with every kindness, and we remained happily together for
the space of a year.

   After this I resolved to fit out a vessel for a mercantile
voyage : accordingly, I stocked a large ship with various
goods and necessary provisions, and said to my sisters,
Will ye rather stay at home during my voyage, or will ye
go with me ? to which they answered, We will accompany
thee during the voyage, for we cannot endure to be separated from thee. I therefore took them with me, and we
set sail ; but first I divided my property into two equal

portions; one of which I took with me, and the other, I
concealed, saying within myself, Perhaps some evil accident may happen to the ship, and our lives may be prolonged; in which case, when we return we shall find that
which will be of service to us. We continued our voyage
by day and night, till at length the vessel pursued a wrong
course, and the captain knew not whither to steer. The
ship had entered a different sea from that which we
wished to cross, and for some time we knew it not; but
for ten days we had a pleasant wind, and after this a city
loomed before us in the distance. We asked the captain
what was the name of this city; and he answered, I know
it not; I have never seen it till this day, nor have I ever
before in the course of my life navigated this sea: but as
we have come hither in safety, ye have nothing to do but
to enter this city and land your goods, and, if ye find
opportunity, sell or exchange there; if not, we will rest
there two days, and take in fresh provisions. So we
entered the port of the city, and the captain landed, and
after a while returned to us, saying, Arise, and go up into
the city, and wonder at that which God hath done unto
his creatures, and pray to be preserved from his anger.
And when we had entered the city, we found all its inhabitants converted into black stones.[1] We were amazed at
the sight, and as we walked through the market streets,
finding the merchandise and the gold and silver remaining
in their original state, we rejoiced, and said, This must
have been occasioned by some wonderful circumstance.
We then separated in the street, each of us attracted from
his companions by the wealth and stuffs in the shops.

[1] Captain Burton supposes that the idea of this and similar stone changes
came from the stone-city Petra.

As for myself, I ascended to the citadel, which I found to be a building of admirable construction ; and, entering the king's palace, I found all the vessels of gold and silver remaining in their places, and the king himself seated in the midst of his chamberlains, and viceroys, and viziers, and clad in apparel of astonishing richness. Drawing nearer to him, I perceived that he was sitting upon a throne, adorned with pearls and jewels, every one of the pearls shining like a star : his dress was embroidered with gold, and around him stood fifty mamlouks, attired in silks of various descriptions, and having in their hands drawn swords. Stupefied at this spectacle, I proceeded and entered the saloon of the harem, upon the walls of which were hung silken curtains ; and here I beheld the queen, attired in a dress embroidered with fresh pearls, and having upon her head a diadem adorned with various jewels, and necklaces of different kinds on her neck. All her clothing and ornaments remained as they were at first, though she herself was converted into black stone. Here, also, I found an open door, and, entering it, I saw a flight of seven steps, by which I ascended to an apartment paved with marble, furnished with gold-embroidered carpets, and containing a sofa of alabaster, ornamented with pearls and jewels ; but my eyes were first attracted by a gleam of light, and when I approached the spot whence it proceeded, I found a brilliant jewel of the size of an ostrich's egg, placed upon a small stool, diffusing light like that of a candle. The coverings of the sofa above mentioned were of various kinds of silk, the richness of which would surprise every beholder ; and I looked at them with wonder. In this apartment I likewise observed some lighted candles, and reflected that there must then have been some person

there to light them. I passed thence to another part of
the palace, and continued to explore the different apartments, forgetting myself in the amazement of my mind at
all these strange circumstances, and immersed in thoughts
respecting what I beheld, until the commencement of
night, when I would have departed, but could not find
the door; so I returned to the place in which were the
lighted candles, and there I laid myself upon the sofa, and,
covering myself with the quilt, repeated some words of
the Koran, and endeavored to compose myself to sleep;
but I could not. I continued restless; and at midnight I
heard a recitation of the Koran, performed by a melodious
and soft voice; upon which I arose, and, looking about,
saw a closet with an open door, and I entered it, and
found that it was an oratory, wherein was a prayer-niche
with two wax candles burning and lamps hanging from the
ceiling. In it, also, was spread a prayer-carpet, whereon
sat a youth fair to see; and before him on its stand was
a copy of the Koran, from which he was reading. Wondering that he had escaped the fate of the other inhabitants of the city, I saluted him; and he raised his eyes,
and returned my salutation: and then I said to him, I
conjure thee by the truth of that which thou art reading in
the Book of God that thou answer the question which I
am about to ask thee: whereupon he smiled, and replied,
Do thou first acquaint me with the cause of thine entrance
into this place, and then I will answer thy question: so I
told him my story, and inquired of him the history of this
city. Wait a little, said he; and he closed the Koran,
and, having put it in a bag of satin, seated me by his side.
As I now beheld him, his countenance appeared like the
full moon, and his whole person exhibited such perfect

elegance and loveliness, that a single glance at him drew from me a thousand sighs, and kindled a fire in my heart. I repeated my request that he would give me an account of the city; and, replying, I hear and obey, he thus addressed me.

Know that this city belonged to my father and his family and subjects; and he is the king whom thou hast seen converted into stone : and the queen whom thou hast seen is my mother. They were all Magi, worshipping fire in the place of the Almighty King ; and they swore by the fire, and the light, and the shade, and the heat, and the revolving orb. My father had no son, till, in his declining years, he was blessed with me, whom he reared until I attained to manhood. But, happily for me, there was in our family an old woman, far advanced in age, who was a Mohammedan, believing in God and his apostle in her heart, though she conformed with my family in outward observances : and my father confided in her on account of the faithfulness and modesty that he had observed in her character, and showed her great favor, firmly believing that she held the same faith as himself ; therefore, when I had passed my infancy, he committed me to her care, saying, Take him, and rear him, and instruct him in the ordinances of our faith, and educate him, and serve him in the best manner. The old woman accordingly received me, but took care to instruct me in the Mohammedan faith, teaching me the laws of purification, and the divine ordinances of ablution, together with the forms of prayer ; after which she made me commit to memory the whole of the Koran. She then charged me to keep my faith a secret from my father, lest he should kill me ; and I did so ; and a few days after the old woman died. The inhabitants of the city had now increased in their impiety and arrogance, and in their dereliction of the truth; and while they were in this state, they heard a crier proclaim with a voice like thunder, so as to be audible to both the near and distant, O inhabitants of this city, abstain from the worship of fire, and worship the Almighty King! The people were struck with consternation, and, flocking to my father, the king of the city, said to him, What is this alarming voice which hath astounded us by its terrible sound? but he answered them, Let not the voice terrify you, nor let it turn you from your faith: and their hearts inclined to his words; so they persevered in the worship of fire, and remained obstinate in their impiety during another year, until the return of the period at which they had heard the voice the first time. It was then heard a second time; and again, in the next year, they heard it a third time; but still they persisted in their evil ways, until, drawing down upon themselves the abhorrence and indignation of Heaven, one morning, shortly after daybreak, they were converted into black stones, together with their beasts and all their cattle. Not one of the inhabitants of the city escaped, excepting me; and from the day on which this catastrophe happened I have continued occupied as thou seest, in prayer and fasting, and reading the Koran: but I have become weary of this solitary state, having no one to cheer me with his company.

On hearing these words, I said to him, Wilt thou go with me to the city of Bagdad, and visit its learned men and lawyers, and increase thy knowledge? If so, I will be thy handmaid, though I am the mistress of my family, and have authority over a household of men. I have here a ship laden with merchandise, and destiny hath driven us

to this city, in order that we might become acquainted
with these events : our meeting was predestined. In this
manner I continued to persuade him until he gave his consent. I slept that night at his feet, unconscious of my
state through excessive joy ; and in the morning we arose,
and, entering the treasuries, took away a quantity of the
lighter and most valuable of the articles that they contained, and descended from the citadel into the city, where
we met the slaves and the captain, who were searching for
me. They were rejoiced at seeing me, and to their questions respecting my absence, I replied by informing them
of all that I had seen, and related to them the history of
the young man, and the cause of the transmutation of the
people of the city, and of all that had befallen them, which
filled them with wonder. But when my two sisters saw
me with the young man, they envied me on his account,
and malevolently plotted against me.

We embarked again, and I experienced the utmost happiness, chiefly owing to the company of the young man,
and after we had waited a while till the wind was favorable,
we spread our sails and departed. My sisters sat with me
and the young man ; and, in their conversation with me,
said, O our sister, what dost thou propose to do with this
handsome youth ? I answered, I desire to take him as my
husband ; and, turning to him, and approaching him, I
said, O my master, I wish to make a proposal to thee, and
do not thou oppose it. He replied, I hear and obey ; and
I then looked toward my sisters, and said to them, This
young man is all that I desire, and all the wealth that is
here is yours. Excellent, they replied, is thy determination : yet still they designed evil against me. We continued our voyage with a favorable wind, and, quitting the

sea of peril, entered the sea of security, across which we proceeded for some days, until we drew near to the city of Balsora, the buildings of which loomed before us at the approach of evening ; but as soon as we had fallen asleep, my sisters took us up in our beds, both myself and the young man, and threw us into the sea. The youth, being unable to swim, was drowned : God recorded him among the company of the martyrs ; while I was registered among those whose life was yet to be preserved ; and accordingly, as soon as I awoke and found myself in the sea, the providence of God supplied me with a piece of timber, upon which I placed myself, and the waves cast me upon the shores of an island.

During the remainder of the night I walked along this island, and in the morning I saw a neck of land, bearing the marks of a man's feet, and uniting with the main land. The sun having now risen, I dried my clothes in its rays, and proceeded along the path that I had discovered until I drew near to the shore upon which stands the city, when I beheld a snake approaching me, and followed by a serpent which was endeavoring to destroy it : the tongue of the snake was hanging from its mouth in consequence of excessive fatigue, and it excited my compassion ; so I took up a stone and threw it at the head of the serpent, which instantly died : the snake then extended a pair of wings, and soared aloft into the sky, leaving me in wonder at the sight. At the time of this occurrence I had become so fatigued, that I now laid myself down and slept ; but I awoke after a little while, and found a damsel seated at my feet, and gently rubbing them with her hands ; upon which I immediately sat up, feeling ashamed that she should perform this service for me, and said to her, Who art thou, and what dost thou want? How soon hast thou forgotten me! she exclaimed: I am she to whom thou hast just done a kindness, by killing my enemy: I am the snake whom thou savedst from the serpent; for I am a Fairy, and the serpent was a Genie at enmity with me; and none but thou delivered me from him: therefore, as soon as thou didst this, I flew to the ship from which thy sisters cast thee, and transported all that it contained to thy house: I then sunk it; but as to thy sisters, I transformed them by enchantment into two black bitches; for I knew all that they had done to thee: the young man, however, is drowned. Having thus said, she took me up, and placed me with the two black bitches on the roof of my house: and I found all the treasures that the ship had contained collected in the midst of my house: nothing was lost. She then said to me, I swear by that which was engraved upon the seal of Solomon,[1] that, if thou do not inflict three hundred lashes upon each of these bitches every day, I will come and transform thee in the like manner: so I replied, I hear and obey; and have continued ever since to inflict upon them these stripes, though pitying them while I do so.

The caliph heard this story with astonishment, and then said to the second lady, And what occasioned the stripes of which thou bearest the marks? She answered as follows: —

[1] This was the hundreth name of God, the Hebrew *Shem Hampporash*. It is often alluded to as giving miraculous power to those who know it.

The Story of the Second of the Three Ladies of Bagdad.

O PRINCE of the Faithful, my father, at his death, left considerable property; and soon after that event I married to one of the wealthiest men of the age, who, when I had lived with him a year, died, and I inherited from him eighty thousand pieces of gold, the portion that fell to me according to the law; with part of which I made for myself ten suits of clothing, each of the value of a thousand pieces of gold. And as I was sitting one day, there entered my apartment an old woman, disgustingly ugly, who saluted me, and said, I have an orphan daughter whose marriage I am to celebrate this night, and I would have thee obtain a reward and recompense in heaven by thy being present at her nuptial fête; for she is broken-hearted, having none to befriend her but God, whose name be exalted. She then wept, and kissed my feet; and, being moved with pity and compassion, I assented, upon which she desired me to prepare myself, telling me that she would come at the hour of nightfall and take me; and so saying, she kissed my hand and departed.

I arose immediately, and attired myself, and when I had completed my preparations, the old woman returned, saying, O my mistress, the ladies of the city have arrived, and I have informed them of thy coming, and they are waiting with joy to receive thee: so I put on my outer garments, and, taking my female slaves with me, proceeded until we arrived at a street in which a soft wind was delightfully playing, where we saw a gateway overarched with a marble vault, admirably constructed, forming the entrance to a

palace which rose from the earth to the clouds.   On our
arrival here, the old woman knocked at the door, and,
when it was opened, we entered a carpeted passage, illuminated by lamps and candles, and decorated with jewels
and precious metals.   Through this passage we passed
into a saloon of unequalled magnificence, furnished with
mattresses covered with silk, lighted with hanging lamps
and by candles, and having at its upper end a couch of
alabaster, decorated with pearls and jewels, and canopied
by curtains of satin, from which there came forth a lady
beautiful as the moon, who exclaimed to me, Most welcome art thou, O my sister : thou delightest me by thy
company, and refreshest my heart.   She then sat down
again, and said to me, O my sister, I have a brother who
hath seen thee at a fête : he is a young man, more handsome than myself, and, his heart being violently inflamed
with thy love, he that bribed this old woman to go to thee,
and to employ this artifice in order to obtain for me an
interview with thee.   He desireth to marry thee according
to the ordinance of God and his Apostle, and in that which
is lawful and no disgrace.   When I heard these words, and
saw myself thus confined in the house so that I could not
escape, I replied, I hear and obey : and the lady, rejoicing
at my consent, clapped her hands [1] and opened a door,
upon which there came out from it a young man so sur-
passingly handsome, that my heart immediately inclined
to him.   No sooner had he sat down than the cadi and
four witnesses entered, and saluted us, and proceeded to
perform the ceremony of the marriage contract between
me and the young man ; which having done, they departed ;

[1] Bells are not used in the East, and servants are called by clapping of
hands.

and when they had retired, the young man looked toward me, and said, May our night be blessed. He then informed me that he desired to impose a covenant upon me, and, bringing a copy of the Koran, said, Swear that thou wilt not indulge a preference, nor at all incline, to any man but me: and when I had sworn to this effect, he rejoiced exceedingly, and embraced me; and the love of him took entire possession of my heart.

We lived together in the utmost happiness for the space of a month, after which I begged that he would allow me to go to the bazar, in order to purchase some stuffs for dress, and, having obtained his permission, went thither in company with the old woman,[1] and seated myself at the shop of a young merchant with whom she was acquainted, and whose father, as she informed me, had died, and left him great wealth. She desired him to show me his most costly stuffs; and while he was occupied in doing so, she began to utter various flattering expressions in praise of him; but I said to her, We have no concern with the praises that thou bestowest upon him; we desire only to make our purchase, and to return home. Meanwhile he produced to us what we wanted, and we handed him the money; he refused, however, to take it, saying, It is an offering of hospitality to you for your visit this day: whereupon I said to the old woman, If he will not take the money, return to him his stuff. But he would not receive it again, and exclaimed, By Allah, I will take nothing from you: all this is a present from me for a single kiss, which I shall value more than the entire contents of my shop. What will a kiss profit thee? asked the old woman. Then

[1] In the East no young woman, married or single, may walk in the street alone.

turning to me, she said, O my daughter, thou hast heard
what the youth hath said : no harm will befall thee if he
give thee a kiss, and thou shalt take what thou wantest.
Dost thou not know, said I, that I have taken an oath?
She answered, Let him kiss thee, then, without thy speaking, and so it will be of no consequence to thee, and thou
shalt take back thy money. Thus she continued to palliate
the matter until I put my head (as it were) into the bag,
and consented : so I covered my eyes and held the edge
of my veil in such a manner as to prevent the passengers
from seeing me, whereupon he put his mouth to my cheek
beneath the veil ; but instead of merely kissing me, he
lacerated my cheek by a violent bite. I fell into a swoon
from the pain, and the old woman laid me on her lap till I
recovered, when I found the shop closed, and the old
woman uttering expressions of grief, and saying, What God
hath averted would have been a greater calamity ; let us
return home, and do thou feign to be ill, and I will come
to thee and apply a remedy that shall cure the wound, and
thou wilt quickly be restored.

After remaining there some time longer, I arose, and, in
a state of great uneasiness and fear, returned to the house,
and professed myself unwell ; upon which my husband
came in to me, and said, What hath befallen thee, O my
mistress, during this excursion? I answered, I am not
well. And what is this wound, said he, that is upon thy
cheek, and in the soft part ? I answered, When I asked
thy permission, and went out to-day to purchase some stuff
for dress, a camel loaded with fire-wood drove against me
in the crowd, and tore my veil, and wounded my cheek, as
thou seest ; for the streets of this city are narrow. To-
morrow, then, he exclaimed, I will go to the governor, and

make a complaint to him, and he shall hang every seller of fire-wood in the city. By Allah, said I, burden not thyself by any injury to any one ; for the truth is, that I was riding upon an ass, which took fright with me, and I fell upon the ground, and a stick lacerated my cheek. If it be so, then, he replied, I will go to-morrow to Giafar the Barmecide, and relate the matter to him, and he shall kill every ass-driver in this city. Wilt thou, said I, kill all those men on my account, when this which befell me was decreed by God ? Undoubtedly, he answered ; and, so saying, he seized me violently, and then sprang up and uttered a loud cry, upon which the door opened, and there came forth from it seven black slaves, who dragged me from my bed, and threw me down in the middle of the apartment ; whereupon he ordered one of them to hold me by the shoulders and to sit upon my head ; and another to sit upon my knees and to hold my feet. A third then came, with a sword in his hand, and said, O my lord, shall I strike her with the sword, and cleave her in twain, that each of these may take a half and throw it into the Tigris [1] for the fish to devour ? For such is the punishment of her who is unfaithful to her oath and to the laws of love. My husband answered, Strike her, O Saad ; and the slave, with the drawn sword in his hand, said, Repeat the profession of the faith, and reflect what thou wouldst have to be done, that thou mayest give thy testamentary directions, for this. is the end of thy life. Good slave, I replied, release me for a while that I may do so ; and I raised my head, and, weeping as I spoke, addressed my husband with these verses :

[1] Arabic, the *Hiddekex Dajlah.* Cf. the Book of Genesis.

You render me lovelorn, and remain at ease. You make my wounded
    eyelids to be restless, and you sleep.
Your abode is between my heart and my eyes; and my heart will not
    relinquish you, nor my tears conceal my passion.
You made, a covenant with me that you would remain faithful; but
    when you had got possession of my heart you deceived me.
Will you not pity my love for you and my moaning? Have you your-
    self been secure from misfortunes?
I conjure you, by Allah, if I die, that you write upon my tombstone,
    This was a slave of love.
That, perchance, some mourner who hath felt the same flame may pass
    by the lover's grave and pity her.

But on hearing these verses, and witnessing my weeping,
he became more incensed, and replied in the words of this
couplet:

I reject not the beloved of my heart from weariness; her own guilty
    conduct is the cause of her punishment.
She desired that another should share with me her love; but the faith
    of my heart inclineth not to partnership.

I continued to weep, and to endeavor to excite his compassion, saying within myself, I will humble me before
him, and address him with soft words, that he at least may
refrain from killing me, though he take all that I possess;
but he cried out to the slave, Cleave her in twain; for she
is no longer of any value to us. So the slave approached
me, and I now felt assured of my death, and committed
myself to God; but suddenly the old woman came and
threw herself at my husband's feet, and kissing them, exclaimed, O my son, by the care with which I nursed thee,
I conjure thee to pardon this damsel, for she hath committed no offence that deserveth such a punishment: thou
art young, and I fear the effect of the imprecations that
she may utter against thee: and after she had thus ad-

dressed him, she wept, and continued to importune him, until, at length, he said, I pardon her, but must cause her to bear upon her person such marks of her offence as shall last for the remainder of her life. So saying, he commanded the slaves to strip off my vest, and, taking a stick cut from a quince-tree, he beat me upon my back and my sides until I became insensible from the violence of the blows, and despaired of my life. He then ordered the slave to take me away as soon as it was night, accompanied by the old woman, and to throw me into my house in which I formerly resided. They accordingly executed their lord's commands, and when they had deposited me in my house, I applied myself to the healing of my wounds; but, after I had cured myself, my sides still bore the appearance of having been beaten with sticks. I continued to apply remedies for four months before I was restored, and then repaired to view the house in which this event had happened; but I found it reduced to ruin, and the whole street pulled down; the site of the house I found occupied by mounds of rubbish, and I knew not the cause.

Under these circumstances, I went to reside with this my sister, who is of the same father as myself, and I found with her these two bitches. Having saluted her, I informed her of all that had befallen me; to which she replied, Who is secure from the afflictions of fortune? Praise be to God, who terminated the affair with safety to thy life! She then related to me her own story and that of her sisters, and I remained with her, and neither of us ever mentioned the subject of marriage. Afterward we were joined by this our other sister, the cateress, who every day goes out to purchase for us whatever we happen to want.

Conclusion of the Story of the Ladies of Bagdad.

THE caliph was astonished at this story, and ordered it to be recorded in a book as an authentic history, and deposited the book in his library. He then said to the first lady, Knowest thou where the Fairy who enchanted thy sister is to be found? She answered, O Prince of the Faithful, she gave me a lock of her hair, and said, When thou desirest my presence, burn a few of these hairs, and I will be with thee quickly, though I should be beyond Mount Caucasus. Bring then the hair, said the caliph. The lady, therefore, produced it; and the caliph taking it, burned a portion of it, and, when the odor had diffused itself, the palace shook, and they heard a sound of thunder, and lo, the Fairy appeared before them. She was a Mohammedan, and therefore greeted the caliph by saying, Peace be on thee, O caliph of God! to which he replied, On you be peace, and the mercy of God, and his blessings! She then said, Know that this lady hath conferred on me a benefit for which I am unable to requite her; for she rescued me from death by killing my enemy; and I, having seen what her sisters had done to her, determined to take vengeance upon them; therefore I transformed them by enchantment into two bitches; and, indeed, I had wished rather to kill them, fearing lest they should trouble her; but now, if thou desire their restoration, O Prince of the Faithful, I will restore them, as a favor to thee and to her; for I am one of the true believers. Do so, said the caliph; and then we will enter upon the consideration of the affair of the lady who hath been beaten, and examine her case, and if her veracity be established, I will take vengeance for

her upon him who hath oppressed her.   The Fairy replied,
O Prince of the Faithful, I will guide thee to the discovery
of him who acted thus to this lady, and oppressed her, and
took her property : he is thy nearest relation.   She then
took a cup of water, and having pronounced a spell over it,
sprinkled the faces of the two bitches, saying, Be restored
to your original human forms! whereupon they became
again two young ladies.   Extolled be the perfection of
their Creator! Having done this, the Fairy said, O Prince
of the Faithful, he who beat the lady is thy son Amin, who
had heard of her beauty and loveliness : and she proceeded
to relate what had happened.   The caliph was astonished,
and exclaimed, Praise be to God for the restoration of these
two bitches, which hath been effected through my means!
and immediately he summoned before him his son Amin,
brother of Al-Maiamun,[1] and inquired of him the history of
the lady ; and he related to him the truth.   He then sent
for cadies and witnesses, and the first lady and her two sisters who had been transformed into bitches he married to
the three mendicants who had related that they were the
sons of kings ; and these he made chamberlains of his
court, appointing them all that they required, and allotting
them apartments in the palace of Bagdad.   The lady who
had been beaten he restored to his son Amin, giving her a
large property, and ordering that the house should be re-
built in a more handsome style.   Lastly, the lady cateress
he took as his own wife ; he admitted her at once to his
own apartment, and, on the following day, he appointed
for her a separate lodging for herself, with female slaves
to wait upon her : he also allotted to her a regular income;
and afterward built for her a palace.

---

[1] Both these sons are historical characters; which we can hardly suppose
this wife to be.   The sons both became caliphs.

THE STORY OF THE HUMPBACK.[1]

THERE was in ancient times, in the city of Balsora, a
tailor who enjoyed an ample income, and was fond
of sport and merriment. He was in the habit of going
out occasionally with his wife, that they might amuse themselves with strange and diverting scenes; and one day they
went forth in the afternoon, and, returning home in the
evening, met a humpbacked man, whose aspect was such
as to excite laughter in the angry, and to dispel anxiety
and grief: so they approached him to enjoy the pleasure
of gazing at him, and invited him to return with them to
their house, and to join with them in a carousal that night.

He assented to their proposal; and after he had gone with
them to the house, the tailor went out to the market, night
having then approached. He bought some fried fish, and
bread, and limes, and sweetmeats, and, returning with them,
placed the fish before the humpback; and they sat down
to eat; and the tailor's wife took a large piece of fish and
crammed the humpback with it, and, closing his mouth
with her hand, said, By Allah, thou shalt not swallow it
but by gulping it at once, and I will not give thee time to
chew it. He therefore swallowed it; but it contained a
large and sharp bone, which stuck across in his throat, his
destiny having so determined, and he expired. The tailor

---

[1] This amusing story has been widely imitated, in various nations.

exclaimed, There is no strength nor power but in God, the High, the Great! Alas, that this poor creature should not have died but in this manner by our hands! Wherefore this idling? exclaimed the woman. And what can I do? asked her husband. Arise, she answered, and take him in thy bosom, and cover him with a silk napkin: I will go out first, and do thou follow me, this very night, and say, This is my son, and this is his mother; and we are going to convey him to the physician, that he may give him some medicine.

No sooner had the·tailor heard these words than he arose and took the humpback in his bosom. His wife, accompanying him, exclaimed, O my child! may Allah preserve thee! Where is the part in which thou feelest pain; and where hath this small-pox[1] attacked thee? So every one who saw them said, They are conveying a child smitten with the small-pox. Thus they proceeded, inquiring, as they went, for the abode of the physician; and the people directed them to the house of a physician who was a Jew; and they knocked at the door, and there came down to them a black slave-girl, who opened the door, and beheld a man carrying (as she imagined) a child, and attended by its mother; and she said, What is your business? We have a child here, answered the tailor's wife, and we want the physician to see him: take, then, this quarter of a piece of gold, and give it to thy master, and let him come down and see my son; for he is ill. The girl, therefore, went up, and the tailor's wife, entering the vestibule, said to her husband, Leave the humpback here, and let us take our-

---

[1] Small-pox: *judri*, "small stones," from the hard, gravelly feeling of the pustules. — *Rodwell*, p. 20. The disease is supposed to have originated in Central Africa, and to have passed to Arabia in Mohammed's time.

selves away. And the tailor, accordingly, set him up against the wall, and went out with his wife.

The slave-girl, meanwhile, went in to the Jew, and said to him, Below in the house is a sick person, with a woman and a man; and they have given me a quarter of a piece of gold for thee, that thou mayest prescribe for them what may suit his case. And when the Jew saw the quarter of a piece of gold, he rejoiced, and, arising in haste, went down in the dark; and in doing so, his foot struck against the lifeless humpback. O Ezra! he exclaimed; O heavens and the ten commandments! O Aaron, and Joshua, son of Nun! It seemeth that I have stumbled against this sick person, and he hath fallen down the stairs and died! And how shall I go forth with one killed from my house? O Ezra's ass! He then raised him, and took him up from the court of the house to his wife, and acquainted her with the accident. And why sittest thou here idle? said she; for if thou remain thus until daybreak our lives will be lost: let me and thee, then, take him up to the terrace, and throw him into the house of our neighbor, the Mohammedan; for he is the steward of the sultan's kitchen, and often do the cats come to his house, and eat of the food which they find there; as do the mice too: and if he remain there for a night, the dogs will come down to him from the terraces and eat him up entirely. So the Jew and his wife went up, carrying the humpback, and let him down by his hands and feet to the pavement, placing him against the wall; which having done, they descended.

Not long had the humpback been thus deposited when the steward returned to his house and opened the door, and, going up with a lighted candle in his hand, found a son of Adam standing in the corner next the kitchen;

upon which he exclaimed, What is this ? By Allah, the
thief that hath stolen our goods is none other than a son
of Adam, who taketh what he findeth of flesh or grease,
even though I keep it concealed from the cats and the
dogs ; and if I killed all the cats and dogs of the quarter it
would be of no use ; for he cometh down from the terraces !
and so saying, he took up a great mallet and struck him
with it, and then, drawing close to him, gave him a second
blow with it upon the chest, when the humpback fell down,
and he found that he was dead ; whereupon he grieved,
and said, There is no strength nor power but in God !
And he feared for himself, and exclaimed, Curse upon the
grease and the flesh, and upon this night, in which the
destiny of this man hath been accomplished by my hand !
Then, looking upon him, and perceiving that he was a
humpback,[1] he said, Is it not enough that thou art humpbacked, but must thou also be a robber, and steal the flesh
and the grease ? O Protector, cover me with thy gracious
shelter ! And he lifted him upon his shoulders, and
descended and went forth from his house, toward the close
of the night, and stopped not until he had conveyed him
to the commencement of the market street, where he
placed him upon his feet by the side of a shop at the
entrance of a lane, and there left him and retired.

Soon after there came a Christian, the sultan's broker,
who, in a state of intoxication, had come forth to visit the
bath ; and he advanced, staggering, until he drew near to
the humpback, when he turned his eyes and beheld one
standing by him. Now some persons had snatched off his

---

[1] In the East and in Southern Europe a humpbacked person is looked on
with aversion. Burton says it is because they have sharper wits than their
neighbors.

turban early in the night, and when he saw the humpback
standing there, he concluded that he intended to do the
same ; so he clinched his fist and struck him on the neck.
Down fell the humpback upon the ground, and the Christian called out to the watchman of the market, while, still
in the excess of his intoxication, he continued beating the
humpback, and attempting to throttle him. As he was
thus employed, the watchman came, and finding the
Christian kneeling upon the Mohammedan and beating
him, said, Arise, and quit him ! He arose, therefore, and
the watchman, approaching the humpback, saw that he
was dead, and exclaimed, How is it that the Christian
dareth to kill the Mohammedan ? Then seizing the
Christian, he bound his hands behind him, and took him
to the house of the judge ; the Christian saying within
himself, O heavens, O Virgin ! how have I killed this man ?
And how quickly did he die from a blow of the hand !
Intoxication had departed, and reflection had come.

The humpback and the Christian passed the remainder
of the night in the house of the judge, and the judge
ordered the executioner to proclaim the Christian's crime,
and set up a gallows, and stationed him beneath it. The
executioner then came and threw the rope round his neck,
and was about to hang him, when the sultan's steward
pushed through the crowd, seeing the Christian standing
beneath the gallows, and the people made way for him,
and he said to the executioner, Do it not ; for it was I who
killed him. Wherefore didst thou kill him ? said the judge.
He answered, I went into my house last night, and saw
that he had descended from the terrace and stolen my goods ;
so I struck him with a mallet upon his chest, and he died,
and I carried him out, and conveyed him to the market

street, where I set him up in such a place, at the entrance
of such a lane. Is it not enough for me to have killed a
Mohammedan, that a Christian should be killed on my
account? Hang, then, none but me. The judge, therefore, when he heard these words, liberated the Christian
broker, and said to the executioner, Hang this man, on the
ground of his confession. And he took off the rope from
,the neck of the Christian and put it round the neck of
the steward, and, having stationed him beneath the gallows,
was about to hang him, when the Jewish physician pushed
through the crowd, and called out to the executioner, saying to him, Do it not ; for none killed him but I ; and the
case was this : he came to my house to be cured of a
disease, and as I descended to him I struck against him
with my foot, and he died ; kill not the steward, therefore,
but kill me. So the judge gave orders to hang the Jewish
physician ; and the executioner took off the rope from the
steward's neck and put it round the neck of the Jew. But,
lo, the tailor came, and, forcing his way among the people,
said to the executioner, Do it not ; for none killed him but
I ; and it happened thus : I was out amusing myself during the day, and as I was returning at the commencement
of the night I met this humpback in a state of intoxication,
with a tambourine, and singing merrily ; and I stopped to
divert myself by looking at him, and took him to my house.
I then bought some fish, and we sat down to eat, and my
wife took a piece of fish and a morsel of bread, and crammed
them into his mouth, and he was choked, and instantly
died. Then I and my wife took him to the house of the
Jew, and the girl came down and opened the door, and while
she went up to her master, I set up the humpback by the
stairs, and went away with my wife : so when the Jew

came down and stumbled against him, he thought that he
had killed him. And he said to the Jew, Is this true?
He answered, Yes. The tailor then, looking toward the
judge, said to him, Liberate the Jew, and hang me. And
when the judge heard this, he was astonished at the case
of the humpback, and said, Verily this is an event that
should be recorded in books! And he said to the executioner, Liberate the Jew, and hang the tailor on account
of his own confession. So the executioner led him forward,
saying, Dost thou put forward this and take back that;
and shall we not hang one? And he put the rope round
the neck of the tailor.

Now the humpback was the sultan's buffoon, and the
sultan could not bear him to be out of his sight; and when
the humpback had got drunk, and been absent that night
and the next day until noon, the king inquired respecting
him of some of his attendants; and they answered him, O
our lord, the judge hath taken him forth dead, and gave
orders to hang the person who killed him, and there came
a second and a third person, each saying, None killed him
but I : and describing to the judge the cause of his killing
him. When the king, therefore, heard this, he called out
to the chamberlain, and said to him, Go down to the judge,
and bring them all hither before me. So the chamberlain
went down, and found that the executioner had almost put
to death the tailor, and he called out to him, saying, Do it
not : and informed the judge that the case had been re-
ported to the king. And he took him, and the humpback
borne with him, and the tailor, and the Jew, and the Christian, and the steward, and went up with them all to the
king; and when the judge came into the presence of the
king, he kissed the ground, and related to him all that

had happened. And the king was astonished and was moved with merriment, at hearing this tale ; and he commanded that it should be written in letters of gold. He then said to those who were present, Have ye ever heard anything like the story of this humpback ? And upon this the Christian advanced, and said, O king of the age, if thou permit me, I will relate to thee an event that hath occurred to me more wonderful, and strange, and exciting, than the story of the humpback. Tell us, then, thy story, said the king. And the Christian related as follows : —

The Story told by the Christian Broker.

Know, O king of the age, that I came to this country with merchandise, and destiny stayed me among your people. I was born in Cairo, and am one of its Copts, and there I was brought up. My father was a broker ; and when I had attained to manhood, he died, and I succeeded to his business ; and as I was sitting one day, lo, a young man of most handsome aspect, and clad in a dress of the richest description, came to me, riding upon an ass,[1] and when he saw me he saluted me ; whereupon I rose to him, to pay him honor, and he produced a handkerchief containing some sesame, and said, What is the value of an ardebb[2] of this ? I answered him, A hundred pieces of silver.[3] And he said to me, Take the carriers and the measurers, and repair to the Khan of Jawali, near the Victory Gate; there wilt thou find me. And he left me and went his way,

---

[1] The reader will remember how often characters in the Bible are spoken of as riding on asses. They are still much used in the East for the saddle.

[2] A measure of about five bushels.

[3] Those are *dirhems*, or drachms, equal to about sixpence.

after having given me the handkerchief with the sample of the sesame. So I went about to the purchasers; and the price of each ardebb amounted to a hundred and twenty pieces of silver; and I took with me four carriers, and went to him. I found him waiting my arrival; and when he saw me he rose and opened a magazine, and we measured its contents, and the whole amounted to fifty ardebbs. The young man then said, Thou shalt have for every ardebb ten pieces of silver as brokerage; and do thou receive the price and keep it in thy care: the whole sum will be five thousand, and thy share of it five hundred; so there will remain for me four thousand and five hundred; and when I shall have finished the sale of the goods contained in my storerooms, I will come to thee and receive it. I replied, It shall be as thou desirest. And I kissed his hand and left him. Thus there accrued to me on that day a thousand pieces of silver, besides my brokerage.

He was absent from me a month, at the expiration of which he came again, and said to me, Where is the money? I rose and invoked blessings on him, and said, O my lord, wilt thou not take thy money? Whence the hurry?[1] said he, keep it until I come to thee to receive it. And I remained expecting him; but he was absent from me another month; after which he came again, and said, Where is the money? Whereupon I arose and saluted him, and said to him, Wilt thou eat something with us? He, however, declined, and said, Keep the money until I shall have gone and returned to receive it from thee. He then departed; and I arose and prepared for him the money, and sat expecting him; but again he absented him-

---

[1] The reference is to an Arabic proverb: "Patience is from the Protector (Allah); hurry is from Hell," — a proverb which most Arabs live up to.

self from me for a month, and then came and said, After
this day I will receive it from thee. And he departed, and
I made ready the money for him as before, and sat waiting
his return. Again, however, he remained a month absent
from me, and I said within myself, Verily this young man
is endowed with consummate liberality! After the month
he came, attired in rich clothing, and resembling the full
moon, appearing as if he had just come out of the bath,
with red cheek and fair forehead, and a mole like a globule
of ambergris. When I beheld him, I kissed his hand, and
invoked a blessing upon him, and said to him, O my master, wilt thou not take thy money? Have patience with
me, he answered, until I shall have transacted all my affairs,
after which I will receive it from thee. And so saying, he
departed; and I said within myself, By Allah, when he
cometh I will entertain him as a guest, on account of the
profit which I have derived from his money; for great
wealth hath accrued to me from it.

At the close of the year he returned, clad in a dress
richer than the former; and I swore to him that he should
alight to be my guest. On the condition, he replied, that
thou expend nothing of my money that is in thy possession.
I said, Well; and having seated him, prepared what was
requisite of meats and drinks and other provisions, and
placed them before him, saying, In the name of Allah!
And he drew near to the table, and put forth his left hand,
and thus ate with me: so I was surprised at him; and when
we had finished he washed his hand, and I gave him a napkin with which to wipe it. We then sat down to converse,
and I said, O my master, dispel a trouble from my mind.
Wherefore didst thou eat with thy left hand? Probably
something paineth thee in thy right hand? On hearing

these words, he stretched forth his arm from his sleeve, and behold, it was maimed — an arm without a hand! And I wondered at this; but he said to me, Wonder not, nor say in thy heart that I ate with thee with my left hand from a motive of self-conceit; for rather to be wondered at is the cause of the cutting off of my right hand. And what, said I, was the cause of it? He answered thus:

Know that I am from Bagdad: my father was one of the chief people of that city; and when I had attained the age of manhood, I heard the wanderers, and travellers, and merchants conversing respecting the land of Egypt, and their words remained in my heart until my father died, when I took large sums of money, and prepared merchandise consisting of the stuffs of Bagdad and of Mosul, and similar precious goods, and, having packed them up, journeyed from Bagdad; and God decreed me safety until I entered this your city.

I entered Cairo, continued the young man, and deposited the stuffs in the Khan of Mesrour, and, having unbound my packages and put them in the magazines, gave to the servant some money to buy for us something to eat, after which I slept a little; and when I arose, I went to the street between the palaces. I then returned and passed the night; and in the morning following, I opened a bale of stuff, and said within myself, I will arise, and go through some of the market streets, and see the state of the mart. So I took some stuff, and made some of my servants carry it, and proceeded until I arrived at the Bezestein of Chaharkass, where the brokers came to me, having heard of my arrival, and took from me the stuff, and cried it about for sale; but the price bidden amounted not to the prime cost. And upon this the sheikh of the brokers said to me,

O my master, I know a plan by which thou mayest profit ;
and it is this : that thou do as other merchants, and sell
thy merchandise upon credit for a certain period, employ-
ing a scrivener, and a witness, and a money-changer, and
receive a portion of the profits every Thursday and Monday ; so shalt thou make of every piece of silver two ; and
besides that, thou wilt be able to enjoy the amusements
afforded by Egypt and its Nile. The advice is judicious,
I replied ; and accordingly I took the brokers with me to
the khan, and they conveyed the stuffs to the Bezestein,
where I sold it to the merchants, writing a bond in their
names, which I committed to the money-changer, and taking from him a corresponding bond. I then returned to
the khan, and remained there some days ; and every day I
took for my breakfast a cup of wine, and mutton and sweetmeats prepared for me, until the month in which I became
entitled to the receipt of the profits, when I seated myself
every Thursday and Monday at the shops of the merchants,
and the money-changer went with the scrivener and brought
me the money.

Thus did I until one day I went to the bath and returned
to the khan, and entering my lodging, took for my breakfast a cup of wine, and then slept ; and when I awoke I ate
a fowl, and perfumed myself with essence, and repaired to
the shop of a merchant named Bedreddin the Gardener,
who, when he saw me, welcomed me, and conversed with
me a while in his shop ; and as we were thus engaged, lo,
a female came and seated herself by my side. She wore a
headkerchief inclined on one side, and the odors of sweet
perfumes were diffused from her, and she captivated my
reason by her beauty and loveliness as she raised her izar
and I beheld her black eyes. She saluted Bedreddin, and

he returned her salutation, and stood conversing with her; and when I heard her speech, love for her took entire possession of my heart. She then said to Bedreddin, Hast thou a piece of stuff woven with pure gold thread? And he produced to her a piece; and she said, May I take it and go, and then send thee the price? But he answered, It is impossible, O my mistress; for this is the owner of the stuff, and I owe him a portion of the profit. Woe to thee! said she; it is my custom to take of thee each piece of stuff for a considerable sum of money, giving thee a gain beyond‘ thy‘ wish, and then to send thee the price. Yes, he rejoined, but I am in absolute want of the price this day. And upon this she took the piece and threw it back to him upon his breast, saying, Verily your class knows not how to respect any person's rank! And she arose and turned away. I felt then as if my soul went with her, and, rising upon my feet, I said to her, O my mistress, kindly bestow a look upon me, and retrace thine honored steps. And she returned, and smiled and said, For thy sake I return. And she sat opposite me upon the seat of the shop; and I said to Bedreddin, What is the price that thou hast agreed to give for this piece? He answered, Eleven hundred pieces of silver. And I said to him, Thy profit shall be a hundred pieces of silver: give me then a paper, and I will write for thee the price upon it. I then took the piece of stuff from him, and wrote upon the paper with my own hand, and gave the piece of stuff to the lady, saying to her, Take it and go; and if thou wilt, bring the price to me in the market; or, if thou wilt, it shall be my present to thee. She replied, God recompense thee, and bless thee with my property, and make thee my husband: and may God accept this prayer! O my mistress, said I, let this piece of stuff be thine, and

another like it, and permit me to see thy face.   And upon
this she raised her veil ; and when I beheld her face, the
sight drew from me a thousand sighs, and my heart was
entangled by her love, so that I no longer remained master
of my reason.   She then lowered the veil again, and took
the piece of stuff, saying, O my master, leave me not desolate.   So she departed, while I continued sitting in the
market street until past the hour of afternoon prayer, with
wandering mind, overpowered by love.   In the excess of
my passion, before I rose I asked the merchant respecting
her ; and he answered me, She is a rich lady, the daughter
of a deceased emir, who left her great property.

I then took leave of him and returned to the khan, and
the supper was placed before me ; but reflecting upon her,
I could eat nothing.   I laid myself down to rest, but sleep
came not to me, and I remained awake until the morning,
when I arose and put on a suit of clothing different from
that which I had worn the day before ; and, having drunk a
cup of wine, and eaten a few morsels as my breakfast, repaired again to the shop of the merchant, and saluted him,
and sat down with him.   The lady soon came, wearing a
dress more rich than the former, and attended by a slave-
girl ; and she seated herself, and saluted me instead of Bedreddin, and said, with an eloquent tongue, which I had
never heard surpassed in softness or sweetness, Send with
me some one to receive the twelve hundred pieces of
silver, the price of the piece of stuff.   Wherefore, said I,
this haste ![1]   She replied, May we never lose thee !   And
she handed to me the price ; and I sat conversing with her,
and made a sign to her, which she understood, intimating
my wish to visit her ; whereupon she arose in haste, ex-

[1] The same proverb is referred to as before.

pressing displeasure at my hint. My heart clung to her, and I followed in the direction of her steps through the market street; and lo, a slave-girl came to me, and said, O my master, answer the summons of my mistress. Wondering at this, I said, No one here knoweth me. How soon, she rejoined, hast thou forgotten her! My mistress is she who was to-day at the shop of the merchant Bedreddin. So I went with her until we arrived at the money-changer's; and when her mistress, who was there, beheld me, she drew me to her side, and said, O my beloved, thou hast wounded my heart, and love of thee hath taken possession of it; and, from the time that I first saw thee, neither sleep, nor food, nor drink hath been pleasant to me. I replied, And more than that do I feel; and the state in which I am needs no complaint to testify it. Then shall I visit thee, O my beloved, she asked, or wilt thou come to me? for our marriage must be a secret. I am a stranger, I answered, and have no place of reception but the khan; therefore, if thou wilt kindly permit me to go to thine abode, the pleasure will be perfect. Well, she replied; but to-night is the eve of Friday, and let nothing be done till to-morrow, when, after thou hast joined in the prayers, do thou mount thine ass, and inquire for the Habbaniah[1]; and when thou hast arrived there, ask for the house called the Mansion of Barakat the Chief, known by the surname of Abou-Shamah; for there do I reside; and delay not; for I shall be anxiously expecting thee.

On hearing this, I rejoiced exceedingly, and we parted; and I returned to the khan in which I lodged. I passed the whole night sleepless, and was scarcely sure that the daybreak had appeared when I arose and changed my

---

[1] Name of a street in Cairo.

clothes, and, having perfumed myself with essences and
sweet scents, took with me fifty pieces of gold in a handkerchief, and walked from the Khan of Mesrour to the
Gate of Zawili, where I mounted an ass, and said to its
owner, Go with me to the Habbaniah. And in less than
the twinkling of an eye he set off, and soon he stopped at
a by-street called Darb El Munakiri, when I said to him,
Enter the street, and inquire for the mansion of the chief.
He was absent but a little while, and, returning, said,
Alight. Walk on before me, said I, to the house. And
he went on until he had led me to the house; whereupon
I said to him, To-morrow come to me hither to convey me
back. In the name of Allah, he replied : and I handed to
him a quarter of a piece of gold, and he took it and departed. I then knocked at the door, and there came forth
to me two young virgins in whom the forms of womanhood
had just developed themselves, resembling two moons, and
they said, Enter ; for our mistress is expecting thee, and
she hath not slept last night from her excessive love for
thee. I entered an upper saloon with seven doors ; around
it were latticed windows looking upon a garden, in which
were fruits of every kind, and running streams and singing
birds : it was plastered with royal gypsum, in which a man
might see his face reflected; its roof was ornamented with
gilding, and surrounded by inscriptions [1] in letters of gold
upon a ground of ultramarine ; it comprised a variety of
beauties, and shone in the eyes of beholders ; the pavement was of colored marbles, having in the midst of it a
fountain, with four snakes of red gold casting forth water
from their mouths like pearls and jewels at the corners of

[1] The walls of houses in Damascus are thus adorned. So is the palace of
the Alhambra.

the pool; and it was furnished with carpets of colored silk, and mattresses.

Having entered, I seated myself; and scarcely had I done so when the lady approached me. She wore a crown set with pearls and jewels, and her hands and feet were stained with henna, and her bosom ornamented with gold. As soon as she beheld me she smiled in my face, and embraced me, saying, Is it true that thou hast come to me, or is this a dream? I am thy slave, I answered; and she said, Thou art welcome. Verily, from the time when I first saw thee, neither sleep hath been sweet to me nor hath food been pleasant! In such case have *I* been, I replied; and we sat down to converse; but I hung down my head towards the ground in bashfulness : and not long had I thus remained, when a repast was placed before me, consisting of the most exquisite dishes, as fritters soaked in honey, and hashes, and fowls stuffed with sugar and pistachio nuts. I ate with her until we were satisfied, when they brought the basin and ewer, and I washed my hands ; after which we perfumed ourselves with rose-water infused with musk, and we sat down again to converse, expressing to each other our mutual passion; and her love took such possession of me that all the wealth I possessed seemed worthless in comparison. In this manner we continued to enjoy ourselves until, night approaching, the female slave brought supper and wine, a complete service, and we drank until midnight. When morning came I arose, and, having thrown to her the handkerchief containing the pieces of gold, I took leave of her and went out ; but as I did so she wept, and said, O my master, when shall I see again this lovely face? I answered her, I will be with thee at the commencement of the night. And when I went forth I found the owner of the ass, who had brought me the day before, waiting for me at the door; and I mounted, and returned with him to the Khan of Mesrour, where I alighted, and gave to him half a piece of gold, saying to him, Come hither at sunset. He replied, On the head be thy command.

I entered the khan and ate my breakfast, and then went forth to collect the price of my stuffs; after which I returned. I had prepared for my wife a roasted lamb, and purchased some sweetmeat; and I now called the porter, described to him the house, and gave him his hire. Having done this, I occupied myself again with my business until sunset, when the owner of the ass came, and I took fifty pieces of gold and put them into a handkerchief. Entering the house, I found that they had wiped the marble, and polished the vessels of copper and brass, and filled the lamps, and lighted the candles, and dished the supper, and strained the wine; and when my wife saw me, she threw her arms around my neck, and said, Thou hast made me desolate by thine absence! The tables were then placed before us, and we ate until we were satisfied, and the slave-girls took away the first table and placed before us the wine; and we sat drinking, and eating of the dried fruits, and making merry until midnight. We then slept until morning, when I arose and handed her the fifty pieces of gold, as before, and left her.

Thus I continued to do for a long time, until I was without a denar or a dirham. Then, one morning I walked forth into the street, and proceeded thence to the Gate of Zawili, where I found the people crowding together, so that the gate was stopped up by their number; and, as destiny willed; I saw there a trooper, and, unintentionally pressing against him, my hand came in contact with his pocket, and Satan tempted me on and I felt it, and found that it contained a purse ; and I caught hold of the purse and took it from his pocket. But the trooper felt that his pocket was lightened, and putting his hand into it, found nothing; upon which he looked aside at me, and raised his hand with the mace, and struck me upon my head. I fell to the ground, and the people surrounded us and seized the bridle of the trooper's horse, saying, On account of the crowd dost thou strike this young man such a blow ? But he called out to them, and said, This is a robber! On hearing this I feared. The people around me said, This is a comely young man, and hath taken nothing. While some, however, believed this, others disbelieved ; and, after many words, the people dragged me along, desiring to liberate me ; but, as it was predestined, there came at this moment the judge and other magistrates entering the gate, and, seeing the people surrounding me and the trooper, the judge said, What is the news ? The trooper answered, By Allah, O emir, this is a robber : I had in my pocket a blue purse containing twenty pieces of gold, and he took it while I was pressed by the crowd. Was any one with thee ? asked the judge. The trooper answered, No. And the judge called out to the chief of his servants, saying, Seize him, and search him. So he seized me, and protection was withdrawn from me ; and the judge said to him, Strip him of all that is upon him. And when he did so, they found the purse in my clothes : and the judge, taking it, counted the money, and found it to be twenty pieces of gold, as the trooper had said : whereupon he was enraged, and called out to his attendants, saying, Bring him forward. They, therefore, brought me before him, and he said to me, O young man, tell the truth : didst thou steal this purse? And I hung down my head toward the ground, saying within myself, If I answer that I did not steal it, it will be useless, for he hath produced it from my clothes ; and if I say I stole, I fall into trouble. I then raised my head, and said, Yes, I took it. And when the judge heard these words, he wondered, and called witnesses, who presented themselves, and gave their testimony to my confession. All this took place at the Gate of Zawili. The judge then ordered the executioner to cut off my hand ; and he cut off my right hand;[1] but the heart of the trooper was moved with compassion for me, and he interceded for me that I should not be killed : so the judge left me and departed. The people, however, continued around me, and gave me to drink a cup of wine; and the trooper gave me the purse, saying, Thou art a comely youth, and it is not fit that thou shouldst be a thief. And I took it from him.

The trooper then left me and departed, after having given me the purse, and I went my way; but first I wrapped my hand in a piece of rag, and put it in my bosom. My condition thus altered, and my countenance pallid in consequence of my sufferings, I walked to the mansion, and, in a disordered state of mind, threw myself upon the bed. My wife, seeing my complexion thus changed, said to me, What hath pained thee, and wherefore do I see thee thus altered? I answered her, My head acheth, and I am not well. And on hearing this she was vexed, and became ill on my account, and said, Burn not my heart, O my master! Sit up, and raise thy head, and tell me what hath happened

[1] This is the punishment prescribed in the Koran for one who steals an article worth four dinars. The practice is now out of use.

to thee this day; for I read a talc in thy face. Abstain from speaking to me, I replied. And she wept, and said, It seemeth that thou art tired of us; for I see thee to be conducting thyself in a manner contrary to thy usual habit. Then she wept again, and continued addressing me, though I made her no reply, until the approach of night, when she placed some food before me; but I abstained from it, fearing that she should see me eat with my left hand, and said, I have no desire to eat at present. She then said again, Tell me what hath happened to thee this day, and wherefore I see thee anxious and broken-hearted. I answered, I will presently tell thee at my leisure. And she put the wine toward me, saying, Take it; for it will dispel thine anxiety; and thou must drink, and tell me thy story. I replied, therefore, If it must be so, give me to drink with thy hand. And she filled a cup and drank it; and then filled it again and handed it to me, and I took it from her with my left hand.

Having thus said, I wept; and when she saw me do so, she uttered a loud cry, and said, What is the reason of thy weeping? Thou hast burned my heart! And wherefore didst thou take the cup with thy left hand? I answered her, I have a boil upon my right hand. Then put it forth, said she, that I may open it for thee. It is not yet, I replied, the proper time for opening it; and continue not to ask me; for I will not put it forth at present. I then drank the contents of the cup, and she continued to hand me the wine until intoxication overcame me, and I fell asleep in the place where I was sitting; upon which she discovered that my right arm was without a hand, and, searching me, saw the purse containing the gold.

Grief, such as none else experienceth, overcame her at

the sight; and she suffered incessant torment on my
account until the morning, when I awoke, and found that
she had prepared for me a dish composed of four boiled
fowls, which she placed before me. She then gave me to
drink a cup of wine; and I ate and drank, and put down
the purse, and was about to depart; but she said, Whither
wouldst thou go? I answered, To a place, to dispel somewhat of the anxiety which oppresseth my heart. Go not,
she said; but rather sit down again. So I sat down, and
she said to me, Hath thy love of me become so excessive
that thou hast expended all thy wealth upon me, and lost
thy hand! I take thee, then, as witness against me, and
God also is witness, that I will never desert thee; and
thou shalt see the truth of my words. Immediately,
therefore, she sent for witnesses, who came; and she
said to them, Write my contract of marriage to this young
man, and bear witness that I have received the dowry.
And they did as she desired them; after which she said,
Bear witness that all my property which is in this chest,
and all my mamlouks and female slaves, belong to this
young man. Accordingly, they declared themselves witnesses of her declaration, and I accepted the property, and
they departed after they had received their fees. She
then took me by my hand, and, having led me to a closet,
opened a large chest, and said to me, See what is contained in this chest. I looked, therefore; and lo, it was
full of handkerchiefs; and she said, This is thy property,
which I have received from thee; for every time that thou
gavest me a handkerchief containing fifty pieces of gold,
I wrapped it up, and threw it into this chest: take, then,
thy property; for God hath restored it to thee, and thou
art now of high estate. Fate hath afflicted thee on my

account, so that thou hast lost thy right hand, and I am unable to compensate thee : if I should sacrifice my life, it would be but a small thing, and thy generosity would still have surpassed mine. She then added, Now take possession of thy property. So I received it; and she transferred the contents of her chest to mine, adding her property to mine which I had given her. My heart rejoiced, my anxiety ceased, and I approached and kissed her, and made myself merry by drinking with her ; after which she said again, Thou has sacrificed all thy wealth and thy hand through love of me, and how can I compensate thee ? By Allah, if I gave my life for love of thee, it were but a small thing, and I should not do justice to thy claims upon me. She then wrote a deed of gift transferring to me all her apparel, and her ornaments of gold and jewels, and her houses and other possessions ; and she passed that night in grief on my account, having heard my relation of the accident that had befallen me.

Thus we remained less than a month, during which time she became more and more infirm and disordered ; and she endured no more than fifty days before she was numbered among the people of the other world. So I prepared her funeral, and deposited her body in the earth, and, having caused recitations of the Koran to be performed for her, and given a considerable sum of money in alms for her sake, returned from the tomb. I found that she had possessed abundant wealth, and houses and lands, and among her property were the storerooms of sesame of which I sold to thee the contents of one ; and I was not prevented from settling with thee during this period but by my being busied in selling the remainder, the price of which I have not yet entirely received. Now I desire of

thee that thou wilt not oppose me in that which I am
about to say to thee, since I have eaten of thy food : I give
thee the price of the sesame, which is in thy hands.   This
which I have told thee was the cause of my eating with
my left hand.

I replied, Thou hast treated me with kindness and generosity : and he then said, Thou must travel with me to
my country ; for I have bought merchandise of Cairo and
Alexandria.   Wilt thou accompany me ?   I answered, Yes ;
and promised him that I would be ready by the first day
of the following month.   So I sold all that I possessed, and,
having bought merchandise with the produce, travelled with
the young man to this thy country, where he sold his merchandise and bought other in its stead, after which he
returned to the land of Egypt ; but it was my lot to remain
here, and to experience that which hath befallen me this
night during my absence from my native country.   Now
is not this, O king of the age, more wonderful than the
story of the humpback ?

The king replied, Ye must be hanged, all of you !   And
upon this the sultan's steward advanced toward the king,
and said, If thou permit me, I will relate to thee a story
that I happened to hear just before I found this humpback ; and if it be more wonderful than the events relating
to him, wilt thou grant us our lives ?   The king answered,
Tell thy story ; and he began thus : —

The Story Told by the Sultan's Steward.

I was last night with a party who celebrated a recitation
of the Koran, for which purpose they had assembled the
professors of religion and law ; and when these reciters

had accomplished their task, the servants spread a repast, comprising among other dishes a zirbaja.[1] We approached, therefore, to eat of the zirbaja; but one of the company drew back, and refused to partake of it : we conjured him ; yet he swore that he would not eat of it : and we pressed him again ; but he said, Press me not ; for I have suffered enough from eating of this dish. And when we had finished, we said to him, By Allah, tell us the reason of thine abstaining from eating of the zirbaja. He replied, Because I cannot eat of it unless I wash my hands forty times with kali, and forty times with cyperus, and forty times with soap; altogether, a hundred and twenty times. And upon this, the giver of the entertainment ordered his servants, and they brought water and the other things which this man required : so he washed his hands as he had described, and advanced, though with disgust, and, having seated himself, stretched forth his hand as one in fear, and put it into the zirbaja, and began to eat, while we regarded him with the utmost wonder. His hand trembled, and when he put it forth we saw that his thumb was cut off, and he ate with his four fingers : we therefore said to him, We conjure thee by Allah to tell us how was thy thumb maimed : was it thus created by God, or hath some accident happened to it ? O my brothers, he answered, not only have I lost this thumb, but also the thumb of the other hand ; and each of my feet is in like manner deprived of the great toe : but see ye ; and, so saying, he uncovered the stump of the thumb of the other hand, and we found it like the right ; and so also his feet, destitute of the great toes. At the sight of this our wonder increased, and we said to him, We are impatient to hear thy story, and thine

[1] A kind of spoon-meat, dressed with vinegar, cumin-seed, and hot spices.

account of the cause of the amputation of thy thumbs and great toes, and the reason of thy washing thy hands a hundred and twenty times.   So he said :

Know that my father was a great merchant, the chief of the merchants of the city of Bagdad in the time of the Caliph Haroun Alrashid ; but he was ardently addicted to the drinking of wine and hearing the · lute ; and when he died he left nothing.   I buried him, and caused recitations of the Koran to be performed for him, and, after I had mourned for him days and nights, I opened his shop, and found that he had left in it but few goods, and that his debts were many : however, I induced his creditors to wait, and calmed their minds, and betook myself to selling and buying from week to week, and so paying the creditors.

Thus I continued to do for a considerable period, until I had discharged all the debts and increased my capital ; and as I was sitting one day, I beheld a young lady, than whom my eye had never beheld any more beautiful, decked with magnificent ornaments and apparel, riding on a mule, with a slave before her and a slave behind her ; and she stopped the mule at the entrance of the market street, and entered, followed by a eunuch, who said to her, O my mistress, enter, but inform no one who thou art, lest thou open the fire of indignation upon us.   The eunuch then further cautioned her ; and when she looked at the shops of the merchants, she found none more handsome than mine ; so, when she arrived before me, with the eunuch following her, she sat down upon the seat of my shop and saluted me ; and I never heard speech more charming than hers, or words more sweet.   She then drew aside the veil from her face, and I directed at her a glance which drew from me a sigh ; my heart was captivated by her love, and I continued repeatedly gazing at her face. She then said to me, O youth, hast thou any handsome stuffs ? O my mistress, I answered, thy slave is a poor man ; but wait until the other merchants open their shops, and then I will bring thee what thou desirest. So I conversed with her, drowned in the sea of her love, and bewildered by my passion for her, until the merchants had opened their shops, when I arose and procured all that she wanted, and the price of these stuffs was five thousand pieces of silver : and she handed them all to the eunuch, who took them ; after which, they both went out from the market street, and the slaves brought to her the mule, and she mounted, without telling me whence she was, and I was ashamed to mention the subject to her : consequently, I became answerable for the price to the merchants, incurring a debt of five thousand pieces of silver.

I went home, intoxicated with her love, and they placed before me the supper, and I ate a morsel ; but reflections upon her beauty and loveliness prevented my eating more. I desired to sleep, but sleep came not to me ; and in this condition I remained for a week. The merchants de-manded of me their money ; but I prevailed upon them to wait another week ; and after this week the lady came again, riding upon a mule, and attended by a eunuch and two other slaves ; and, having saluted me, said, O my master, we have been tardy in bringing to thee the price of the stuffs : bring now the money-changer,[1] and receive it. So the money-changer came, and the eunuch gave him

---

[1] A money-changer is very frequently employed to examine the money which a purchaser offers; and, if it be old, to weigh it. The money-changers are mostly Jews and Christians.

the money, and I took it, and sat conversing with her until the market was replenished and the merchants opened their shops, when she said to me, Procure for me such and such things. Accordingly, I procured for her what she desired of the merchants, and she took the goods and departed without saying anything to me respecting the price. When she had gone, therefore, I repented of what I had done ; for I had procured for her what she demanded for the price of a thousand pieces of gold ; and as soon as she had disappeared from my sight, I said within myself, What kind of love is this ? She hath brought me five thousand pieces of silver, and taken goods for a thousand pieces of gold ! I feared that the result would be my bankruptcy and the loss of the property of others, and said, The merchants know none but me, and this woman is no other than a cheat, who hath imposed upon me by her beauty and loveliness : seeing me to be young, she hath laughed at me, and I asked her not where was her residence.

I remained in a state of perplexity, and her absence was prolonged more than a month. Meanwhile the merchants demanded of me their money, and so pressed me that I offered my possessions for sale, and was on the brink of ruin ; but as I was sitting absorbed in reflection, suddenly she alighted at the gate of the market street, and came in to me. As soon as I beheld her my solicitude ceased, and I forgot the trouble with which I had suffered. She approached, and addressed me with her agreeable conversation, and said, Produce the scales and weigh thy money : and she gave me the price of the goods which she had taken, with a surplus ; after which she amused herself by talking with me, and I almost died with joy and happiness.

She then said to me, Hast thou a wife? I answered, No;
for I am not acquainted with any woman; and wept. So
she asked me, What causeth thee to weep? And I answered, A thought that hath come into my mind; and
taking some pieces of gold, gave them to the eunuch, requesting him to grant me his mediation in the affair, upon
which he laughed, and said, She is in love with thee more
than thou art with her, and hath no want of the stuffs, but
hath done this only from her love of thee; propose to her,
therefore, what thou wilt; for she will not oppose thee in
that which thou wilt say. Now she observed me giving
the pieces of gold to the eunuch, and returned, and resumed her seat; and I said to her, Show favor to thy
slave, and pardon me for that which I am about to say.
I then acquainted her with the feelings of my heart,
and my declaration pleased her, and she consented
to my proposal, saying, This eunuch will come with
my letter, and do thou what he shall tell thee; and she
arose and departed.

I went to the merchants, and delivered to them their
money, and all profited excepting myself; for when she
left me I mourned for the interruption of our intercourse,
and I slept not during the whole of the next night: but a
few days after her eunuch came to me, and I received him
with honor, and asked him respecting his mistress. He
answered, She is sick; and I said to him, Disclose to me
her history. He replied, The Lady Zobeide, the wife of
Haroun Alrashid, brought up this damsel, and she is one
of her slaves; she had desired of her mistress to be allowed
the liberty of going out and returning at pleasure, and the
latter gave her permission; she continued, therefore, to do
so until she became a chief confidant; after which she

spoke of thee to her mistress, and begged that she would
marry her to thee : but her mistress said, I will not do it
until I see this young man ; and if he have a desire for
thee, I will marry thee to him. We therefore wish to introduce thee immediately into the palace ; and if thou enter
without any one's having knowledge of thy presence, thou
wilt succeed in accomplishing thy marriage with her ; but
if thy plot be discovered, thy head will be struck off. What,
then, sayest thou ? I answered, Good ; I will go with
thee, and await the event that shall befall me there. As
soon, then, as this next night shall have closed in, said the
eunuch, repair to the mosque which the Lady Zobeide hath
built on the bank of the Tigris, and there say thy prayers,
and pass the night. Most willingly, I replied.

Accordingly, when the time of nightfall arrived, I went
to the mosque, and said my prayers there, and passed the
night ; and as soon as the morning began to dawn, I saw
two eunuchs approaching in a small boat conveying some
empty chests, which they brought into the mosque. One
of them then departed, and the other remained ; and I
looked attentively at him, and lo, it was he who had been
our intermediary ; and soon after the damsel, my companion, came up to us. I rose to her when she approached,
and embraced her ; and she kissed me and wept ; and, after
we had conversed together for a little while, she took me
and placed me in a chest, and locked it upon me. The
slaves then brought a quantity of stuffs, and filled with
them the other chests, which they locked, and conveyed,
together with the chest in which I was inclosed, to the
boat, accompanied by the damsel ; and, having embarked
them, they plied the oars, and proceeded to the palace of
the honored Lady Zobeide. The intoxication of love now

ceased in me, and reflection came in its place; I repented of what I had done, and prayed God to deliver me from my dangerous predicament.

Meanwhile, they arrived at the gate of the caliph, where they landed, and took out all the chests, and conveyed them into the palace: but the chief of the door-keepers, who had been asleep when they arrived, was awoke by the sounds of their voices, and cried out to the damsel, saying, The chests must be opened, that I may see what is in them; and he arose, and placed his hand upon the chest in which I was hidden. My reason abandoned me, my heart almost burst from my body, and my limbs trembled; but the damsel said, These are the chests of the Lady Zobeide, and if thou open and turn them over, she will be incensed against thee, and we shall all perish. They contain nothing but clothes dyed of various colors, excepting this chest upon which thou hast put thy hand, in which there are also some bottles filled with the water of Zemzem,[1] and if any of the water run out upon the clothes it will spoil their colors. Now I have advised thee, and it is for thee to decide; so do what thou wilt. When he heard, therefore, these words, he said to her, Take the chests and pass on; and the eunuchs immediately took them up, and, with the damsel, conveyed them into the palace; but in an instant I heard a person crying out, and saying, The caliph! the caliph!

I was bereft of my reason, and seized with a colic from excessive fear; I almost died, and my limbs were affected with a violent shaking. The caliph cried out to the damsel, saying to her, What are these chests? She answered, O my lord (may God exalt thy dominion!), these chests contain clothes of my mistress, Zobeide. Open them, said the

---

[1] The holy well of Mecca.

caliph, that I may see the clothes. When I heard this I felt sure of my destruction. The damsel could not disobey his command, but she replied, O Prince of the Faithful, there is nothing in these chests but clothes of the Lady Zobeide, and she hath commanded me not to open them to any one. The caliph, however, said, The chests must be opened, all of them, that I may see their contents : and immediately he called out to the eunuchs to bring them before him. I therefore felt certain that I was on the point of destruction. They then brought before him chest after chest, and opened each to him, and he examined the contents ; and when they brought forward the chest in which I was inclosed I bade adieu to life, and prepared myself for death ; but, as the eunuchs were about to open it, the damsel said, O Prince of the Faithful, verily this chest containeth things especially appertaining to women, and it is proper, therefore, that it should be opened before the Lady Zobeide ; and when the caliph heard her words, he ordered the eunuchs to convey all the chests into the interior of the palace. The damsel then hastened and ordered two eunuchs to carry away the chest in which I was hidden, and they took it to an inner chamber and went their way ; whereupon she quickly opened it, and made a sign to me to come out ; so I did as she desired, and entered a closet that was before me, and she locked the door upon me, and closed the chest ; and when the eunuchs had brought in all the chests, and had gone back, she opened the door of the closet, and said, Thou hast nothing to fear ! May God refresh thine eye ! Come forth now, and go up with me, that thou mayest have the happiness of kissing the ground before the Lady Zobeide.

I therefore went with her, and beheld twenty other female

slaves, high-bosomed virgins, and among them was Lady
Zobeide, who was scarcely able to walk from the weight of
the robes and ornaments with which she was decked. As
she approached, the female slaves dispersed from around
her, and I advanced to her, and kissed the ground before
her. She made a sign to me to sit down : so I seated myself before her ; and she began to ask me questions respecting my condition and lineage ; to all of which I gave
such answers that she was pleased, and said, By Allah, the
care which we have bestowed on the education of this damsel hath not been in vain. She then said to me, Know
that this damsel is esteemed by us as though she were really
our child, and she is a trust committed to thy care by God.
Upon this, therefore, I again kissed the ground before her,
well pleased to marry the damsel ; after which she commanded me to remain with them ten days. Accordingly,
I continued with them during this period ; but I knew
nothing meanwhile of the damsel ; certain of the maids
only bringing me my dinner and supper, as my servants.
After this, however, the Lady Zobeide asked permission of
her husband, the Prince of the Faithful, to marry her maid,
and he granted her request, and ordered that ten thousand
pieces of gold should be given to her.

The Lady Zobeide, therefore, sent for the cadi and witnesses, and they wrote my contract of marriage to the
damsel ; and the maids then prepared sweetmeats and
exquisite dishes, and distributed them in all the apartments. Thus they continued to do for a period of ten
more days ; and after the twenty days had passed, they
conducted the damsel into the bath, preparatively to my
being introduced to her as her husband. They then
brought to me a repast comprising a basin of zirbaja

sweetened with sugar, perfumed with rose-water infused
with musk, and containing different kinds of fricandoed
fowls, and a variety of other ingredients, such as astonished the mind ; and, by Allah, when this repast was
brought, I instantly commenced upon the zirbaja, and ate
of it as much as satisfied me, and wiped my hand, but forgot to wash it. I remained sitting until it became dark ;
when the maids lighted the candles, and the singing girls
approached with the tambourines, and they continued to
display the bride, and to give presents of gold, until she
had perambulated the whole of the palace ; after which
they brought her to me and disrobed her ; and as soon as
I was left alone with her I threw my arms around her
neck, scarcely believing in our union ; but as I did so, she
perceived the smell of the zirbaja from my hand, and immediately uttered a loud cry : whereupon the female slaves
ran in to her from every quarter.

I was violently agitated, not knowing what was the
matter ; and the slaves who had come in said to her, What
hath happened to thee, O our sister ? Take away from me,
she exclaimed to them, this madman, whom I imagined to
be a man of sense ! What indication of my insanity hath
appeared to thee ? I asked. Thou madman, said she, wherefore hast thou eaten of the zirbaja, and not washed thy
hand ? By Allah, I will not accept thee for thy want of
sense, and thy disgusting conduct ! And so saying, she
took from her side a whip, and beat me with it upon my
back until I became insensible from the number of the
stripes. She then said to the other maids, Take him to
the magistrate of the city police, that he may cut off his
hand with which he ate the zirbaja without washing it
afterward. On hearing this, I exclaimed, There is no

strength nor power but in God! Wilt thou cut off my hand on account of my eating a zirbaja and neglecting to wash it? And the maids who were present entreated her, saying to her, O our sister, be not angry with him for what he hath done this time. But she replied, By Allah, I must cut off something from his extremities! And immediately she departed, and was absent from me ten days : after which she came again, and said to me, O thou black-faced! am I not worthy of thee? How didst thou dare to eat the zirbaja and not wash thy hand? And she called to the maids, who bound my hands behind me, and she took a sharp razor, and cut off both my thumbs and both my great toes, as ye see, O companions ; and I swooned away. She then sprinkled upon my wounds some powder, by means of which the blood was stanched ; and I said, I will not eat of a zirbaja as long as I live unless I wash my hands forty times with kali, and forty times with cyperus, and forty times with soap ; and she exacted of me an oath that I would not eat of this dish unless I washed my hands as I have described to you. Therefore, when this zirbaja was brought, my color changed, and I said within myself, This was the cause of the cutting off of my thumbs and great toes ; so, when ye compelled me, I said, I must fulfil the oath which I have sworn.

I then said to him (continued the sultan's steward), And what happened to thee after that? He answered, When I had thus sworn to her, she was appeased, and I was admitted into her favor ; and we lived happily together for a considerable time ; after which she said, The people of the caliph's palace know not that thou hast resided here with me, and no strange man excepting thee hath entered it ; nor didst thou enter but through the assistance of the

Lady Zobeide. She then gave me fifty thousand pieces of gold, and said to me, Take these pieces of gold, and go forth and buy for us a spacious house. So I went forth, and purchased a handsome and spacious house, and removed thither all the riches that she possessed, and all that she had treasured up, and her dresses and rarities. This was the cause of the amputation of my thumbs and great toes. So we ate (said the sultan's steward), and departed ; and after this the accident with the humpback happened to me : this is all my story ; and peace be on thee.

The king said, This is not more pleasant than the story of the humpback : nay, the story of the humpback is more pleasant than this ; and ye must all of you be crucified. The Jew, however, then came forward, and having kissed the ground, said, O king of the age, I will relate to thee a story more wonderful than that of the humpback ; and the king said, Relate thy story ; so he commenced thus : —

The Story Told by the Jewish Physician.

THE most wonderful of the events that happened to me in my younger days was this : I was riding in Damascus, where I learned and practised my art ; and while I was thus occupied, one day there came to me a mamlouk from the house of the governor of the city : so I went forth with him, and accompanied him to the abode of the governor. I entered, and beheld at the upper end of a saloon a sofa of alabaster overlaid with plates of gold, upon which was reclining a sick man : he was young ; and a person more comely had not been seen in his age. Seating myself at his head, I ejaculated a prayer for his restoration ; and he made a sign to me with his eye. I then said to him, O my master, stretch forth to me thy hand : whereupon he put forth to me his left hand ; and I was surprised at this, and said within myself, What self-conceit ! I felt his pulse, however, and wrote a prescription for him, and continued to visit him for a period of ten days, until he recovered his strength ; when he entered the bath, and washed himself, and came forth : and the governor conferred upon me a handsome dress of honor, and appointed me superinten- dent of the hospital of Damascus.[1] But when I went with him into the bath, which they had cleared of all other visitors for us alone, and the servants had brought the clothes, and taken away those which he had pulled off within, I perceived that his right hand had been cruelly amputated ; at the sight of which I wondered, and grieved for him ; and looking at his skin, I observed upon him marks of beating with sticks, which caused me to wonder more. The young man then turned toward me, and said, O doctor of the age, wonder not at my case ; for I will relate to thee my story when we have gone out from the bath : and when we had gone forth, and arrived at the house, and had eaten some food, and rested, he said to me, Hast thou a desire to divert thyself in the supper-room ? I answered, Yes : and immediately he ordered the slaves to take up thither the furniture, and to roast a lamb and bring us some fruit. So the slaves did as he commanded them : they brought the fruit, and when we had eaten, I said to him, Relate to me thy story : and he replied, O doctor of the age, listen to the relation of the events which have befallen me.

[1] This was the first Moslem hospital. It was founded in the year 706-7, A.D. It is called the Maristan; but is now empty and a ruin.

Know that I am of the children of Mosul. My paternal grandfather died, leaving ten male children, one of whom was my father: he was the eldest of them; and they all grew up and married ; and my father was blest with me ; but none of his nine brothers was blessed with children. So I grew up among my uncles, who delighted in me exceedingly ; and when I had attained manhood, I was one day with my father in the chief mosque of Mosul. The day was Friday ; and we performed the congregational prayers ; and all the people went out, excepting my father and my uncles, who sat conversing together respecting the wonders of various countries, and the strange sights of different cities, until they mentioned Egypt ; when one of my uncles said, The travellers assert that there is not on the face of the earth a more agreeable country than Egypt with its Nile : and my father added, He who hath not seen Cairo hath not seen the world : its soil is gold ; its Nile is a wonder ; its women are like the black-eyed virgins of Paradise ; its houses are palaces ; and its air is temperate ; its odor surpassing that of aloes-wood, and cheering the heart : and how can Cairo be otherwise when it is the metropolis of the world ? Did ye see its gardens in the evening (he continued), with the shade obliquely extending over them, ye would behold a wonder, and yield with ecstasy to their attractions.

When I heard these descriptions of Egypt, my mind became wholly engaged by reflections upon that country ; and after they had departed to their homes I passed the night sleepless, from my excessive longing toward it, and neither food nor drink was pleasant to me. A few days after, my uncles prepared to journey thither, and I wept before my father that I might go with them, so that he prepared a stock of merchandise for me, and I departed in their company; but he said to them, Suffer him not to enter Egypt, but leave him at Damascus, that he may there sell his merchandise.

I took leave of my father, and we set forth from Mosul, and continued our journey until we arrived at Aleppo, where we remained some days; after which we proceeded thence until we came to Damascus; and we beheld it to be a city with trees, and rivers, and fruits, and birds, as though it were a paradise, containing fruits of every kind. We took lodgings in one of the khans, and my uncles remained there until they had sold and bought; and they also sold my merchandise, gaining, for every piece of silver, five, so that I rejoiced at my profit. My uncles then left me and repaired to Egypt, and I remained, and took up my abode in a handsome mansion, such as the tongue cannot describe; the monthly rent of which was two pieces of gold.

Here I indulged myself with eating and drinking, squandering away the money that was in my possession; and as I was sitting one day at the door of the mansion a damsel approached me, attired in clothing of the richest description, such as I had never seen surpassed in costliness, and I invited her to come in; whereupon, without hesitation, she entered; and I was delighted at her compliance, and closed the door upon us both. She then uncovered her face and took off her izar, and I found her to be so surprisingly beautiful that love for her took possession of my heart : so I went and brought a repast consisting of the most delicious viands and fruit, and everything else that was requisite for her entertainment, and we ate together. I gave to her ten pieces of gold ; but she swore that she would not accept them from me, and said, Expect me again, O my beloved, after three days : at the hour of sunset I will be with thee ; and do thou prepare for us, with these pieces of gold, a repast similar to this which we have just enjoyed. She then gave me ten pieces of gold, and took leave of me, and departed, taking my reason with her. And after the three days had expired she came again, decked with embroidered stuffs and ornaments, and other attire more magnificent than those which she wore on the former occasion. I had prepared for her what was required previously to her arrival; so we now ate and drank as before ; and in the morning she gave me again ten pieces of gold, promising to return to me after three more days. I therefore made ready what was requisite, and after the three days she came attired in a dress still more magnificent than the first and second, and said to me, O my master, am I beautiful? Yea, verily, I answered. Wilt thou give me leave, she rejoined, to bring with me a damsel more beautiful than myself, and younger than I, that she may sport with us and we may make merry with her? For she hath requested that she may accompany me, and pass the night in frolicking with us. And so saying, she gave me twenty pieces of gold, desiring me to prepare a more plentiful repast, on account of the lady who was to come with her : after which she bade me adieu, and departed.

Accordingly, on the fourth day, I procured what was requisite, as usual, and soon after sunset she came, accompanied by a girl wrapped in an izar, and they entered and seated themselves. I was rejoiced, and I lighted the candles, and welcomed them with joy and exultation. They then took off their outer garments, and when the new damsel uncovered her face, I perceived that she was like the full moon : I had never beheld a person more beautiful. I arose immediately, and placed before them the food and drink, and we ate and drank, while I continued caressing the new damsel, and filling the wine-cup for her, and drinking with her : but the first lady was affected with a secret jealousy. By Allah, she said, verily this girl is beautiful! Is she not more charming than I ? Yea, indeed, I answered. Soon after this I fell asleep, and when I awoke in the morning, I found my hand defiled with blood, and, opening my eyes, perceived that the sun was risen ; so I attempted to rouse the girl, whereupon her head rolled from her body. The other damsel was gone, and I concluded, therefore, that she had done this from her jealousy ; and after reflecting a while, I arose, and took off my clothes, and dug a hole in the house, in which I deposited the murdered damsel, afterward covering her remains with earth, and replacing the marble pavement as it was before. I then dressed myself again, and, taking the remainder of my money, went forth, and repaired to the owner of the house, and paid him a year's rent, saying to him, I am about to journey to my uncles in Egypt.

So I departed to Egypt, where I met with my uncles, and they were rejoiced to see me. I found that they had concluded the sale of their merchandise, and they said to me, What is the cause of thy coming? I answered, I had a longing desire to be with you, and feared that my money would not suffice me. For a year I remained with them, enjoying the pleasures of Egypt and its Nile ; and I dipped my hand into the residue of my money, and expended it prodigally in eating and drinking until the time approached of my uncles' departure, when I fled from them : so they said, Probably he hath gone before us and returned to

Damascus : and they departed. I then came forth from
my concealment, and remained in Cairo three years, squandering away my money until scarcely any of it remained :
but, meanwhile I sent every year the rent of the mansion
at Damascus to its owner ; and after the three years my
heart became contracted, for nothing remained in my possession but the rent for the year.

I therefore journeyed back to Damascus, and alighted
at the house. The owner was rejoiced to see me, and I
entered it, and cleansed it of the blood of the murdered
damsel, and, removing a cushion, I found beneath this the
necklace that she had worn that night. I took it up and
examined it, and wept a while. After this I remained in
the house two days, and on the third day I entered the
bath and changed my clothes. I now had no money left ;
and I went one day to the market, where (the devil sug-
gesting it to me in order to accomplish the purpose of
destiny) I handed the necklace of jewels to a broker ; and
he rose to me, and seated me by his side : then, having
waited until the market was replenished, he took it and
announced it for sale secretly, without my knowledge.
The price bidden for it amounted to two thousand pieces
of gold ; but he came to me and said, This necklace is of
brass, of the counterfeit manufacture of the Franks,[1] and
its price hath amounted to a thousand pieces of silver. I
answered him, Yes ; we had made it for a woman, merely
to laugh at her, and my wife has inherited it, and we desire
to sell it : go, therefore, and receive the thousand pieces
of silver. Now when the broker heard this, he perceived
that the affair was suspicious, and went and gave the neck-

---

[1] Meaning Europeans generally. Their name has been such in the East
since the Crusades, in which the French took a leading part.

lace to the chief of the market, who took it to the judge, and said to him, This necklace was stolen from me, and we have found the thief, clad in the dress of the sons of the merchants. And before I knew what had happened, the officers had surrounded me, and they took me to the judge, who questioned me respecting the necklace. I told him, therefore, the same story that I had told to the broker ; but he laughed, and said, This is not the truth : and instantly his people stripped me of my outer clothing, and beat me with sticks all over my body, until, through the torture that I suffered from the blows, I said I stole it ; reflecting that it was better I should say I stole it than confess that its owner was murdered in my abode ; for then they would kill me to avenge her : and as soon as I had said so, they cut off my hand, and scalded the stump with boiling oil,[1] and I swooned away. They then gave me to drink some wine, by swallowing which I recovered my senses ; and I took my amputated hand, and returned to the mansion ; but its owner said to me, Since this hath happened to thee, leave the house and look for another abode ; for thou art accused of an unlawful act. O my master, I replied, give me two or three days' delay, that I may seek for a lodging : and he assented to this, and departed and left me. So I remained alone, and sat weeping, and saying, How can I return to my family with my hand cut off ? He who cut it off knoweth not that I am innocent : perhaps, then, God will bring about some event for my relief.

I sat weeping violently ; and when the owner of the house had departed from me, excessive grief overcame me,

---

[1] This was the old surgical practice, before the more modern practice of tying up the arteries.

and I was sick for two days; and on the third day, suddenly the owner of the house came to me, with some officers of the police, and the chief of the market, and accused
me again of stealing the necklace. So I went out to them,
and said, What is the news? whereupon, without granting
me a moment's delay, they bound my arms behind me, and
put a chain around my neck, saying to me, The necklace
which was in thy possession hath proved to be the property
of the governor of Damascus, its vizier and its ruler : it hath
been lost from the governor's house for a period of three
years, and with it was his daughter. When I heard these
words from them, my limbs trembled, and I said within
myself, They will kill me! my death is inevitable! By
Allah, I must relate my story to the governor ; and if he
please he will kill me, or if he please he will pardon me.
And when we arrived at the governor's abode, and they had
placed me before him, and he beheld me, he said, Is this
he who stole the necklace and went out to sell it? Verily
ye have cut off his hand wrongfully. He then ordered
that the chief of the market should be imprisoned, and
said to him, Give to this person the compensatory fine for
his hand, or I will hang thee and seize all thy property.
And he called out to his attendants, who took him and
dragged him away.

I was now left with the governor alone, after they had,
by his permission, loosed the chain from my neck, and
untied the cords which bound my arms ; and the governor,
looking toward me, said to me, O my son, tell me thy story
and speak truth. How did this necklace come into thy possession? So I replied, O my lord, I will tell thee the truth :
and I related to him all that had happened to me with the
first damsel, and how she had brought to me the second,

and murdered her from jealousy; on hearing which he shook his head, and covered his face with his handkerchief, and wept. Then, looking toward me, he said, Know, O my son, that the elder damsel was my daughter: I kept her closely: and when she had attained a fit age for marriage, I sent her to the son of her uncle in Cairo; but he died, and she returned to me. It was then that she met thee, and brought to thee her younger sister. They were sisters by the same mother, and much attached to each other; and when the event which thou hast related occurred to the elder, she imparted her secret to her sister, who asked my permission to go out with her; after which the elder returned alone; and when I questioned her respecting her sister, I found her weeping for her, and she answered, I know no tidings of her: but she afterward informed her mother, secretly, of the murder which she had committed; and her mother privately related the affair to me; and she continued to weep for her incessantly, saying, By Allah,[1] I will not cease to weep for her until I die. Thy account, O my son, is true; for I knew the affair before thou toldest it me. See, then, O my son, what hath happened: and now I request of thee that thou wilt not oppose me in that which I am about to say; and it is this: I desire to marry thee to my youngest daughter; for she is not of the same mother as they were: she is a virgin, and I will receive from thee no dowry, but will assign to you both an allowance; and thou shalt be to me as an own son. I replied, Let it be as thou desirest, O my master. How could I expect to attain unto such hap-

---

[1] This frequent reference to God, — which will be observed all through the Arabian Nights, — is now avoided by the better-educated Turks. But it still holds with the vulgar.

piness ?   The governor then sent immediately a courier
to bring the property which my father had left me (for he
had died since my departure from him), and now I am
living in the utmost affluence.

I wondered, said the Jew, at his history; and after I
had remained with him three days, he gave me a large
sum of money; and I left him to set forth on a journey;
and, arriving in this country, my residence here pleased
me, and I experienced this which hath happened to me
with the humpback.

The king, when he heard this story, said, This is not
more wonderful than the story of the humpback, and ye
must all of you be hanged, and especially the tailor, who is
the source of all the mischief.   But he afterward added, O
tailor, if thou tell me a story more wonderful than that of
the humpback, I will forgive you your offences.   So the
tailor advanced, and said : —

The Story Told by the Tailor.

Know, O king of the age, that what hath happened to
me is more wonderful than the events which have happened to all the others.   Before I met the humpback, I
was, early in the morning, at an entertainment given to
certain tradesmen of my acquaintance, consisting of tailors,
and linen-drapers, and carpenters, and others ; and when
the sun had risen, the repast was brought for us to eat ;
and lo, the master of the house came in to us, accompanied
by a strange and handsome young man, of the inhabitants
of Bagdad.   He was attired in clothes of the handsomest
description, and was a most comely person, excepting that
he was lame ; and as soon as he had entered and saluted

us, we rose to him ; but when he was about to seat himself, he observed among us a barber, whereupon he refused to sit down, and desired to depart from us. We and the master of the house, however, prevented him, and urged him to seat himself ; and the host conjured him, saying, What is the reason of thy entering, and then immediately departing ? By Allah, O my master, replied he, offer me no opposition : for the cause of my departure is this barber, who is sitting with you. And when the host heard this, he was exceedingly surprised, and said, How is it that the heart of this young man, who is from Bagdad, is troubled by the presence of this barber ? We then looked toward him, and said, Relate to us the cause of thy displeasure against this barber ; and the young man replied, O company, a surprising adventure happened to me with this barber in Bagdad, my city ; and he was the cause of my lameness, and of the breaking of my leg; and I have sworn that I will not sit in any place where he is present, nor dwell in any town where he resides. I quitted Bagdad and took up my abode in this city, and I will not pass the next night without departing from it. Upon this we said to him, We conjure thee by Allah to relate to us thy adventure with him ; and the countenance of the barber turned pale when he heard us make this request. The young man then said :

Know, O good people, that my father was one of the chief merchants of Bagdad ; and God, whose name be exalted, blessed him with no son but myself ; and when I grew up, and had attained to manhood, my father was admitted to the mercy of God, leaving me wealth, and servants, and other dependents ; whereupon I began to attire myself in clothes of the handsomest description, and to feed upon the most delicious meats. Now God, whose perfection be extolled, made me to be a hater of women ; and so I continued, until, one day, I was walking through the streets of Bagdad, when a party of them stopped my way. I therefore fled from them, and, entering a by-street which was not a thoroughfare, I reclined upon a stone bench at its further extremity. Here I had

been seated but a short time when lo, a window opposite the place where I sat was opened, and there looked out from it a damsel like the full moon, such as I had never in my life beheld. She had some flowers, which she was watering, beneath the window ; and she looked to the right and left, and then shut the window and disappeared from before me. Fire had been shot into my heart, and my mind was absorbed by her; my hatred of women was turned into love, and I continued sitting in the same place until sunset, in a state of distraction, from the violence of my passion, when lo, the cadi of the city came riding along, with slaves before him and servants behind him, and alighted, and entered the house from which the damsel had looked out; so I knew that he must be her father.

I then returned to my house, sorrowful, and fell upon my bed full of anxious thoughts; and my female slaves came in to me, seated themselves around me, not knowing what was the matter with me; and I acquainted them not with my case, nor returned any answers to their questions: and my disorder increased. The neighbors, therefore, came to cheer me with their visits; and among those who visited me was an old woman, who, as soon as she saw me, discovered my state; whereupon she seated herself at my head, and addressing me in a kind manner, said, O my son, tell me what hath happened to thee? So I related to her my story, and she said, O my son, this is the daughter of the Cadi of Bagdad, and she is kept in close confinement: the place where thou sawest her is her apartment, and her father occupies a large saloon below, leaving her alone, and often do I visit her: thou canst obtain an interview with her only through me: so brace up thy nerves. When I heard, therefore, what she said, I took courage, and fortified my heart, and my family rejoiced that day. I rose up firm in limb, and hoping for complete restoration; and the old woman departed; but she returned with her countenance changed, and said, O my son, ask not what she did when I told her of thy case; for she said, If thou abstain not, O ill-omened old woman, from this discourse, I will treat thee as thou deservest : but I must go to her a second time.

On hearing this, my disorder increased ; after some days, however, the old woman came again, and said, O my son, I desire of thee a reward for good tidings. My soul returned to my body at these words, and I replied, Thou shalt receive from me everything that thou canst wish. She then said, I went yesterday to the damsel, and when she beheld me with broken heart and weeping eye, she said to me, O my aunt, wherefore do I see thee with contracted heart ? And when she had thus said, I wept, and answered, O my daughter and mistress, I came to thee yesterday from visiting a youth who loveth thee, and he is at the point of death on thy account : and, her heart being moved with compassion, she asked, Who is this youth of whom thou speakest ? I answered, He is my son, and the child that is dear to my soul : he saw thee at the window some days ago, while thou wast watering thy flowers, and when he beheld thy face he became distracted with love for thee. I informed him of the conversation that I had with thee the first time, upon which his disorder increased, and he took to his pillow ; he is now dying, and there is no doubt of his fate. And upon this her countenance became pale, and she said, Is this all on my account ? Yea, by Allah, I answered ; and what dost thou order me to do ? Go to him, said she, convey to him my salutation, and tell him that my love is greater than his, and on Friday next, before the congregational prayers, let him come hither ; I will give orders to open the door to him, and to bring him up to me, and I will have a short interview with him, and he shall return before my father comes back from the prayers.

When I heard these words of the old woman, the anguish which I had suffered ceased; my heart was set at rest, and I gave her the suit of clothes which I was then wearing, and she departed, saying to me, Cheer up thy heart. I replied, I have no longer any pain. The people of my house, and my friends, communicated one to another the good news of my restoration to health, and I remained thus until the Friday, when the old woman came in to me, and asked me respecting my state; so I informed her that I was happy and well. I then dressed and perfumed myself, and sat waiting for the people to go to prayers, that I might repair to the damsel; but the old woman said to me, Thou hast yet more than ample time, and if thou go to the bath and shave, especially for the sake of obliterating the traces of thy disorder, it will be more becoming. It is a judicious piece of advice, replied I; but I will shave my head first, and then go into the bath.

So I sent for a barber to shave my head, saying to the boy, Go to the market and bring me a barber, one who is a man of sense, little inclined to impertinence, that he may not make my head ache by his chattering. And the boy went, and brought this sheikh, who, on entering, saluted me, and when I had returned his salutation, he said to me, May God dispel thy grief and thine anxiety, and misfortunes and sorrows! I responded, May God accept thy prayer! He then said, Be cheerful, O my master, for health hath returned to thee. Dost thou desire to be shaved, or to be bled? for it hath been handed down, on the authority of Ibn Abbas, that the Prophet said, Whoso shorteneth his hair on Friday, God will avert from him seventy diseases; and it hath been handed down, also, on the same authority, that the Prophet said, Whoso is cupped on Friday will not be secure from the loss of sight and from frequent disease. Abstain, said I, from this useless discourse, and come immediately, and shave my head, for I am weak. And he arose, and, stretching forth his hand, took out a handkerchief, and opened it, and lo, there was in it an astrolabe [1] consisting of seven plates ; and he took it, and went into the middle of the court, where he raised his head toward the sun, and looked for a considerable time, after which he said to me, Know that there have passed, of this our day, which is Friday, and which is the tenth of the month Saffar, of the year 263 [2] of the Flight of the Prophet — upon whom be the most excellent of blessings and peace ! — and the ascendant star of which, according to the required rules of the science of computation, is the planet Mars — seven degrees and six minutes ; and it happeneth that Mercury hath come in conjunction with that planet ; and this indicateth that the shaving of hair is now a most excellent operation ; and it hath indicated to me, also, that thou desirest to confer a benefit upon a person ; and fortunate is he ! but after that, there is an announcement that presenteth itself to me respecting a matter which I will not mention to thee.

By Allah, I exclaimed, thou hast wearied me, and dissipated my mind, and augured against me, when I required thee only to shave my head ; arise, then, and shave it, and prolong not thy discourse to me. But he replied, By Allah, if thou knewest the truth of the case, thou wouldst demand of me a further explication, and I counsel thee to do this day as I direct thee, according to the calculations deduced

---

[1] The astrolabe was the instrument by which the altitude of the heavenly bodies was observed. A fragment of one was found in the palace of Sennacherib.

[2] November 2, A.D. 876.

from the stars: it is thy duty to praise God, and not to
oppose me; for I am one who giveth thee good advice, and
who regardeth thee with compassion : I would that I were
in thy service for a whole year, that thou mightest do me
justice; and I desire not any pay from thee for so doing.
When I heard this, I said to him, Verily thou art killing
me this day, and there is no escape for me. O my master,
he replied, I am he whom the people call The Silent, on
account of the paucity of my speech, by which I am distinguished above my brothers; for my eldest brother is
named Bacbouc; and the second, Heddah; and the third,
Bacbac; and the fourth is named Alcouz; and the fifth,
Anaschar; and the sixth is named Shacabac; and the
seventh brother is named the Silent; and he is myself.

Now, when this barber thus overwhelmed me with his
talk, I felt as if my gall-bladder had burst, and said to the
boy, Give him a quarter of a piece of gold, and let him
depart from me for the sake of Allah; for I have no need
to shave my head. But the barber, on hearing what I said
to the boy, exclaimed, What is this that thou hast said, O
my lord? By Allah, I will accept from thee no pay unless
I serve thee; and serve thee I must; for to do so is incumbent on me, and to perform what thou requirest; and I
care not if I receive from thee no money. If thou knowest
not my worth, I know thine : and thy father — may Allah
have mercy upon him ! — treated us with beneficence; for
he was a man of generosity. By Allah, thy father sent
for me one day, like this blessed day, and when I went to
him he had a number of his friends with him, and he said
to me, Take some blood from me. So I took the astrolabe,
and observed the altitude for him, and found the ascendant
of the hour to be of evil omen, and that the letting of blood

would be attended with trouble : I therefore acquainted
him with this, and he conformed to my wish, and waited
until the arrival of the approved hour, when I took the
blood from him. He did not oppose me ; but, on the contrary, thanked me ; and in like manner all the company
present thanked me ; and thy father gave me a hundred
pieces of gold for services similar to the letting of blood.
May God, said I, show no mercy to my father for knowing
such a man as thou ! and the barber laughed, and exclaimed,
There is no Deity but God ! Mohammed is God's Apostle !
Extolled be the perfection of him who changeth others,
but is not changed ! I did not imagine thee to be otherwise
than a man of sense ; but thou hast talked nonsense in
consequence of thine illness. God hath mentioned, in his
Excellent Book, those who restrain their anger, and who
forgive men ; but thou art excused in every case. I am
unacquainted, however, with the cause of thy haste ; and
thou knowest that thy father used to do nothing without
consulting me : and it hath been said, that the person to
whom one applies for advice should be trusted : now, thou
wilt find no one better acquainted with the affairs of the
world than myself, and I am standing on my feet to serve
thee. I am not displeased with thee, and how, then, art
thou displeased with me ? But I will have patience with
thee on account of the favors which I received from thy
father. By Allah, said I, thou hast wearied me with thy
discourse, and overcome me with thy speech ! I desire
that thou shave my head and depart from me.

I gave vent to my rage, and would have arisen, even if
he had wetted my head, when he said, I knew that displeasure with me had overcome thee ; but I will not be
angry with thee, for thy sense is weak, and thou art a

youth : a short time ago I used to carry thee on my shoulder, and take thee to the school. Upon this, I said to him, O my brother, I conjure thee by the requisitions of Allah, depart from me that I may perform my business, and go thou thy way. Then I rent my clothes ; and when he saw me do this, he took the razor, and sharpened it, and continued to do so until my soul almost parted from my body : then advancing to my head, he shaved a small portion of it ; after which he raised his hand, and said, O my Lord, haste is from the devil. Leave, said I, that which doth not concern thee ! Thou hast contracted my heart and troubled my mind. I fancy that thou art in haste, he rejoined. I replied, Yes ! yes ! yes ! Proceed slowly, said he ; for verily haste is from the devil, and it giveth occasion to repentance and disappointment ; and he, upon whom be blessing and peace, hath said, The best of affairs is that which is commenced with deliberation : and, by Allah, I am in doubt as to thine affair ; I wish, therefore, that thou wouldst make known to me what thou art hasting to do ; and it may be good, for I fear it is otherwise.

There now remained to the appointed time three hours ; and he threw the razor from his hand in anger, and, taking the astrolabe, went again to observe the sun ; then, after he had waited a long time, he returned, saying, There remain to the hour of prayer three hours, neither more nor less. For the sake of Allah, said I, be silent, for thou hast crumbled my liver ! and thereupon he took the razor, and sharpened it, as he had done the first time, and shaved another portion of my head. Then, stopping again, he said, I am in anxiety on account of thy hurry : if thou wouldst acquaint me with the cause of it, it would be better for thee ; for thou knowest that thy father used to do nothing without consulting me.

I perceived now that I could not avoid his importunity, and said within myself, The time of prayer is almost come, and I desire to go before the people come out from the service: if I delay a little longer, I know not how to gain admission to her. I therefore said to him, Be quick, and cease from this chattering and impertinence; for I desire to repair to an entertainment with my friends. But when he heard the mention of the entertainment, he exclaimed, The day is a blessed day for me! I yesterday conjured a party of my intimate friends to come and feast with me, and forgot to prepare for them anything to eat; and now I have remembered it. Alas for the disgrace that I shall experience from them! So I said to him, Be in no anxiety on this account, since thou hast been told that I am going to-day to an entertainment; for all the food and drink that is in my house shall be thine if thou use expedition in my affair, and quickly finish shaving my head. May God recompense thee with every blessing! he replied : describe to me what thou hast for my guests, that I may know it. I have, said I, five dishes of meat, and ten fowls fricandoed, and a roasted lamb. Cause them to be brought before me, he said, that I may see them. So I had them brought to him, and he exclaimed, Divinely art thou gifted! How generous is thy soul! But the incense and perfumes are wanting. I brought him, therefore, a box containing perfumes, and aloes-wood, and ambergris, and musk worth fifty pieces of gold. The time had now become contracted, like my own heart; so I said to him, Receive this, and shave the whole of my head, by the existence of Mohammed, God favor and preserve him! But he replied, By Allah, I will not take it until I see all that it contains. I therefore ordered the boy, and he opened the box to him; whereupon the barber threw down the astrolabe from his hand, and, seating himself upon the ground, turned over the perfumes, and incense, and aloes-wood in the box until my soul almost quitted my body.

He then advanced, and took the razor, and shaved another small portion of my head; after which he said, By Allah, O my son, I know not whether I should thank thee or thank thy father; for my entertainment to-day is entirely derived from thy bounty and kindness, and I have no one among my visitors deserving of it; for my guests are Zeitoun the bath-keeper, and Salia the wheat-seller, and Oukal the bean-seller, and Akrasha the grocer, and Homeid the dustman, and Akarish the milk-seller, and each of these hath a peculiar dance which he performeth, and peculiar verses which he reciteth; and the best of their qualities is that they are like thy servant, the mamlouk, who is before thee; and I, thy slave, know neither loquacity nor impertinence. As to the bath-keeper, he saith, If I go not to the feast, it cometh to my house! and as to the dustman, he is witty and full of frolic: often doth he dance, and say, News with my wife is not kept in a chest! and each of my friends hath jests that another hath not; but the description is not like the actual observation. If thou choose, therefore, to come to us, it will be more pleasant both to thee and to us; relinquish, then, thy visit to thy friends, of whom thou hast told us that thou desirest to go to them; for the traces of disease are yet upon thee, and probably thou art going to a people of many words, who will talk of that which concerneth them not; or probably there will be among them one impertinent person; and thy soul is already disquieted by disease. I replied, If it be the will of God, that shall be on some other day; but he said, It will be more proper that thou first join my party of friends, that thou mayest enjoy their conviviality, and delight thyself with their salt. Act in accordance with the saying of the poet :

Defer not a pleasure when it can be had; for fortune often destroyeth our plans.

Upon this I laughed from a heart laden with anger, and said to him, Do what I require, that I may go in the care of God, whose name be exalted, and do thou go to thy friends, for they are waiting thine arrival. He replied, I desire nothing but to introduce thee into the society of these people; for verily they are of the sons of that class among which is no impertinent person; and if thou didst but behold them once, thou wouldst leave all thine own companions. May God, said I, give thee abundant joy with them, and I must bring them together here some day. If that be thy wish, he rejoined, and thou wilt first attend the entertainment of thy friends this day, wait until I take this present with which thou hast honored me and place it before my friends, that they may eat and drink without waiting for me, and then I will return to thee, and go with thee to thy companions; for there is no false delicacy between me and my companions that should prevent my leaving them: so I will return to thee quickly, and repair with thee whithersoever thou goest. Upon this I exclaimed, There is no strength nor power but in God, the High, the Great. Go thou to thy companions, and delight thy heart with them, and leave me to repair to mine, and to remain with them this day, for they are waiting my arrival. But he said, I will not leave thee to go alone. The place to which I am going, said I, none can enter except myself. I suppose then, he rejoined, that thou hast an appointment

to-day with some female : otherwise thou wouldst take me
with thee ; for I am more deserving than all other men,
and will assist thee to attain what thou desirest. I fear
that thou art going to visit some strange woman, and that
thy life will be lost ; for in this city of Bagdad no one can
do anything of this kind, especially on such a day as this ;
seeing that the judge of Bagdad is a terrible, sharp sword.
Woe to thee, O wicked old man! I exclaimed; what are
these words with which thou addressest me ? And upon
this he kept a long silence.

The time of prayer had now arrived, and the time of the
prayer was near, when he had finished shaving my head;
so I said to him, Go with this food and drink to thy friends,
and I will wait for thee until thou return, and thou shalt
accompany me : and I continued my endeavors to deceive
him, that he might go away ; but he said to me, Verily
thou art deceiving me, and wilt go alone, and precipitate
thyself into a calamity from which there will be no escape
for thee: by Allah! by Allah! then, quit not this spot
until I return to thee and accompany thee, that I may
know what will be the result of thine affair. I replied,
Well : prolong not thine absence from me. And he took
the food, and drink, and other things which I had given
him, but intrusted them to a porter to convey them to his
abode, and concealed himself in one of the by-streets. I
then immediately arose. The mueddins on the minarets
had chanted the Selam of Friday ; and I put on my clothes
and went forth alone, and, arriving at the by-street, stopped
at the door of the house where I had seen the damsel ;
and lo, the barber was behind me, and I knew it not. I
found the door open, and entered ; and immediately the
master of the house returned from the prayers, and entered

the saloon, and closed the door; and I said within myself, How did this devil discover me?

Now it happened just at this time, for the fulfilment of God's purpose to rend the veil of protection before me, that a female slave belonging to the master of the house committed some offence, in consequence of which he beat her, and she cried out, whereupon a male slave came in to liberate her; but he beat him also, and he likewise cried out, and the barber concluded that he was beating me; so he cried, and rent his clothes, and sprinkled dust upon his head, shrieking, and calling out for assistance. He was surrounded by people, and said to them, My master hath been killed in the house of the cadi! Then running to my house, crying out all the while, and with a crowd behind him, he gave the news to my family; and I knew not what he had done when they approached, crying, Alas for our master! The barber all the while being before them, with his clothes rent, and a number of the people of the city with them. They continued shrieking, the barber shrieking at their head, and all of them exclaiming, Alas for our slain! Thus they advanced to the house in which I was confined; and when the cadi heard of this occurrence, the event troubled him, and he arose and opened the door, and, seeing a great crowd, he was confounded, and said, O people, what is the news? The servants replied, Thou hast killed our master. O people, rejoined he, what hath your master done unto me that I should kill him, and wherefore do I see this barber before you? Thou hast just now beaten him with sticks, said the barber, and I heard his cries. What hath he done that I should kill him? repeated the cadi. And whence, he added, came he, and whither would he go? Be not an old man of malevolence, exclaimed the barber, for I know the story, and the reason of his entering thy house, and the truth of the whole affair: thy daughter is in love with him, and he is in love with her; and thou hast discovered that he had entered thy house, and hast ordered thy young men, and they have beaten him. By Allah, none shall decide between us and thee excepting the caliph; or thou shalt bring forth to us our master, that his family may take him, and oblige me not to enter and take him forth from you; haste then thyself to produce him.

Upon this the cadi was withheld from speaking, and became utterly abashed before the people; but presently he said to the barber, If thou speak truth, enter thyself, and bring him forth. So the barber advanced, and entered the house; and when I saw him do so, I sought for a way to escape; but I found no place of refuge excepting a large chest, which I observed in the same apartment in which I then was; I therefore entered this, and shut down the lid, and held in my breath. Immediately after, the barber ran into the saloon, and, without looking in any other direction than that in which I had concealed myself, came thither; then turning his eyes to the right and the left, and seeing nothing but the chest, he raised it upon his head, whereupon my reason forsook me. He quickly descended with it, and I, being now certain that he would not quit me, opened the chest, and threw myself upon the ground. My leg was broken by the fall; and when I came to the door of the house, I found a multitude of people: I had never seen such a crowd as was there collected on that day; so I began to scatter gold among them to divert them, and while they were busied in picking it up, I ran through the by-streets of Bagdad, followed by this barber, and wherever I entered he entered after me, crying, They would have plunged me into affliction on account of my master! Praise be to God who aided me against them, and delivered my master from their hands! Thou continuedst, O my master, to be excited by haste for the accomplishment of thine evil design, until thou brought-est upon thyself this event ; and if God had not blessed thee with me, thou hadst not escaped from this calamity into which thou hast fallen ; and they might have involved thee in a calamity from which thou wouldst never have escaped. Beg, therefore, of God, that I may live for thy sake, to liberate thee in future. By Allah, thou hast almost destroyed me by thine evil design, desiring to go alone ; but we will not be angry with thee for thine igno-rance, for thou art endowed with little sense, and of a hasty disposition. Art thou not satisfied, replied I, with that which thou hast done, but wilt thou run after me through the market streets ? And I desired death to liberate me from him, but I found it not ; and in the excess of my rage I ran from him, and, entering a shop in the midst of the market, implored the protection of its owner ; and he drove away the barber from me.

I then seated myself in a magazine belonging to him, and said within myself, I cannot now rid myself of this barber ; but he will be with me night and day, and I can-not endure the sight of his face. So I immediately sum-moned witnesses, and wrote a document, dividing my property among my family, and appointing a guardian over them, and ordered him to sell the house and all the im-movable possessions, charging him with the care of the old and young, and set forth at once on a journey in order to escape from this rascal. I then arrived in your country,

where I took up my abode, and have remained a considerable time; and when ye invited me, and I came unto you, I
saw this vile rascal among you, seated at the upper end of
the room. How, then, can my heart be at ease, or my sitting
in your company be pleasant to me, with this fellow, who
hath brought these events upon me, and been the cause of
the breaking of my leg?

The young man still persevered in his refusal to remain
with us; and when we had heard this story we said to the
barber, Is this true which this young man hath said of
thee? By Allah, he answered, it was through my intelli-
gence that I acted thus toward him; and had I not done
so, he had perished; myself only was the cause of his
escape; and it was through the goodness of God, by my
means, that he was afflicted by the breaking of his leg,
instead of being punished by the loss of his life. Were I
a person of many words, I had not done him this kindness;
and now I will relate to you an event that happened to me,
that ye may believe me to be a man of few words, and less
of an impertinent than my brothers; and it was this : —

The Barber's Story of Himself.

I WAS living in Bagdad, in the reign of the Prince of the
Faithful Mountasir Billah, who loved the poor and indigent,
and associated with the learned and virtuous ; and it happened, one day, that he was incensed against ten persons,
in consequence of which he ordered the chief magistrate
of Bagdad to bring them to him in a boat. I saw them,
and I said within myself, These persons have assembled
for nothing but an entertainment, and, I suppose, will pass
their day in this boat eating and drinking ; and none shall

be their companion but myself; so I embarked, and mixed
myself among them; and when they had landed on the
opposite bank, the guards of the judge came with chains,
and put them upon their necks, and put a chain upon my
neck also. Now this, O people, is it not a proof of my
generosity, and of my paucity of speech? For I determined not to speak. They took us, therefore, all together,
in chains, and placed us before Mountasir Billah, the Prince
of the Faithful; whereupon he gave orders to strike off
the heads of the ten; and the executioner struck off the
heads of the ten, and I remained. The caliph then turning
his eyes, and beholding me, said to the executioner, Wherefore dost thou not strike off the heads of all the ten? He
answered, I have beheaded every one of the ten. I do not
think, rejoined the caliph, that thou hast beheaded more
than nine; and this who is before me is the tenth. But
the executioner replied, By thy beneficence, they are ten.
Count them, said the caliph. And they counted them;
and lo, they were ten. The caliph then looked toward me,
and said, What hath induced thee to be silent on this occasion? and how hast thou become included among the men
of blood? And when I heard the address of the Prince of
the Faithful, I said to him, Know, O Prince of the Faithful,
that I am the Sheikh El Samit, or The Silent; I possess,
of science, a large stock; and as to the gravity of my understanding, and the quickness of my apprehension, and
the paucity of my speech, they are unbounded; my trade
is that of a barber; and yesterday, early in the morning, I
saw these ten men proceeding to the boat; whereupon I
mixed myself with them, and embarked with them, thinking that they had met together for an entertainment; but
soon it appeared that they were criminals; and the guards

came to them, and put chains upon their necks, and upon my neck, also, they put a chain; and from the excess of my generosity I was silent, and spoke not : my speech was not heard on that occasion, on account of the excess of my generosity ; and they proceeded with us until they stationed us before thee, and thou gavest the order to strike off the heads of the ten, and I remained before the executioner, and acquainted you not with my case. Was not this great generosity which compelled me to accompany them to slaughter? But throughout my life I have acted in this excellent manner.

When the caliph heard my words, and knew that I was of a very generous character, and of few words, and not inclined to impertinence as this young man, whom I delivered from horrors, asserteth, he said, Hast thou brothers? I answered, Yes : five. And are thy five brothers, said he, like thyself, distinguished by science, and knowledge, and paucity of speech ? I answered, They lived not so as to be like me ; thou hast disparaged me by thy supposition, O Prince of the Faithful, and it is not proper that thou shouldst compare my brothers to me ; for through the abundance of their speech, and the smallness of their generous qualities, each of them experienced a defect: the first was lame ; the second blind ; the third one-eyed ; the fourth cropped of his ears ; and the fifth had both his lips cut off: and think not, O Prince of the Faithful, that I am a man of many words: nay, I must prove to thee that I am a man of a more generous character than they ; and each of them met with a particular adventure, in consequence of which he experienced a defect : if thou please, I will relate their stories to thee.

The Barber's Story of his First Brother.

Know, O Prince of the Faithful, that the first (who was named Bacbouc) was the lame one. He practised the art of a tailor in Bagdad, and used to sew in a shop which he hired of a man possessing great wealth, who lived over the shop, and who had, in the lower part of his house, a mill. And as my lame brother was sitting in his shop one day, sewing, he raised his head, and saw a woman like the rising full moon, at a projecting window of the house, looking at the people passing by ; and as soon as he beheld her, his heart was entangled by her love. He passed that day gazing at her, and neglecting his occupation, until the evening ; and on the following morning he opened his shop, and sat down to sew ; but every time that he sewed a stitch he looked toward the window ; and in this state he continued, sewing nothing sufficient to earn a piece of silver.

On the third day he seated himself again in his place, looking toward the woman ; and she saw him. She disappeared from before him, and sent to him her slave girl, with a wrapper containing a piece of red flowered silk ; and the girl coming to him, said to him, My mistress saluteth thee, and desireth thee to cut out for her, with the hand of skill, a tunic of this piece, and to sew it beautifully. So he answered, I hear and obey : and he cut out for her the tunic, and finished the sewing of it on that day ; and on the following day the slave girl came to him again, and said to him, My mistress saluteth thee. She then placed before him a piece of yellow satin, and said to him, My mistress desireth thee to cut out for her, of this piece, two pairs of trowsers, and to make them this day.

He replied, I hear and obey. Salute her with abundant salutations, and say to her, Thy slave is submissive to thine order, and command him whatsoever thou wilt. He then busied himself with the cutting out, and used all diligence in sewing the two pairs of trowsers ; and presently the woman looked out at him from the window and saluted him by a sign, now casting down her eyes, and now smiling in his face, so that he imagined he should soon obtain admission to her. After this she disappeared from before him, and the slave girl came to him; so he delivered to her the two pairs of trowsers, and she took them and departed. Now all this was a trick of the woman to punish my brother for taking a look at her. She told her husband, the master of the house, and the next day came to my brother, bringing some linen, and said to him, Cut out and make this into shirts for me. He replied, I hear and obey ; and ceased not from his work until he had cut out twenty shirts by the time of nightfall, without having tasted food. The man then said to him, How much is thy hire for this ? but my brother answered not ; and the damsel made a sign to him that he should receive nothing, though he was absolutely in want of a single copper coin.[1] For three days he continued scarcely eating or drinking anything, in his diligence to accomplish his work, and when he had finished it he went to deliver the shirts.

Now the husband of the young woman had said to her, How shall we contrive when he cometh for his money that I may take him, and drag him before the judge? She replied, Let me then play him a trick, and involve him in a disgrace for which he shall be paraded throughout this

---

[1] Captain Burton, who knows the language of all countries, takes our American phrase, and says, " he was destitute even to a *red cent.*"

city as an example to others : and my brother knew nothing of the craftiness of women. Accordingly, at the
approach of evening, the slave girl came to him, and,
taking him by the hand, returned with him to her mistress, who said to him, Verily, O my master, I have been
longing for thee. And her words were not finished when
the young woman's husband came in from his neighbor's
house, and, seizing my brother, exclaimed to him, By
Allah, I will not loose thee but in the presence of the
chief magistrate of the police. My brother humbled himself before him ; but, without listening to him, he took
him to the house of the judge, who flogged him with
whips, and mounted him upon a camel, and conveyed him
through the streets of the city, the people crying out,
This is the recompense of him who breaketh into the
harems of others ! and he fell from the camel, and his leg
broke ; so he became lame. The judge then banished
him from the city; and he went forth, not knowing whither
to turn his steps ; but I, though enraged, overtook him,
and brought him back ; and I have taken upon myself to
provide him with meat and drink unto the present day.

The caliph laughed at my story, and exclaimed, Thou
hast spoken well : but I replied, I will not accept this
honor until thou hast listened to me while I relate to thee
what happened to the rest of my brothers ; and think me
not a man of many words.

The Barber's Story of his Second Brother.

As to my second brother (the blind man, Bacbac, the
Gobbler), who was also surnamed Kuffeh, or empty-head,
fate and destiny impelled him one day to a large house,
and he knocked at the door, hoping that its master would

answer him, and that he might ·beg of him a trifle. The
owner called out, Who is at the door? but my brother
answered not; and then heard him call with a loud voice,
Who is this? Still, however, he returned him no answer;
and he heard the sound of his footsteps approaching until
he came to the door and opened it, when he said to him
What dost thou desire? My brother answered, Something for the sake of God, whose name be exalted! Art
thou blind? said the man; and my brother answered, Yes.
Then give me thy hand, rejoined the master of the house;
so my brother stretched forth to him his hand, and the
man took him into the house, and led him up from staircase
to staircase until he had ascended to the highest platform
of the roof, my brother thinking that he was going to give
him some food or money: and when he had arrived at this
highest terrace of his house, the owner said, What dost
thou desire, O blind man? I desire something, he answered again, for the sake of God, whose name be exalted!
May God, replied the man, open to thee some other way!
What is this? exclaimed my brother: couldst thou not tell
me so when I was below? Thou vilest of the vile! retort-
ed the other: why didst thou not ask of me something for
the sake of God when thou heardest my voice the first time,
when thou wast knocking at the door? What, then, said
my brother, dost thou mean to do to me? The man of the
house answered, I have nothing to give to thee. Then
take me down the stairs, said my brother. The man replied, The way is before thee. So my brother made his
way to the stairs, and continued descending until there
remained between him and the door twenty steps, when
his foot slipped and he fell, and, rolling down, broke his
head.

He went forth, not knowing whither to direct his steps,
and presently there met him two blind men, his companions, who said to him, What hath happened to thee this
day? My brother, therefore, related to them the event
that had just befallen him ; and then said to them, O my
brothers, I desire to take a portion of the money now in
our possession, to expend it upon myself. Now the owner
of the house which he had just before entered had followed
him to acquaint himself with his proceedings, and, without
my brother's knowledge, he walked behind him until the
latter entered his abode, when he went in after him, still
unknown. My brother then sat waiting for his companions ; and when they came in to him, he said to them,
Shut the door and search the room, lest any stranger have
followed us. When the intruder, therefore, heard what he
said, he arose and clung to a rope that was attached to the
ceiling ; and the blind men went feeling about the whole
of the chamber, and, finding no one, returned and seated
themselves by my brother, and brought forth their money
and counted it ; and lo, it was more than ten thousand
pieces of silver. Having done this, they laid it in a corner
of the room, and each of them took of the surplus of that
sum as much as he wanted, and they buried the ten
thousand pieces of silver in the earth ; after which they
placed before themselves some food, and sat eating ; but
my brother heard the sound of a stranger by his side, and
said to his friends, Is there a stranger among us ? Then
stretching forth his hand, it grasped the hand of the
intruder ; whereupon he cried out to his companions, saying, Here is a stranger ! and they fell upon him with
blows until they were tired, when they shouted out, O
Believers ! a thief hath come in upon us, and desireth to

take our property! and immediately a number of persons collected around them.

Upon this the stranger, whom they accused of being a thief, shut his eyes, feigning to be blind like themselves, so that no one who saw him doubted him to be so; and shouted, O Believers! I demand protection of Allah and the sultan! I demand protection of Allah and the judge! I demand protection of Allah and the emir! for I have important information to give to the emir! and before they could collect their thoughts, the officers of the judge surrounded them and took them all, including my brother, and conducted them before their master. The judge said, What is your story? and the stranger replied, Hear my words, O judge; the truth of our case will not become known to thee but by means of beating; and if thou wilt, begin by beating me before my companions. The judge therefore said, Throw down this man and flog him with whips; and accordingly they threw him down and flogged him: and when the stripes tortured him, he opened one of his eyes; and after they had continued the flogging a little longer, he opened his other eye; upon which the judge exclaimed, What meaneth this conduct, O thou villain? Grant me indemnity, replied the man, and I will acquaint thee: and the judge having granted his request, he said, We four pretend that we are blind, and, intruding among other people, enter their houses and see their women, and employ stratagems to corrupt them and to obtain money from them. We have acquired, by this means, vast gain, amounting to ten thousand pieces of silver; and I said to my companions, Give me my due, two thousand and five hundred, and they arose against me and beat me, and took my property. I beg protection, therefore, of Allah and of thee ; and thou art more deserving of my share than they. If thou desire to know the truth of that which I have said, flog each of them more than thou hast flogged me, and he will open his eyes.

So the judge immediately gave orders to flog them ; and the first of them who suffered was my brother. They continued beating him until he almost died ; when the judge said to them, O ye scoundrels! do ye deny the gracious gift of God, feigning yourselves to be blind! My brother exclaimed, Allah! Allah! Allah! there is none among us who seeth! They then threw him down again, and ceased not to beat him until he became insensible, when the judge said, Leave him until he shall have recovered, and then give him a third flogging : and, in the mean time, he gave orders to flog his companions, to give each of them more than three hundred stripes : while the seeing man said to them, Open your eyes, or they will flog you again after this time. Then addressing himself to the judge, he said, Send with me some person to bring thee the property ; for these men will not open their eyes, fearing to be disgraced before the spectators. And the judge sent with him a man, who brought him the money ; and he took it, and gave to the informer, out of it, two thousand and five hundred pieces of silver, according to the share which he claimed, in spite of the others (retaining the rest), and banished from the city my brother and the two other men ; but I went forth, O Prince of the Faithful, and, having overtaken my brother, asked him respecting his sufferings ; and he acquainted me with that which I have related unto thee. I then brought him back secretly into the city, and allotted him a supply of food and drink as long as he lived.

The caliph laughed at my story, and said, Give him a

present, and let him go; but I replied, I will receive nothing until I have declared to the Prince of the Faithful
what happened to the rest of my brothers, and made it
manifest to him that I am a man of few words : whereupon
the caliph said, Crack our ears, then, with thy ridiculous
stories, and continue to us thy disclosure of vices and
misdeeds. So I proceeded thus : —

The Barber's Story of his Third Brother.

MY third brother, O Prince of the Faithful, was the
one-eyed (named Alcouz): he was a butcher in Bagdad,
and both sold meat and reared lambs ; and the great and
the rich had recourse to him to purchase of him their meat,
so that he amassed great wealth, and became possessor of
cattle and houses. Thus he continued to prosper for a
long time ; and as he was in his shop one day, there
accosted him an old man with a long beard, who handed
to him some money, saying, Give me some meat for it.
So he took the money and gave him the meat ; and when
the old man had gone away, my brother looked at the
money which he had paid him, and seeing that it was of
a brilliant whiteness, put it aside by itself. This old man
continued to repair to him during a period of five months,
and my brother always threw his money into a chest by
itself ; after which period he desired to take it out for the
purpose of buying some sheep, but, on opening the chest,
he found all the contents converted into white paper,
clipped round ; and he slapped his face and cried out ;
whereupon a number of people collected around him, and
he related to them his story, at which they were astonished.

He then went again, as usual, into his shop, and having

killed a ram, and hung it up within the shop, he cut off
some of the meat and suspended it outside, saying within
himself, Perhaps now this old man will come again, and
if so, I will seize him: and very soon after the old man
approached with his money; upon which my brother arose,
and, laying hold upon him, began to cry out, O Believers!
come to my aid, and hear what this scoundrel hath done
unto me! But when the old man heard his words, he said
to him, Which will be more agreeable to thee, that thou
abstain from disgracing me, or that I disgrace thee before
the public? For what wilt thou disgrace me? said my
brother. The old man answered, For thy selling human
flesh for mutton. Thou liest, thou accursed! exclaimed
my brother. None is accursed, rejoined the old man, but
he who hath a man suspended in his shop. My brother
said, If it be as thou hast asserted, my property and blood
shall be lawful to thee: and immediately the old man exclaimed, O ye people here assembled! verily this butcher
slaughtereth human beings, and selleth their flesh for mutton; and if ye desire to know the truth of my assertion,
enter his shop! So the people rushed upon his shop, and
beheld the ram converted into a man, hung up; and they
laid hold upon my brother, crying out against him, Thou
infidel! thou scoundrel! and those who had been his dear-
est friends turned upon him and beat him; and the old
man gave him a blow upon his eye, and knocked it out.
The people then carried the carcass, and took with them
my brother, to the chief magistrate of the police; and the
old man said to him, O emir, this man slaughtereth human
beings, and selleth their flesh for mutton; and we have
therefore brought him to thee: arise, then, and perform
the requisition of God, whose might and glory be extolled!

Upon this the magistrate thrust back my brother from him, and, refusing to listen to what he would have said, ordered that five hundred blows of a staff should be inflicted upon him, and took all his property. Had it not been for the great amount of his wealth, he had put him to death. He then banished him from the city.

My brother, therefore, went forth in a state of distraction, not knowing what course to pursue; but he journeyed onward until he arrived at a great city, where he thought fit to settle as a shoemaker: so he opened a shop, and sat there working for his subsistence. And one day he went forth on some business, and hearing the neighing of horses, he inquired respecting the cause, and was told that the king was going forth to hunt; whereupon he went to amuse himself with the sight of the procession; but the king happening to look on one side, his eye met that of my brother, and immediately he hung down his head, and exclaimed, I seek refuge with God from the evil of this day! He then turned aside the bridle of his horse and rode back, and all his troops returned with him; after which he ordered his pages to run after my brother and to beat him; and they did so; giving him so severe a beating that he almost died; and he knew not the cause. He returned to his abode in a miserable plight, and afterward went and related his misfortune to one of the king's attendants, who laughed at the recital until he fell backward, and said to him, O my brother, the king cannot endure the sight of a one-eyed person, and especially when the defect is that of the left eye; for in this case he faileth not to put the person to death.

When my brother heard these words he determined to fly from that city; and forthwith departed from it, and

repaired to another city, where there was no king. Here
he remained a long time ; and after this, as he was meditating upon his adventure in the former city, he went out
one day to amuse himself, and heard again the neighing of
horses behind him ; upon which he exclaimed, The decree
of God hath come to pass ! and ran away, seeking for a
place in which to conceal himself ; but he found none,
until, continuing his search, he saw a door set up as a bar-
ricade : so he pushed this, and it fell down ; and, entering
the door-way, he beheld a long passage, into which he
advanced. Suddenly, however, two men laid hold upon
him, and exclaimed, Praise be to God who hath enabled us
to take thee, O thou enemy of God ! For these three
nights thou hast suffered us to enjoy neither quiet nor
sleep, and we have found no repose : nay, thou hast given
us a foretaste of death ! O men, said my brother, what
hath happened unto you ? They answered, Thou keepest
a watch upon us, and desirest to disgrace us, and to disgrace the master of the house ! Is it not enough for thee
that thou hast reduced him to poverty, thou and thy companions ? Produce now the knife wherewith thou threaten-
est us every night. And so saying, they searched him,
and found upon his waist the knife with which he cut the
shoe-leather. O men, he exclaimed, fear God in your
treatment of me, and know that my story is wonderful.
They said, What then is thy story ? So he related it to
them, in the hope that they would liberate him ; but they
believed not what he said ; and, instead of showing him
any regard, they beat him, and tore his clothes ; whereupon, his body becoming exposed to their view, they discovered upon his sides the marks of beating with sticks,
and exclaimed, O wretch ! these scars bear testimony to

thy guilt. They then conducted him before the judge, while he said within himself, I am undone for my transgressions, and none can deliver me but God, whose name be exalted! And when he was brought before the judge, the magistrate said to him, O thou scoundrel! nothing but a heinous crime hath occasioned thy having been beaten with sticks : and he caused a hundred lashes to be inflicted upon him; after which they mounted him upon a camel, and proclaimed before him, This is the recompense of him who breaketh into men's houses! But I had already heard of his misfortunes, and gone forth, and found him; and I accompanied him about the city while they were making this proclamation, until they left him; when I took him, and brought him back secretly into Bagdad, and apportioned him a daily allowance of food and drink.

Ꞇhe Barber's Storo of his ꝼourth Brother.

My fourth brother, Alnaschar,[1] was cropped of his ears, O Prince of the Faithful. He was a pauper, who begged alms by night, and subsisted upon what he thus acquired by day : and our father was a very old man, and he fell sick and died, leaving to us seven hundred pieces of silver, of which each of us took his portion, namely, a hundred pieces. Now my fifth brother, when he had received his share, was perplexed, not knowing what to do with it ; but while he was in this state, it occurred to his mind to buy with it all kinds of articles of glass, and to sell them and make profit : so he bought glass with his hundred pieces

[1] Al-naschar : the name is from Nashr, *sawing.* It is curious that we have the same idea when we speak of old "saws"; the reference being to constant repetition. A fiddler in Italy is called "the saw of the village."

of silver, and put it in a large tray, and sat upon an elevated place to sell it, leaning his back against a wall. And as he sat he meditated, and said within himself, Verily, my whole stock consisteth of this glass : I will sell it for two hundred pieces of silver ; and with the two hundred I will buy other glass, which I will sell for four hundred ; and thus I will continue buying and selling until I have acquired great wealth. Then with this I will purchase all kinds of merchandise, and essences, and jewels, and so obtain vast gain. After that I will buy a handsome house, and mamlouks, and horses, and gilded saddles ; and I will eat and drink ; and I will not leave in the city a single singer but I will have him brought to my house that I may hear his songs. All this he calculated with the tray of glass lying before him. Then, said he, I will send to seek in marriage for me the daughters of kings and viziers, and I will demand as my wife the daughter of the chief vizier ; for I have heard that she is endowed with perfect beauty and surprising loveliness ; and I will give as her dowry a thousand pieces of gold. If her father consent, my wish is attained ; and if he consent not, I will take her by force, in spite of him. Then I will purchase the apparel of kings and sultans, and cause to be made for me a saddle of gold set with jewels ; after which I will ride every day upon a horse, with slaves behind me and before me, and go about through the streets and markets to amuse myself, while the people will salute me and pray for me. Then I will pay a visit to the vizier, who is the father of the maiden, with mamlouks behind me and before me, and on my right and on my left ; and when he seeth me, he will rise to me in humility, and seat me in his own place ; and he himself will sit down below me, be-

cause I am his son-in-law. I will then order one of the
servants to bring a purse containing the pieces of gold
which compose the dowry; and he will place it before the
vizier; and I will add to it another purse, that he may
know my manly spirit and excessive generosity, and that
the world is contemptible in my eye; and when he
addresseth me with ten words, I will answer him with
two. And I will return to my house; and when any person cometh to me from the house of the vizier, I will
clothe him with a rich dress; but if any come with a
present, I will return it; I will certainly not accept it.
Then, on the night of the wedding, I will attire myself in
the most magnificent of my dresses, and sit upon a mattress covered with silk; and when my wife cometh to me,
like the full moon, decked with her ornaments and apparel,
I will command her to stand before me, as stand the
timid and the abject; and I will not look at her on account
of the haughtiness of my spirit and the gravity of my
wisdom; so that the maids will say, O our master and our
lord, may we be thy sacrifice! This, thy wife, or, rather,
thy handmaid, awaiteth thy kind regard, and is standing
before thee: then graciously bestow on her one glance;
for the posture hath become painful to her. Upon this I
will raise my head, and look at her with one glance, and
again incline my head downward; and thus I will do until
the ceremony of displaying her is finished. Then I will
look at her through the corner of my eye, and command
her to remain standing before me, that she may taste the
savor of humiliation, and know that I am the sultan of the
age. Then her mother will say to me, O my master, this
is thy handmaid; have compassion upon her, and be
gracious to her; and she will order her to fill a cup with

wine, and to put it to my mouth. So her daughter will say, O my lord, I conjure thee by the requisitions of God, that thou reject not the cup from thy slave; for verily I am thy slave. But I will make her no reply: and she will urge me to take it, and will say, It must be drunk; and will put it to my mouth; and upon this, I will shake my hand in her face, and spurn her with my foot, and do thus. So saying, he kicked the tray of glass, which, being upon a place elevated above the ground, fell,·and all that was in it broke; there escaped nothing; and he cried out and said, All this is the result of my pride! And he slapped his face and tore his clothes; the passengers gazing at him while he wept, and exclaimed, Ah! O my grief!

The people were now repairing to perform the Friday prayers; and some merely cast their eyes at him, while others noticed him not; but while he was in this state, deprived of his whole property, and weeping without intermission, a woman approached him, on her way to attend the Friday prayers: she was of admirable loveliness; the odor of musk was diffused from her; under her was a mule with a stuffed saddle covered with gold-embroidered silk; and with her was a number of servants; and when she saw the broken glass, and my brother's state, and his tears, she was moved with pity for him, and asked respecting his case. She was answered, He had a tray of glass, by the sale of which to obtain his subsistence, and it is broken, and he is afflicted as thou seest; and upon this she called to one of the servants, saying, Give what thou hast with thee to this poor man. So he gave him a purse, and he took it, and when he had opened it, he found in it five hundred pieces of gold, whereupon he almost died from excessive joy, and offered up prayers for his benefactress.   With the money my brother bought stuffs, praying to begin life again as a merchant in such articles. But see the will of God!

He passed the next night well contented, but when the morning came, he found at the door twenty soldiers, and on his going forth to them, they laid hold upon him, saying, The judge summoneth thee.   So they took him, and conducted him to the judge, who, when he saw him, said to him, Whence obtainedst thou these stuffs?   Grant me indemnity, said my brother; and the judge gave him the handkerchief of indemnity: and my brother related to him all that had befallen him, adding, And of that which I have, take thou what thou wilt; but leave me wherewith to procure my food.   The judge thereupon demanded the whole of the money and the stuffs; but fearing that the sultan might become acquainted with the matter, he retained a portion only, and gave the rest to my brother, saying to him, Quit this city or I will hang thee. My brother replied, I hear and obey; and went forth to one of the surrounding cities.   Some robbers, however, came upon him, and stripped and beat him, and cut off his ears; and I, having heard of his situation, went forth to him, taking to him some clothes, and brought him back privily into the city, and supplied him with daily food and drink.

The Barber's Story of his Fifth Brother.[1]

MY fifth brother (Shacabac), O Prince of the Faithful, had his lips cut off. He was in a state of extreme poverty, possessing nothing of the goods of this perishable world; and he went forth one day to seek for something with which to stay his departing spirit, and on his way he beheld a handsome house, with a wide and lofty vestibule, at the door of which were servants, commanding and forbidding; whereupon he inquired of one of the persons standing there, who answered, This house belongeth to a man of the sons of the Barmecides. My brother, therefore, advanced to the door-keepers, and begged them to give him something; and they said, Enter the door of the house, and thou wilt obtain what thou desirest of its master. So he entered the vestibule, and proceeded through it a while until he arrived at a mansion of the utmost beauty and elegance, having a garden in the midst of it, unsurpassed in beauty by anything that had ever been seen: its floors were paved with marble, and its curtains were hanging around. He knew not in which direction to go, but advanced to the upper extremity; and there he beheld a man of handsome countenance and beard, who, on seeing my brother, rose to him, and welcomed him, inquiring re-

[1] From this well-known story comes our phrase "A Barmecide feast." The Barmecides were in fact a noble family of great distinction.

specting his circumstances. He accordingly informed him that he was 'in want; and when the master of the house heard his words, he manifested excessive grief, and, taking hold of his own clothes, rent them, and exclaimed, Am I in the city, and thou in it hungry? It is a thing I cannot endure. Then promising him every kind of happiness, he said, Thou must stay and partake of my salt. But my brother replied, O my master, I have not patience to wait, for I am in a state of extreme hunger.

Upon this, the master of the house called out, Boy, bring the basin and ewer! and he said, O my guest, advance, and wash thy hands. He then performed the same motions as if he were washing his hands, and called to his attendants to bring the table; whereupon they began to come and go as though they were preparing it; after which the master of the house took my brother, and sat down with him at this imaginary table, and proceeded to move his hands and lips as if he were eating, saying to my brother, Eat, and be not ashamed, for thou art hungry, and I know how thou art suffering from the violence of thy hunger. My brother, therefore, made the same motions, as if he also were eating, while his host said to him, Eat, and observe this bread and its whiteness. To this my brother at first made no reply; but observed in his own mind, Verily this is a man who loveth to jest with others: so he said to him, O my master, in my life I have never seen bread more beautifully white than this, or any of sweeter taste. On which the host rejoined, This was made by a female slave of mine whom I purchased for five hundred pieces of gold. He then called out, Boy, bring to us the dish the like of which is not found among the viands of kings ! and, addressing my brother, he said, Eat, O my guest ; for thou art hungry, vehemently so, and in absolute want of food. So my brother began to twist about his mouth, and to chew, as in eating. The master of the house now proceeded to demand different kinds of viands, one after another ; and, though nothing was brought, he continued ordering my brother to eat. Next he called out, Boy, place before us the chickens stuffed with pistachio-nuts ; and said to his guest, Eat that of which thou hast never tasted the like. O my master, replied my brother, verily this dish hath not its equal in sweetness of flavor : and the host thereupon began to put his hand to my brother's mouth as though he were feeding him with morsels, and proceeded to enumerate to him the various different kinds of viands, and to describe their several excellences ; while his hunger so increased that he longed for a cake of barley-bread. The master of the house then said to him, Hast thou tasted anything more delicious than the spices in these dishes ? No, O my master, answered my brother. Eat more then, resumed the host, and be not ashamed. I have eaten enough of the meats, replied the guest. So the man of the house called to his attendants to bring the sweets ; and they moved their hands about in the air as if they were bringing them ; whereupon the host said to my brother, Eat of this dish, for it is excellent ; and of these cakes, by my life! and take this one before the syrup runs from it. May I never be deprived of thee, O my master ! exclaimed my brother, proceeding to inquire of him respecting the abundance of musk in the cake. This, answered the host, is my usual custom in my house : they always put for me, in each of the cakes, a mithkal [1] of

----

[1] About seventy-two grains.

musk, and half a mithkal of ambergris. All this time my
brother was moving his head and mouth, and rolling about
his tongue between his cheeks, as if he were enjoying the
sweets. After this, the master of the house called out to
his attendants, Bring the dried fruits! and again they
moved about their hands in the air as though they were
doing what he ordered; when he said to my brother, Eat
of these almonds, and of these walnuts, and of these raisins,
and so on; enumerating the various kinds of dried fruits;
and added again, Eat, and be not ashamed. O my master,
replied my brother, I have had enough, and have not power
to eat anything more; but the host rejoined, If thou desire,
O my guest, to eat and delight thyself, with more extraordinary dainties, by Allah! by Allah! remain not hungry.

My brother now reflected upon his situation, and upon
the manner in which this man was jesting with him, and
said within himself, By Allah, I will do to him a deed that
shall make him repent before God of these actions! The
man of the house next said to his attendants, Bring us the
wine; and, as before, they made the same motions with
their hands in the air as if they were doing what he commanded; after which he pretended to hand to my brother
a cup, saying, Take this cup, for it will delight thee; and
his guest replied, O my master, this is of thy bounty : and
he acted with his hand as though he were drinking it.
Hath it pleased thee? said the host. O my master,
answered my brother, I have never seen anything more
delicious than this wine. Drink, then, rejoined the master
of the house, and may it be attended with benefit and
health ; and he himself pretended to drink, and to hand a
second cup to my brother, who, after he had affected to
drink it, feigned himself intoxicated, and, taking his host

unawares, raised his hand until the whiteness of his armpit appeared, and struck him such a slap upon his neck that the chamber rang at the blow; and this he followed by a second blow; whereupon the man exclaimed, What is this, thou vilest of the creation? O my master, answered my brother, I am thy slave, whom thou hast graciously admitted into thine abode, and thou hast fed him with thy provisions, and treated him with old wine, and he hath become intoxicated, and committed an outrage upon thee; but thou art of too exalted dignity to be angry with him for his ignorance.

When the master of the house heard these words of my brother, he uttered a loud laugh, and said to him, Verily for a long time have I made game of men, and jested with all persons accustomed to joking and rudeness, but I have not seen among them any who could endure this trick, nor any who had sagacity to conform to all my actions, excepting thee: now, therefore, I pardon thee; and be thou my companion in reality, and never relinquish me. He then gave orders to bring a number of the dishes above mentioned, and he and my brother ate together to satisfaction; after which they removed to the drinking-chamber, where female slaves, like so many moons, sang all kinds of melodies, and played on all kinds of musical instruments. There they drank until intoxication overcame them: the master of the house treated my brother as a familiar friend, became greatly attached to him, and clad him with a costly dress; and on the following morning they resumed their feasting and drinking. Thus they continued to live for a period of twenty years: the man then died, and the sultan seized upon his property, and took possession of it.

My brother, upon this, went forth from the city, a fugi-
tive; and upon his way a party of Arabs came upon him.
They made him a captive; and the man who captured
him tortured him with beating, and said to him, By Allah,
purchase thyself of me by wealth, or I will kill thee: but

my brother, weeping, replied, By Allah, I possess nothing,
O sheïkh of the Arabs; nor do I know the means of obtaining any property: I am thy captive; I have fallen into
thy hands, and do with me what thou wilt. And immediately the tyrannical Bedouin drew forth from his girdle a
broad-bladed knife (such as, if plunged into the neck of a

camel, would cut it across from one jugular vein to the
other), and taking it in his right hand, approached my
poor brother, and cut off with it his lips; still urging his
demand. Now this Bedouin had five handsome children,
who delighted much in my brother's company. And one
day when he was playing with them, and singing to them
the songs of Antar, their father came in upon them; and
when he beheld my brother, he exclaimed, Woe to thee,
thou base wretch! Dost thou desire now to escape
with my children? Then with his knife he inflicted
upon him another wound; after which he mounted him
upon a camel, and having cast him upon a mountain,
left him there and went his way. Some travellers, however, passed by him, and when they discovered him they
gave him food and drink, and acquainted me with his
case; so I went forth to him, and conveyed him back
into the city, and allotted him a sufficient mainte-
nance.

Now I have come unto thee, O Prince of the Faithful, continued the barber, and feared to return to my
house without relating to thee these facts; for to ne-
glect doing so had been an error. Thus thou hast seen
that, although having five brothers, I am of a more
upright character than they. But when the Prince of
the Faithful had heard my story, and all that I had
related to him respecting my brothers, he laughed, and
said, Thou hast spoken truth, O Samit (O silent man);
thou art a person of few words, and devoid of impertinence; now, however, depart from this city, and take
up thine abode in another. So he banished me from
Bagdad; and I journeyed through various countries,
and traversed many regions, until I heard of his death,

and of the succession of another caliph, when, returning
to my city, I met with this young man, unto whom I
did the best of deeds, and who, had it not been for me,
had been slain : yet he hath accused me of that which is
not in my character ; for all that he hath related of me,
with respect to impertinence, and loquacity, and dulness,
and want of taste, is false, O people.

Continuation of the Story told by the Tailor.

THE tailor then proceeded thus : When we heard the
story of the barber, and were convinced of his impertinence and loquacity, and that the young man had been
treated unjustly by him, we seized hold upon him, and put
him in confinement, and, seating ourselves to keep watch
over him, ate and drank ; and the feast was finished in the
most agreeable manner. We remained sitting together
until the call to afternoon prayers, when I went forth and
returned to my house ; but my wife looked angrily at me
and said, Thou hast been all the day enjoying thy pleasure,
while I have been sitting at home sorrowful ; now if thou
go not forth with me and amuse me for the remainder of
the day, thy refusal will be the cause of my separation
from thee. So I took her, and went out with her, and we
amused ourselves until nightfall, when, returning home,
we met this humpback, full of drink, and repeating verses ;
upon which I invited him to come home with us, and he
consented. I then went forth to buy some fried fish, and
having bought it and returned, we sat down to eat ; and
my wife took a morsel of bread and a piece of fish, and put
them into his mouth, and choked him, so that he died ;

whereupon I took him up, and contrived to throw him into the house of this physician, and he contrived to throw him into the house of the steward, and the steward contrived to throw him in the way of the broker. This is the story of what happened to me yesterday. Is it not more wonderful than that of the humpback?

Continuation of the Story of the Humpback.

WHEN the king had heard this story, he ordered certain of his chamberlains to go with the tailor, and to bring the barber ; saying to them, His presence is indispensable, that I may hear his talk, and it may be the cause of the deliverance of you all : then we will bury this humpback decently in the earth, for he hath been dead since yesterday ; and we will make him a monument round his grave, since he hath been the occasion of our acquaintance with these wonderful stories.

The chamberlains and the tailor soon came back, after having gone to the place of confinement and brought the barber, whom they placed before the king ; and when the king beheld him, he saw him to be an old man, past his ninetieth year, of dark countenance, and white beard and eyebrows, with small ears, and long nose, and a haughty aspect. The king laughed at the sight of him, and said to him, O silent man, I desire that thou relate to me somewhat of thy stories. O king of the age, replied the barber, what is the occasion of the presence of this Christian, and this Jew, and this Mohammedan, and this humpback lying dead among you ; and what is the reason of this assembly? Wherefore dost thou ask this? said the king. The barber answered, I ask it in order that the king may

know me to be no impertinent person, nor one who med-
dleth with that which doth not concern him, and that I am
free from the loquacity of which they accused me; for I
am fortunate in my characteristic appellation, since they
have surnamed me The Silent, and, as the poet hath said,

Seldom hast thou seen a person honored with a surname, but thou wilt
find, if thou search, that his character is expressed by it.

The king therefore said, Explain to the barber the case of
this humpback, and what happened to him yesterday evening, and explain to him also what the Christian hath related,
and the Jew, and the steward, and the tailor. So they
repeated to him the stories of all these persons.

The barber thereupon shook his head, saying, By Allah,
this is a wonderful thing! Uncover this humpback, that
I may examine him. And they did so. He then seated
himself at his head, and, taking it up, placed it upon his
lap, and looked at his face, and laughed so violently that
he fell backward, exclaiming, For every death there is a
cause; and the death of this humpback is most wonderful:
it is worthy of being registered in the records, that posterity may be instructed by this event! The king, astonished at his words, said, O Samit, explain to us the reason
of thy saying this. O king, replied the barber, by thy
beneficence, life is yet in the humpback! He then drew
forth from his bosom a pot containing some ointment, and
with this he anointed the neck of the humpback; after
which he covered it up until it perspired; when he took
forth an iron forceps, and put it down his throat, and
extracted the piece of fish with its bone, and all the people
saw them. The humpback now sprang upon his feet, and
sneezed, and, recovering his consciousness, drew his hands

over his face, and exclaimed, There is no deity but God!
Mohammed is God's apostle! God favor and preserve
him! and all who were present were astonished at the
sight, and the king laughed until he became insensible ; as
did also the other spectators. The king exclaimed, By
Allah, this accident is wonderful! I have never witnessed
anything more strange! and added, O Believers! O assembly of soldiers! have ye ever in the course of your lives
seen any one die, and after that come to life? But had not
God blessed him with this barber, the humpback had been
to-day numbered among the people of the other world ; for
the barber hath been the means of restoring him to life.
They replied, This is indeed a wonderful thing!

The king then gave orders to record this event; and
when they had done so, he placed the record in the royal
library ; after which he bestowed dresses of honor upon the
Jew, and the Christian, and the steward; upon each of
them a costly dress : the tailor he appointed to be his own
tailor, granting him regular allowances, and reconciling
him and the humpback with each other. The humpback
he honored with a rich and beautiful dress, and with similar allowances, and appointed him his cup-companion.
Upon the barber, also, he conferred the like favors, rewarding him with a costly dress of honor, regular allowances, and a fixed salary, and appointed him state barber,
and his own cup-companion : so they all lived in the utmost
happiness and comfort until they were visited by the de-
stroyer of delights and the separator of friends, the depop-
ulator of palaces and the garnerer for graves.

THE STORY OF ABOU MOHAMMED THE LAZY.

———❖———

ONE day Haroun Alrashid bade the merchant Abou Mohammed the Lazy tell him his story, and why he was called Abou Mohammed the Lazy.

Abou Mohammed replied, Know, O Prince of the Faithful, that my father died and left my mother poor. She gave to me five pieces of silver, and bade me go to the land of China, that I might trade with them. But when I came to the ship, the ship-master took my money, and agreed to bring me back the profit.

The Sheikh Aboul Muzaffar set forth on the voyage, and with him a company of merchants, and they proceeded without interruption until they arrived at the land of China ; when the sheikh sold and bought, and set forth to return, he and those who were with him, after they had accomplished their desires. But when they had continued out at sea for three days, the sheikh said to his companions, Stay the vessel ! The merchants asked, What dost thou want ? And he answered, Know that the deposit committed to me, belonging to Abou Mohammed the Lazy, I have forgotten : so return with us, that we may buy for him with it something by which he may profit. But they replied, We conjure thee by Allah (whose name be exalted !) that thou take us not back ; for we have traversed a very long distance, and in doing so we have experienced great terrors and exceeding trouble. Still he said, We must return. They therefore said, Receive from us several times as much as the profit of the five pieces of silver, and take us not back. So he assented to their proposal; and they collected for him a large sum of money.

Then they proceeded until they came in sight of an island containing a numerous population, where they cast anchor; and the merchants landed to purchase thence merchandise, consisting of minerals, and jewels, and pearls, and other things. And Aboul Muzaffar saw a man sitting, with a great number of apes before him; and among these was an ape whose hair was plucked off. The other apes, whenever their master was inadvertent, laid hold upon this plucked ape, and beat him, and threw him upon their master; who arose thereat, and beat them, and chained and tormented them, for doing this; and all these apes became enraged in consequence against the other, and beat him again. Now when the Sheikh Aboul Muzaffar saw this ape, he grieved for him, and showed

kindness to him, and said to its owner, Wilt thou sell me
this ape? The man answered, Buy. And the sheikh said,
I have with me, belonging to a lad who is an orphan, five
pieces of silver. Wilt thou sell him to me for that sum?
He answered, I sell him to thee. May God bless thee in
him! Then the sheikh took possession of him, and paid
the money to his owner; and the slaves of the sheikh took
the ape and tied him in the ship.

After this they loosed the sails, and proceeded to another
island, where they cast anchor. And the divers who dived
for minerals, and pearls, and jewels, and other things came
down ; and the merchants gave them money as their hire
for diving. So they dived ; and the ape, seeing them do
this, loosed himself from his cord, leaped from the vessel,
and dived with them ; whereupon Aboul Muzaffar exclaimed,
There is no strength nor power but in God, the High, the
Great. We have lost the ape, with the luck of this poor
youth for whom we bought him! They despaired of the
ape ; but when the party of divers came up, lo, the ape came
up with them, having in his hands precious jewels ; and
he threw them down before Aboul Muzaffar, who wondered
at this, and said, Verily, there is a great mystery in this ape!

Then they loosed, and proceeded to an island called the
Island of the Ethiops, who are a people of the blacks, that
eat the flesh of the sons of Adam. And when the blacks
beheld them, they came to them in boats, and, taking all
that were in the ship, bound their hands behind them, and
conducted them to the king, who ordered them to slaughter
a number of the merchants. So they slaughtered them,
and ate their flesh. The rest of the merchants passed the
night imprisoned, in great misery ; but in the night the ape
arose and came to Aboul Muzaffar, and loosed his chains.
And when the merchants beheld Aboul Muzaffar loosed,

they said, God grant that our liberation may be effected by thy hands, O Aboul Muzaffar! But he replied, Know ye that none liberated me, by the will of God (whose name be exalted!), but this ape; and I have bought my liberty of him for a thousand pieces of gold. So the merchants said, And we in like manner: each of us buyeth his liberty of him for a thousand pieces of gold, if he release us. The ape therefore arose and went to them, and began to loose one after another, until he had loosed them all from their chains; and they repaired to the ship, and embarked in it, and found it safe, nothing being lost from it.

They loosed immediately, and continued their voyage, and Aboul Muzaffar said, O merchants, fulfil the promise that ye have given to the ape. They replied, We hear and obey. And each of them paid him a thousand pieces of gold. Aboul Muzaffar also took forth from his property a thousand pieces of gold; and a great sum of money was thus collected for the ape. They then continued their voyage until they arrived at the city of Balsora; whereupon their companions came to meet them; and when they had landed, Aboul Muzaffar said, Where is Abou Mohammed the Lazy? The news therefore reached my mother, and while I was lying asleep, my mother came to me and said, O my son, the Sheikh Aboul Muzaffar hath arrived, and come to the city: arise then, and repair to him and salute him, and ask him what he hath brought for thee: perhaps God (whose name be exalted!) hath blessed thee with something. So I replied, Lift me from the ground, and support me, that I may go forth and walk to the bank of the river. I walked on, stumbling upon my skirts, until I came to the Sheikh Aboul Muzaffar; and when he beheld me, he said to me, Welcome to him whose money was the means of my liberation and the

liberation of these merchants, by the will of God, whose
name be exalted! He then said to me, Take this ape; for
I bought him for thee; go with him to thy house, and wait
until I come to thee. I therefore took the ape before me,
and went, saying within myself, By Allah, this is none
other than magnificent merchandise! I entered my house,
and said to my mother, Every time that I lie down to
sleep, thou desirest me to arise to traffic: see then with
thine eye this merchandise. Then I sat down; and while
I was sitting, lo, the slaves of Aboul Muzaffar approached
me, and said to me, Art thou Abou Mohammed the Lazy?
I answered them, Yes. And behold, Aboul Muzaffar
approached, following them. I rose to him, and kissed his
hands, and he said to me, Come with me to my house.
So I replied, I hear and obey. I proceeded with him until
I entered the house, when he ordered his slaves to bring
the money; and they brought it, and he said, O my son,
God hath blessed thee with this wealth as the profit of the
five pieces of silver. They then carried it in the chests
upon their heads, and he gave me the keys of those chests,
saying to me, Walk before the slaves to thy house; for all
this wealth is thine.

I therefore went to my mother, and she rejoiced at this,
and said, O my son, God hath blessed thee with this abundant wealth; so give over this laziness, and go down into
the market street, and sell and buy. Accordingly, I relinquished my lazy habits, and opened a shop in the market
street, and the ape sat with me upon my mattress: when
I ate he ate with me; and when I drank he drank with
me; and every day he absented himself from me from
morning until noon, when he came, bringing with him a
purse containing a thousand pieces of gold, and he put it
by my side and sat down. Thus he ceased not to do for a

long time, until abundant wealth had accrued to me ; whereupon I bought, O Prince of the Faithful, possessions and
houses, and planted gardens, and purchased mamlouks, and
male black slaves, and female slaves.

And it happened one day that I was sitting, and the ape
was sitting with me upon the mattress, and lo, he looked
to the right and left; whereat I said within myself, What
is the matter with this ape ? And God caused the ape to
speak with an eloquent tongue, and he said, O Abou Mohammed! On hearing this, I was violently terrified; but
he said, Fear not. I will acquaint thee with my condition.
I am a Marid of the Genii ; but I came to thee on account
of thy poverty, and now thou knowest not the amount of
thy wealth ; and I have a want for thee to perform, the
accomplishment of which will be productive of good to
thee. What is it ? I asked. He answered, I desire to
marry thee to a damsel like the full moon. And how so ?
said I. To-morrow, he answered, attire thyself in thy rich
clothing, mount thy mule with the saddle of gold, and
repair with me to the market of the sellers of fodder :
there inquire for the shop of the shereef, and seat thyself
by him, and say to him, I have come to thee as a suitor,
desiring thy daughter. And if he say to thee, Thou hast
not wealth, nor rank, nor descent, give him a thousand
pieces of gold ; and if he say to thee, Give me more, do so,
and excite his cupidity for money. So I replied, I hear
and obey : to-morrow I will do this, if it be the will of God,
whose name be exalted!

Accordingly, when I arose in the morning, I put on the
richest of my apparel, mounted the mule with the saddle
of gold, and having gone to the market of the sellers of
fodder, inquired for the shop of the shereef, and found him
sitting in his shop. I therefore alighted and saluted him,

and seated myself with him. I had with me ten of my black slaves and mamlouks; and the shereef said, Perhaps thou hast some business with us which we may have the pleasure of performing. So I replied, Yes; I have some business with thee. And what is it? he asked. I answered, I have come unto thee as a suitor, desiring thy daughter. He replied, Thou hast not wealth, nor rank, nor descent. And upon this I took forth and presented to him a purse containing a thousand pieces of red gold, saying to him, This is my rank and descent; and he whom may God favor and preserve hath said, An excellent rank is [that conferred by] wealth.

When the shereef heard these words, he hung down his head for a while toward the ground; after which he raised his head, and said to me, If it must be, I desire of thee three thousand pieces of gold besides. So I replied, I hear and obey. I immediately sent one of the mamlouks to my house, and he brought me the money that the shereef had demanded; and when the shereef saw this come to him, he arose from the shop, and said to his young men, Close it. Then he invited his companions from the market to his house, and, having performed the contract of my marriage to his daughter, said to me, After ten days I will introduce thee to her.

I returned to my house full of joy, and in privacy informed the ape of that which had happened to me; whereupon he said, Excellently hast thou done. And when the time appointed by the shereef approached, the ape said to me, I have a want for thee to perform: if thou accomplish it for me, thou shalt obtain of me what thou wilt. And what is thy want? said I. He answered, At the upper end of the saloon in which thou wilt pay thy first visit to the daughter of the shereef is a closet, upon the door of which is a ring of brass, and the keys are beneath the ring. Take them and open the door. Thou wilt find a chest of iron, at the corners of which are four talismanic flags ; in the midst is a basin filled with money, and by its side are eleven serpents, and in the basin is tied a white cock with a cleft comb ; and there is also a knife by the side of the chest. Take the knife, and kill with it the cock, tear in pieces the flags, and empty the chest ; and after that go forth to the bride. This is what I require of thee. And I replied, I hear and obey.

I then went to the house of the shereef, and, entering the saloon, I looked toward the closet which the ape had described to me. And when I was left alone with the bride, I wondered at her beauty and loveliness, and her justness of stature and form ; for she was such that the tongue cannot describe her beauty and loveliness. I was exceedingly delighted with her ; and when midnight came, and the bride slept, I arose, took the keys, and opened the closet, and, taking the knife, I killed the cock, threw down the flags, and overturned the chest ; whereupon the damsel awoke, and saw that the closet was opened, and the cock killed ; and she exclaimed, There is no strength nor power but in God, the High, the Great ! The Marid hath taken me ! And her words were not ended when the Marid encompassed the house, and snatched away the bride. Upon this a clamor ensued ; and lo, the shereef approached, slapping his face, and said, O Abou Mohammed, what is this deed that thou hast done unto us ? Is this the recompense that we receive from thee ? I made this talisman in this closet through my fear for my daughter from this accursed wretch ; for he was desirous of taking this damsel during a period of six years, and could not do so. But thou shalt no longer remain with us : so go thy way.

I therefore went forth from the house of the shereef, and, having returned to my own abode, searched for the ape; but I found him not, nor saw any trace of him : so I knew that he was the Marid who had taken my wife, and that he had practised a stratagem against me, so that I had acted thus with the talisman and the cock which prevented his taking her.

I lay down, but could not sleep, hearing a voice. So I said to the person who addressed me, By the Object of thy worship, acquaint me who thou art! Whereupon the invisible speaker assumed the form of a man, and replied, Fear not; for thy kind conduct hath become known to us, and we are a tribe of the believing Genii. Art thou Abou Mohammed the Lazy? I replied, Yes. And he said, But fear not on account of this affair : we will convey thee to thy wife, and we will slay the Marid; for thy kindness is not lost upon us. He then uttered a great cry, with a terrible voice ; and lo, a troop approached him, and he required of them respecting the ape; upon which one of them answered, I know his abode. He said, Where is his abode? And he answered, In the City of Brass, upon which the sun riseth not.

And we flew together, by the strength of his wings, to the City of Brass. I alighted from behind him, and walked on until I arrived at the city, when I saw that its wall was of brass ; and I went round about it, hoping to find a gate to it ; but I found none.

But at last I entered with the water into a grotto beneath the earth, and, rising thence, beheld myself in the midst of the city, and found the damsel herself sitting upon a couch of gold, with a canopy of brocade over her, and round the canopy was a garden containing trees of gold, the fruits of which were of precious jewels, such as rubies and chrysolites, and pearls and coral. And when the dam-

sel saw me, she knew me ; and, having saluted me first,
she said to me, O my master, who brought thee to this
place ? So I informed her of the events that had happened ; and she replied, Know that this accursed wretch,
from the excess of his affection for me, hath acquainted
me with that which will injure him and that which will
profit him, and hath informed me that there is in this city
a talisman with which, if he desired to destroy all who are
in the city, he could destroy them; and whatsoever he
should order his Afrites to do, they would comply with his
command ; and that talisman is upon a pillar. And where,
said I, is the pillar ? She answered, In such a place. And
what is that talisman? I asked. She answered, It is the
figure of an eagle, and upon it is an inscription which I
know not. Take it and place it before thee, and take a
censer with fire, and throw into it a little musk, whereupon there will arise from it a smoke which will attract the
Afrites. If thou do so, they will all present themselves
before thee ; not one of them will remain absent ; and
they will obey thy command, and do whatsoever thou shalt
order them. Arise, therefore, and do that, and may the
blessing of God (whose name be exalted !) attend the act.
So I replied, I hear and obey.

I arose and went to that pillar, and did all that she
desired me to do, and the Afrites came and presented
themselves before me, each of them saying, At thy service, O my master ! Whatsoever thou commandest us to
do, we will do it. I therefore said to them, Chain the
Marid who brought this damsel from her abode. And
they replied, We hear and obey. They repaired immediately to that Marid and chained him, making his bonds
tight ; and returned to me, saying, We have done what
thou hast commanded us. And I ordered them to return.

I then went back to the damsel, and, having acquainted her with what had happened, said, O my wife, wilt thou go with me! She answered, Yes. And I went forth with her by the subterranean grotto by which I had entered; and we proceeded until we came to the party who had directed me to her; when I said to them, Direct me to a route that shall lead me to my country.

Accordingly, they guided me and walked with me to the shore of the sea, and placed us on board a ship; and the wind was favorable, and the ship conveyed us on until we arrived at the city of Balsora. And when the damsel entered the house of her father, her family saw her, and rejoiced exceedingly at her return. I then fumigated the eagle with musk, and lo, the Afrites approached me from every quarter, saying, At thy service, and what dost thou desire us to do? And I commanded them to transport all that was in the City of Brass, of money, and minerals, and jewels, to my house, which was in Balsora; and they did so. After that I commanded them to bring the ape; and they brought him in an abject and despicable state: whereupon I said to him, O accursed, why didst thou act perfidiously to me? And I ordered them to put him in a bottle of brass. So they put him into a narrow bottle of brass, and stopped it over him with lead. And I resided with my wife in joy and happiness. I have now, O Prince of the Faithful, of precious treasures, and extraordinary jewels, and abundant wealth, what cannot be expressed by numbers nor confined by limits; and if thou desire anything, of wealth or aught else, I will command the Genii to bring it to thee immediately. All this I have received from the bounty of God, whose name be exalted!

And the Prince of the Faithful wondered at this story extremely.

THE STORY OF GANEM THE SON OF AYOUB,[1] THE DISTRACTED SLAVE OF LOVE.

———◆◆◆———

I T hath been told me, O happy king, said Scheherazade, that there was, in ancient times, a certain merchant of Damascus, possessed of wealth, who had a son like the moon at the full, of eloquent tongue, called Ganem the son of Ayoub, the Distracted Slave of Love; and this son had a sister, named Fetnah, on account of her excessive beauty and loveliness. Their father died, leaving them large property, among which were a hundred loads of silk and brocade, and bags of musk, and upon these loads was written, This is intended for Bagdad : it having been his desire to journey to that city.

So when God (whose name be exalted !) had taken his soul, and some time had elapsed, his son took these loads, and journeyed with them to Bagdad. This was in the time of Haroun Alrashid. He took leave of his mother and relations and townspeople before his departure, and went forth, placing his dependence upon God (whose name be exalted !), and God decreed him safety, so that he arrived at Bagdad, whither there travelled in his company a party of merchants. He hired for himself a handsome house, and furnished it with carpets and cushions, and

[1] The name is the same as Job. It is a misfortune that the I of the old texts is generally now read as J by readers of English. Jerusalem should really have no sound of soft G, nor should Job.

suspended curtains in it ; and there he deposited those
loads, together with the mules and camels, and remained
until he had rested himself ; and the merchants of Bagdad,
and its great men, came and saluted him. He then took
a wrapper containing ten pieces of costly stuff, with the
prices written upon them, and went forth with them to the
market of the merchants, who met him and saluted him,
treated him with honor and welcomed him, and seated him
at the shop of the sheikh of the market ; and he sold the
pieces, gaining, for every piece of gold, two. So Ganem
rejoiced, and he proceeded to sell the stuffs by little and
little ; and continued to do so for a whole year.

After this, on the first day of the following year, he
came to the same market, but found its gate shut, and,
inquiring the cause of this, he was answered, One of the
merchants hath died, and all the rest of them have gone to
walk in his funeral procession.[1] Wilt thou then, added
his informant, gain a recompense by walking with them ?
He replied, Yes ; and he asked respecting the place of the
funeral. So they guided him thither ; and he performed
the ablution, and walked with the other merchants until
they arrived at the place of prayer, where they prayed over
the dead. The merchants then walked all together before
the corpse to the burial-ground, Ganem following them,
until the procession arrived at the burial-ground outside
the city, and they proceeded among the tombs until they
came to that in which the corpse was to be deposited.
They found that the family of the deceased had pitched a
tent over the tomb, and placed there the candles and
lamps ; and they buried the dead, and the readers sat
reciting the Koran at the tomb. The merchants sat with

[1] Among Mohammedans it is meritorious to walk in a funeral procession.

them ; and so also did Ganem the son of Ayoub ; but he was overcome by bashfulness, saying within himself, I cannot quit them until I have departed with them. They sat listening to the recitation of the Koran until the period of nightfall, when the servants placed before them the supper and sweetmeats, and they ate till they were satisfied, and washed their hands, and resumed their seats.

The heart of Ganem was now troubled with reflections upon his merchandise, and he was fearful of the thieves, and said within himself, I am a stranger, and suspected of possessing wealth, and if I pass the night far away from my abode the thieves will steal the money and the loads. So, fearing for his property, he arose and went forth from among the company, asking their leave to depart on account of some business that he had to transact, and followed the beaten track until he came to the gate of the city ; but it was then midnight, and he found the gate of the city shut, and saw no one coming or going, and heard not a sound save the barking of the dogs and the howling of the wolves ; whereupon he exclaimed, There is no strength nor power but in God ! I was in fear for my property, and came hither on account of it, and have found the gate shut, and now I have become in fear of my life ! He then returned to seek for himself a place in which to sleep until the morning ; and, finding a private burial-place inclosed by four walls, with a palm-tree within it, and a gateway of hard stone, open, he entered it, and desired to sleep ; but sleep came not to him.

Tremor and gloom overcame him, thus lying among the tombs, and he rose upon his feet, and, opening the door, looked out, and beheld a light gleaming in the distance in the direction of the city gate. He advanced a few

steps, and saw the light approaching in the way which led
to the burial-place in which he was taking refuge; whereupon Ganem feared for himself, and hastily closed the door,
and climbed up into the palm-tree, and concealed himself
in the midst of its branches. The light continued to approach the tomb by little and little until it came very near;
and as he looked attentively at it, he perceived three black
slaves, two of whom were bearing a chest, the other having
in his hand an adze and a lantern; and as they drew near,
one of the two slaves who were bearing the chest said,
What aileth thee, O Sawab? to which the other of the
two replied, What aileth thee, O Cafour?[1] The former rejoined, Were we not here at the hour of nightfall, and did
we not leave the door open? Yes, answered the other,
what thou sayest is true. See then, resumed the first
speaker, it is shut and barred. Upon this the third, who
was carrying the adze and light, and whose name was Bakheet, said, How small is your sense! Know ye not that
the owners of the gardens go forth from Bagdad and repair
hither, and, evening overtaking them, enter this place, and
shut the door upon themselves, through fear, lest the blacks
like ourselves should take them, and roast them, and eat
them? Thou hast spoken truth, they answered; but there
is none among us of less sense than thyself. Verily, he
replied, ye will not believe me until we enter the burial-
place and find some one in it; and I imagine that, if any
one be in it, and have seen the light, he hath betaken himself to the top of the palm-tree.

When Ganem heard these words of the slave, he said
within himself, How cunning is this slave! May Allah
disgrace the blacks for their malice and villany! There

---

[1] Cafour: "Camphor," or white, in grotesque allusion to his blackness.

is no strength nor power but in God, the High, the Great! What will deliver me from this difficulty? The two who were bearing the chest then said to him who had the adze, Climb over the wall, and open to us the door, O Bakheet; for we are fatigued with carrying the chest upon our necks: and if thou open to us the door, we will give thee one of the persons whom we take, and we will fry him for thee excellently, so that not a drop of his fat shall be lost. But he replied, I am afraid of a thing which my little sense hath suggested to me: let us throw over the chest behind the door; for it is our deposit. They said to him, If we throw it, it will break. I am afraid, he rejoined, that there may be within the tomb robbers who slay men and steal their property; for when evening overtaketh them they enter these places to divide what they have taken. O thou of little sense, exclaimed the two others; can they enter here? They then put down the chest, and climbed up the wall, and descended, and opened the door, while the third slave, Bakheet, stood waiting for them with the light, and a basket containing some plaster: after which they seated themselves, having closed the door; and one of them said, O my brother, we are tired with walking, and taking up and putting down, and opening the door and shutting it, and it is now midnight, and we have not strength remaining to open the tomb and to bury the chest; wherefore, we will sit here three hours to rest ourselves, and then arise and accomplish our business: but each of us shall, in the mean time, tell his story, and relate all that hath happened to him from beginning to end. So the first, who carried the light, told his story; but it was of a nature unfit to be here repeated; after which another of the slaves thus began: —

The Story of the Slave Cafour.

Know, O my brothers, that I was, at the commencement of my career, a boy of eight years, and I used to tell one lie to the slave merchants every year, so that they fell out with each other in consequence, and the slave merchant my master, becoming impatient of me, committed me to the broker, desiring him to cry, Who will buy this slave with his fault? He was therefore asked, What is his fault? and answered, He telleth one lie every year. And a merchant approached the broker, and said to him, How much have they bidden for this slave with his fault? He answered, They have bidden six hundred pieces of silver. Then thou shalt have twenty for thyself, replied the merchant. So the broker introduced him to the slave merchant, who received from him the money, and the broker conveyed me to the dwelling of the merchant, and took his brokerage.

The merchant clad me in a dress suitable to my condition, and I continued with him for the remainder of the year, until the new year commenced with prosperity. It was a blessed year, plenteous in the produce of the earth, and the merchants began to give entertainments, every day one taking his turn to do so, until it was my master's turn to give an entertainment in a garden within the city. So he went, and the other merchants also, and he took for them what they required of food and other provisions, and they sat eating, and drinking, and carousing till noon, when my master wanted something from the house, and said, O slave, mount the mule, and go to the house, and bring from thy mistress such a thing, and return quickly.

I obeyed, therefore, and went to the house ; but when I approached it, I shrieked out, and shed tears ; whereupon the people of the quarter assembled together, old and young ; and my master's wife and daughters, hearing my cry, opened the door, and asked me what was the matter. I answered them, My master was sitting beneath an old wall, he and his friends, and it fell upon them ; and when I beheld what happened to them, I mounted the mule and came in haste to inform you. And when his children and wife heard these words, they shrieked, and tore their clothes, and slapped their faces, and the neighbors came to them. Then my master's wife overturned the furniture of the house, one thing upon another, and pulled down its shelves, and broke its shutters and its windows, and smeared its walls with mud and indigo, and said to me, Woe to thee, O Cafour ! Come hither and help me, and demolish these cupboards, and smash these vessels and this China-ware. So I went to her, and destroyed with her the shelves of the house and all that was upon them, and its cupboards and what they contained, and went about over the terraces and through every place until I had laid waste the whole, crying all the while, O my master ! My mistress then went forth, with her face uncovered, and only with her head-veil, and the girls and boys went with her, saying to me, O Cafour, walk on before us, and show us the place where thy master lieth dead beneath the wall, that we may take him forth from under the ruins, and carry him in a bier, and bring him to the house, and convey his corpse in a handsome manner to the burial. So I walked before them, crying, O my master ! and they followed me with their faces and heads uncovered, crying, O our misfortune ! O our calamity ! and there was none among the

men, nor among the women, nor among the children, nor a
maiden, nor an old woman [in the quarter], who did not
accompany us ; and all of them slapped themselves in the
excess of their lamentation. Thus I went with them
through the city ; and the people asking the news, they
informed them of that which they had heard from me ; and
the people exclaimed, There is no strength nor power but
in God, the High, the Great ! We will go to the judge, and
acquaint him. And when they arrived before the judge,
they informed him ; and he mounted, and took with him
laborers, with axes and baskets, and they followed my
footsteps, accompanied by a crowd of people.

I preceded them, weeping and crying out, and throwing
dust upon my head, and slapping my face ; and when I
came to the party in the garden, and my master beheld
me, I slapped my face, and exclaimed, O my mistress !
who will have pity upon me after my mistress ? Would
that I had been her sacrifice ! When my master, therefore, saw me, he was confounded, his countenance became
pale, and he said, What aileth thee, O Cafour, and what is
this predicament, and what is the news ? I answered,
When thou sentest me to the house to bring thee what
thou wantedst, I went thither and entered the house, and
found that the wall of the saloon had fallen, and that the
whole saloon had tumbled down upon my mistress and her
children. And did not thy mistress, said he, escape ? I
answered, No ; not one of them escaped ; and the first of
them that died was my mistress the elder. But did my
youngest daughter escape ? he asked. I answered, No.
And what, said he, hath become of the mule that I ride :
is she safe ? No, O my master, I answered ; for the walls
of the house and the walls of the stable tumbled down

upon all that was in the house ; even upon the sheep, and the geese, and the hens, and all of them became a mass of flesh beneath the ruins ; not one of them escaped. He then said to me, And thy master the elder ? I answered, No ; not one escaped : and now there remain neither house nor inhabitants, nor any trace of them ; and as to the sheep, and the geese, and the hens, the cats and dogs have now eaten them. And when my master heard my words, the light became darkness before his face, and he was no longer master of his senses nor of his reason, and was unable to stand upon his feet : he was paralyzed, and the strength of his back failed him, and he rent his clothes, and plucked his beard, and slapped his face, and threw his turban from his head, and ceased not to slap his face until the blood flowed from it ; and he began to cry, Ah ! O my children ! Ah ! O my wife ! Ah ! O my misfortune ! Unto whom hath happened the like of that which hath happened to me ! The merchants, also, his companions, joined with him in cries and lamentations, and were moved with pity for his case, and rent their clothes : and my master went forth from the garden, beating himself for the calamity that had [as he supposed] befallen him, and re-doubled the blows upon his face, seeming as though he were drunk.

And as the party thus went out from the gate of the garden, they beheld a great dust, and heard tumultuous cries, and, looking in that direction, saw the crowd approaching them. This crowd was the judge and his attendants, and a concourse of people who had come to gratify their curiosity, with the merchant's family behind them, shrieking and crying with violent lamentation and excessive grief ; and the first who accosted my master were

his wife and children. On beholding these, he was confounded, and laughed, and said to them, How are ye; and
what hath happened to you in the house, and what hath
befallen you? And when they saw him, they exclaimed,
Praise be to God for thy safety! And they threw themselves upon him, and his children clung to him, crying out, O our father! Praise be to God for thy
safety, O our father! and his wife said to him, Praise
be to God who hath shown us thy face in safety! and
she was stupefied, and her reason fled from her at that
which she beheld. She then said to him, How didst thou
escape with thy friends? And how, said he, were ye in
the house? We were all well, they answered, in prosperity
and health, and no evil hath befallen our house, save that
thy slave Cafour came to us with his head uncovered and
his clothes rent, crying out, O my master! O my master!
and we said to him, What is the matter, O Cafour? and he
answered, My master was sitting under a wall in the garden, and it fell upon him, and he died. By Allah, replied
my master, he came to me just now crying, O my mistress! O the children of my mistress! and said, My
mistress and her children are all dead!

He then looked aside, and seeing me with my turban falling from my head, while I still cried out and wept violently,
and threw dust upon my head, he called out to me: so I
approached him, and he said to me, Woe to thee, O malevo-
lent slave! O misbegotten wretch! O thou of accursed
race! What events hast thou brought about! But, by
Allah, I will strip off thy skin from thy flesh, and cut thy
flesh from thy bones! By Allah, replied I, thou canst not
do to me anything; for thou boughtest me with my fault,
on this condition, the witnesses testifying that thou bought-

est me with my fault, thou knowing it, and it was, that I
was accustomed to tell one lie every year; and this is but
half a lie : and when the year is complete I will tell the
other half of it ; so it will be an entire lie. But upon this
he cried out at me, O most accursed of slaves ! is this but
half a lie ? Nay, it is an exceeding calamity ! Depart
from me ; for thou art free.[1] By Allah, I replied, if thou
liberate me, I will not liberate thee until the year be complete, and I tell the remaining half of the lie ; and when I
have completed it, then take me to the market, and sell me
as thou boughtest me with my fault ; and liberate me not ;
for I have no trade by means of which to procure my subsistence ; this is a legal proposition that I have stated to
thee, laid down by the lawyers in the chapter of emanci-
pation.   While we were thus talking, the crowd approached,
with the people of the quarter, women and men, come to
mourn, and the judge with his attendants ; and my master
and the other merchants went to the judge, and acquainted
him with the case, and that this was but half a lie ; and
when the people who were present heard this, they were
astonished at this lie, and struck with the utmost wonder ;
and they cursed and reviled me ; while I stood laughing,
and saying, How can my master kill me when he bought
me with this fault ?

So when my master went to the house, he found it in a
state of ruin (and it was I who destroyed the greater part,
and broke in it things worth a large sum of money) ; and
his wife said to him, It was Cafour who broke the vessels

---

[1] The manumission of a slave, without giving him the means of providing for
himself, is considered by Mohammedans as a punishment. Burton says that
when by imperial law the slaves in Scinde were freed, there was great lamentation.

and the China-ware. Upon this his rage increased, and he exclaimed, By Allah, in my life I have never seen such a misbegotten wretch as this slave; yet he calleth it half a lie. What, then, would have been the result had it been a whole lie? In that case he had destroyed a city, or two cities! Then, in the excess of his rage, he went to the judge, who inflicted upon me a severe beating, so that I became insensible, and swooned away; after which my master contrived means of obtaining for me a high price, and I ceased not to excite disturbances in the places into which I was sold, and was transferred from emir to emir, and from grandee to grandee, by sale and purchase, until I entered the palace of the Prince of the Faithful, and now my spirit is broken, and my strength hath failed.

Continuation of the Story of Ganem the Son of Ayoub, the Distracted Slave of Love.

WHEN the other slaves had heard his story, they laughed at it, and said to him, Verily thou art a villain, the son of a villain: thou hast told an abominable lie. The first and second then said to the third slave, Relate to us thy story. O sons of my uncle, he replied, all that hath just been related is nonsense: but my story is long, and this is not a time to tell it; for the morning, O sons of my uncle, is near, and perhaps it may overtake us with this chest still before us, and we shall be disgraced among the public, and our lives be lost: haste then to work, and when we have finished, and returned home, I will relate to you my story. So they put down the light, and dug a trench of the size of the chest between four tombs; Cafour digging, and Sawab removing the earth in baskets, until they had dug to the depth of half a fathom, when they put the chest into the trench, and replaced the earth over it, and went forth from the inclosure, and, having closed the gate, disappeared from before the eyes of Ganem the son of Ayoub.

When, therefore, they had left the place vacant unto Ganem, and he knew that he was alone, his mind became busied respecting the contents of the chest, and he said within himself, What can this chest contain? He waited until daybreak gleamed and shone forth, and then descended from the palm-tree, and removed the earth with his hand until he had uncovered the chest and disengaged it, when he took a stone, and struck with it the lock, and broke it; and lifting up the cover, he looked in, and beheld a damsel asleep, stupefied with bhang, but still breathing: she was of a beautiful and lovely person, and decked with ornaments of gold and necklaces of jewels worth a kingdom, and of a value that no money would equal. When Ganem the son of Ayoub beheld her, he knew that she had been the object of a plot, and, being convinced of this, he pulled her up until he had lifted her out of the chest, and laid her upon her back; and as soon as she scented the breeze, and the air entered her nostrils, and her mouth and throat, she sneezed, and then was choked, and coughed, whereupon theré fell from her throat a round piece of bhang, of such potency that if an elephant smelled it he would sleep from one night to another. She then opened her eyes, and, looking round, said, with an eloquent voice, Woe to thee, O wind! Thou neither satisfiest the thirsty, nor cheerest by thy presence the satisfied with drink! Where is Zahr el Bostan?[1] But no one answered her. Then, looking aside,

[1] Garden-Bloom.

she exclaimed, Where are my slaves? are ye awake? speak! But no one answered her. And she looked round about her, and exclaimed, Alas for me, that I am transported to the tombs! O Thou who knowest the secrets of the breasts, and recompenseth on the day of resurrection! who hath brought me from among the curtains and the veils, and placed me amid four tombs?

While she was saying all this, Ganem stood still; but he now said to her, O my mistress, there are neither veils, nor palaces, nor tombs for thee here: this is none other than thy slave Ganem the son of Ayoub, whom the King, who is omniscient with respect to hidden things, hath impelled hither that he may deliver thee from these troubles, and that the utmost of thy desires may be accomplished unto thee. And he was silent; and when she became convinced of the truth of the case, she exclaimed, I testify that there is no deity but God, and I testify that Mohammed is God's apostle! Then looking toward Ganem, with her hands placed upon her breast, she said to him, with a sweet voice, O auspicious youth! who brought me unto this place? For now I have recovered my senses. O my mistress, he answered, three eunuchs came bearing this chest: and he related to her all that had happened, and how the evening had overtaken him, so that he became the means of her preservation, and that otherwise she had died of suffocation; and he inquired of her respecting her history. O youth, she replied, praise be to God who hath cast me into the hands of one like thee! Rise, therefore, now, and put me into the chest, and go forth to the road, and as soon as thou shalt find any one who lets out asses or other beasts, or a muleteer, hire him to transport this chest, and convey me to thy house; and when I am in thy abode it will be well, and I will relate to thee my story, and acquaint thee with my tale, and good fortune will accrue to thee through my means. So Ganem rejoiced, and he went forth into the desert tract.

The day had begun to gleam, the sun rose in splendor, and the people came walking forth; and Ganem hired a man with a mule, and brought him to the burial-place. He then lifted the chest, after he had put the damsel into it, and, with his heart smitten by love for her, proceeded with her, full of joy, for she was a damsel worth ten thousand pieces of gold, and was decked with ornaments and apparel of enormous value. Scarcely had he found himself at his house when he put down the chest, and opened it, and took forth from it the damsel, who looked, and saw that the place was a handsome dwelling furnished with variegated carpets, and she observed the gay colors and various embellishments, and beheld stuffs packed up, and loads of goods, and other property : so she knew that he was a great merchant, and a man of wealth. She then uncovered her face, and looked at him, and observed him to be a handsome young man, and loved him ; and she said to him, Bring us something to eat. He answered her, On the head and the eye be thy commands : and went to the market, and bought a roasted lamb, and a dish of sweetmeat, and procured some dried fruits, and candles, and wine, and the requisite apparatus for perfumes. Then returning to the house, he took in the things, and when the damsel saw him she laughed, and kissed him, and embraced him, and began to caress him. They then ate and drank until the approach of night, and their love was mutual; for they were both of the same age, and both equal in comeliness; and when the night approached, the Distracted Slave of

Love, Ganem the son of Ayoub, arose and lighted the
candles and lamps, and the chamber glistened; he then
brought forth the wine-service, and prepared the table,
and sat down with her; he filling and handing to her,
and she filling and handing to him, while they both
laughed, and recited verses: their gayety increased, and
they were engrossed by mutual love. Extolled be the perfection of the Uniter of Hearts! Thus they continued
until it was near morning, when sleep overcame them,
and each of them slept apart from the other till morning
came.

Ganem the son of Ayoub then arose and went forth to
the market, and bought what was requisite of vegetables,
and meat, and wine, and other provisions, and brought
them to the house: and he again sat with her to eat, and
they ate until they were satisfied; after which he brought
the wine, and they drank and toyed together till their
cheeks reddened and their eyes became more intensely
black; and Ganem said, O my mistress, have compassion
on the captive of thy love, and him whom thine eyes have
slain! I had remained sound of heart but for thee! Then
he wept a while; and she replied, O my master, and light
of mine eye, by Allah, I love thee and confide in thee; but
I know that thou canst not be united to me. And what
hindereth? said he. She answered, I will this night relate
to thee my story, that thou mayest accept my excuse. But
they continued thus a whole month; and after this, one
night, when Ganem was complaining to her of his passion,
she said to him, I will now explain to thee my case, that
thou mayest know my dignity, and my secret be revealed
to thee, and my excuse become manifest to thee. He replied, Well. And she took hold of a band which confined

a part of her dress, and said to him, O my master, read what is on this border. So he took the border in his hand, and looked at it, and he found worked upon it in gold, I AM THINE AND THOU ART MINE, O DESCENDANT OF THE PROPHET'S UNCLE.[1] And when he had read this, he let fall his hand, and said to her, Reveal to me thy history. She answered, Well: and thus began: —

Know that I am a favorite slave of the Prince of the Faithful, and my name is Kut-ul-Kulub, the Food of Hearts. The Prince of the Faithful, after he had reared me in his palace, and I had grown up, observed my qualities, and the beauty and loveliness with which my Lord had endowed me, and loved me excessively: he took me and lodged me in a private apartment, and appointed me ten female slaves to serve me, and then gave me those ornaments which thou seest with me. After this the caliph went forth one day on a journey to one of the surrounding provinces, and the Lady Zobeide came to one of the female slaves who were in my service, and said, When thy mistress, Kut-ul-Kulub sleepeth, put this piece of bhang into her nose and her drink, and thou shalt receive from me a sum of money that will satisfy thee. The slave replied, Most willingly: and she received the bhang from her, rejoicing on account of the money, and because she had been originally Zobeide's slave; and she insinuated the bhang into me, whereupon I fell upon the floor, with my head bent down to my feet, and seemed to be in another world; and when she could devise no other stratagem, she put me into that chest, and privily summoned the black slaves, and, after having given presents to them and to the door-keepers,

---

[1] The badge shows that she belonged to the harem of the Caliph Haroun, because the Abbaside caliphs were descendants of Abbas, uncle of Mohammed.

sent me with the black slaves on the night when thou wast
reposing at the top of the palm-tree : and they did with
me as thou sawest, and my deliverance was effected
through thy means : then thou broughtest me unto this
place, where thou hast treated me with the utmost kindness. This is my story ; and I know not what hath happened to the caliph during my absence. Know, therefore,
my dignity ; and divulge not my case.

When Ganem the son of Ayoub heard these words of
Kut-ul-Kulub, and discovered that she was the favorite of
the caliph, he drew back, in his awe for the caliph, and sat
alone at one side of the chamber, blaming himself, and
reflecting upon his situation, perplexed by love of her to
whom he could not be united ; and he wept from the
violence of his desire, and the fierceness of his passion and
distraction, and began to complain of fortune and its
injustice. Extolled be the perfection of Him who causeth
the hearts of the generous to be troubled with love, and
endueth not the mean with so much of it as equalleth the
weight of a grain ! And upon this Kut-ul-Kulub rose to
him and embraced him, and kissed him, and, her heart
being entirely captivated by his love, she revealed what she
had hidden of the extent of her passion, and encircled his
neck with her arms, and kissed him again ; but he withdrew from her embrace, in his fear for the caliph. They
then conversed a while, drowned in the sea of mutual love,
and so remained until day, when Ganem arose and went
forth to the market as usual, and procured what was
requisite, and, returning to the house, found Kut-ul-Kulub
weeping : but as soon as she beheld him, she ceased from
her tears, and smiled, and said to him, Thou hast made
me desolate by thine absence, O beloved of my heart ! By

Allah, this hour, during which thou hast been away from me, hath appeared as a year; for I cannot endure thy separation; and see, I have thus shown thee my state, through the violence of my passion. Arise, therefore, now, and mind not what hath happened, but take me as thy wife. But he replied, I seek refuge with Allah! This is a thing that cannot be. How should the dog sit in the place of the lion? What belongeth to my lord is forbidden me to approach. He then tore himself from her, and sat apart; and she increased in love through his refusal. In this manner they passed three long months; and whenever she made any advances to him he withdrew from her, and said, Whatever belongeth to the master is forbidden to the slave. Such was the case of the Distracted Slave of Love, Ganem the son of Ayoub.

Meanwhile, Zobeide, during the absence of the caliph, having acted thus with Kut-ul-Kulub, became perplexed, saying within herself, What shall I say to the caliph when he cometh and inquireth respecting her? and what shall be my answer to him? She then called for an old woman who resided with her, and acquainted her with her secret, and said to her, What shall I do, now that Kut-ul-Kulub is no more. The old woman answered, when she understood the affair, Know, O my mistress, that the return of the caliph is near; but I will send to a carpenter, and desire him to make a wooden image of a corpse, and they shall dig for it a grave, and thou shalt light candles and lamps around it, and command every one who is in the palace to wear black, and order thy female slaves and eunuchs, as soon as they know of the caliph's return from his journey, to raise lamentations in the vestibules, and when he enters and asks the news, they shall answer him, Kut-ul-Kulub is dead; and may God abundantly compensate thee for the loss of her! and from the esteem with which she was regarded by our mistress, she hath buried her in her own palace. So when he heareth this, he will weep, and the event will distress him. Then he will cause the readers to sit up by night at her tomb to perform recitations of the Koran; and if he say within himself, Surely the daughter of my uncle, through her jealousy, hath been led to destroy Kut-ul-Kulub or the distraction of love overpower him, and he give orders to take her forth from the tomb, fear not from that; for if they dig down to the image in the form of a human being, and take it forth, shrouded in costly grave-clothes, and the caliph desire to remove the grave-clothes from it, to behold her, do thou prevent him, and the fear of the world to come will withhold him; and do thou say to him, To behold her corpse uncovered is unlawful. Then he will believe her death, and will return her image to its place, and thank thee for thy conduct, and thou shalt escape, please God, from this difficulty. When the Lady Zobeide, therefore, heard what she said, she approved of it, and bestowed upon her a dress of honor, and commanded her to do this, having given her a sum of money. So the old woman set about the business immediately, and ordered the carpenter to make for her an image as above described, and when it was finished she brought it to the Lady Zobeide, and she shrouded it, and lighted the candles and lamps, and spread the carpets around the tomb, and clad herself in black,[1] ordering the female slaves to do the same; and the news was spread through the palace that Kut-ul-Kulub had died.

---

[1] It has already been noted that the usual mourning color in Mussulman countries is blue. Burton cannot explain the "black" in the text. Black was assumed, however, as the color of the banners of the Abbasides.

Some time after this, the caliph returned from his journey, and went up to his palace : but his mind was occupied only with Kut-ul-Kulub; and seeing the pages, and
eunuchs, and female slaves all clad in black, his heart was
agitated ; and when he entered the palace of the Lady
Zobeide, and beheld her also clad in black, he inquired the
reason of it, and they informed him of the death of Kut-ul-
Kulub.   Upon hearing this he fell down in a swoon ; and
when he recovered, he asked where was her tomb ; and
the Lady Zobeide answered, Know, O Prince of the Faithful, that, on account of the esteem in which she was held
by me, I buried her in my palace.   So the caliph, entering
the palace in his travelling dress, proceeded to visit the
tomb of Kut-ul-Kulub, and found the carpets spread, and
the candles and lamps lighted ; and when he beheld this,
he thanked her for what she had done.   But afterward he
became perplexed, and wavered for some time between
belief and disbelief, until suspicion overcame him, and he
gave orders to open the tomb and to take her out ; when,
however, he saw the grave-clothes, and was about to
remove them that he might behold her, he feared God
(whose name be exalted !), and the old woman said, Restore
her to her place   Then immediately the caliph commanded
to bring the professors of religion and law, and the readers,
and they performed recitations of the whole of the Koran
at her tomb, while he sat by the side of it weeping until
he became insensible.

He continued to frequent the tomb for the space of a
month ; after which it happened that he entered the harem,
after the emirs and viziers had dispersed from before him
to their houses, and he slept a while, and a female slave
sat at his head, and another at his feet ; and after sleep

had overcome him he awoke, and opened his eyes, and heard the damsel who was at his head say to her who was at his feet, Woe to thee, O Keizuran! Wherefore, O Kadib? said the other. Our lord, rejoined the first, is ignorant of what hath happened; so he sitteth up at night at a tomb in which there is nothing but a carved image, the work of the carpenter. And what then, asked the other damsel, hath befallen Kut-ul-Kulub. Her companion answered, Know that our mistress Zobeide sent some bhang by a female slave, and she stupefied her with it, and when the bhang had taken effect upon her, she put her in a chest, and sent her away with Sawab and Cafour, commanding them to throw her into the tomb. Upon this Keizuran said, Woe to thee, O Kadib! Is not the Lady Kut-ul-Kulub dead? Heaven preserve her youth from death! answered Kadib: I heard the Lady Zobeide say that Kut-ul-Kulub was with a young merchant named Ganem of Damascus, and that she had been with him, including this day, four months; and our lord here weepeth and passeth sleepless nights at a tomb in which there is no corpse. Thus they conversed together, while the caliph heard their words; and when they had finished their conversation, and he had become acquainted with the event, that this tomb was a false one, and that Kut-ul-Kulub had been with Ganem the son of Ayoub for the space of four months, he was violently incensed, and arose, and summoned the emirs of his court; whereupon the Vizier Giafar the Barmecide presented himself and kissed the ground before him, and the caliph said to him in anger, Descend, O Giafar, with a body of men, and inquire for the house of Ganem the son of Ayoub, and assault it suddenly, and bring him hither with my female slave Kut-ul-Kulub, and I will assuredly torture him.

Giafar replied, I hear and obey ; and he went forth with his attendants, the judge also accompanying him, and they proceeded until they arrived at Ganem's house. Ganem had just before gone out and brought a pot of meat, and was about to stretch forth his hand to eat of it with Kut-ul-Kulub, when she looked out, and found that the house was beset on all sides, and the vizier and the judge, and the officers of violence, and the mamlouks, with drawn swords, were surrounding it as the black surrounds the pupil of the eye ; and upon this she knew that tidings of her situation had reached the ears of the caliph, her lord, and she made sure of destruction : her countenance became pale, and her beauty changed, and, looking toward Ganem, she said to him, O my beloved, save thyself! How shall I do, said he, and whither shall I flee, when my wealth and means of subsistence are in this house ? But she answered, Delay not, lest thou perish, and thy wealth also be lost. O my mistress, and light of mine eye, rejoined he, how can I contrive to go forth when they are surrounding the house ? Fear not, she answered ; and she pulled off his clothes, and clad him in worn-out, ragged garments, and, taking the pot that had contained the meat, placed it upon his head, and put in it a little bread and a saucer of meat, and said to him, Go forth by the help of this stratagem, and thou hast nothing to fear with respect to me, for I know what I am able to do with the caliph. When Ganem, therefore, heard the words of Kut-ul-Kulub, and the advice which she gave him, he went forth through the midst of them, bearing the pot, and Providence protected him, so that he escaped from the

snares and injuries which menaced him, by the blessing
of his good conscience.

And when the Vizier Giafar arrived at the house, he dismounted from his horse, and entered, and looked at Kut-ul-
Kulub, who had adorned herself, and filled a chest with
gold and ornaments, and jewels and rarities, such as were
light to carry and of great value; and when Giafar came in
to her, she rose upon her feet, and kissed the ground before
him, saying to him, O my master, the Pen hath written what
God hath decreed. But Giafar, when he beheld her situation, replied, By Allah, O my mistress, he gave me no
order but to arrest Ganem, the son of Ayoub. And she
said, Know that he hath packed up some bales of merchandise, and gone with them to Damascus, and I know nothing
more than this ; and I request thee to take care of this chest
for me, and to convey it to the palace of the Prince of the
Faithful. So Giafar answered, I hear and obey: and he
took the chest, and gave orders that it should be conveyed,
together with Kut-ul-Kulub, to the palace of the caliph,
treating her with honor and respect. This took place after
they had plundered the house of Ganem ; and they went to
the caliph ; and Giafar related to him all that had happened :
whereupon the caliph appointed to Kut-ul-Kulub a dark
chamber, and there lodged her, commissioning an old
woman to serve her; for he imagined that Ganem had
acted dishonestly toward her.

He then wrote a letter to the Emir Mohammed, the son
of Suleiman Zeini, who was Viceroy of Damascus, containing as follows : As soon as this letter cometh to thy hands,
thou shalt arrest Ganem the son of Ayoub, and send him
unto me. So when the mandate was brought to him, he
kissed it, and put it upon his head, and caused it to be

proclaimed through the market street, Whosoever desireth
to plunder, let him repair to the house of Ganem the son
of Ayoub. And they came to the house, and found that
the mother of Ganem and his sister had made for them a
tomb, and sat by it weeping; and they laid hold upon them,
and plundered the house, and the mother and sister knew
not the cause: and when they brought them before the
sultan, he inquired of them respecting Ganem the son of
Ayoub; and they answered him, For the space of a year
we have obtained no tidings of him. And they restored
them to their place.

In the meantime, Ganem the son of Ayoub, the Distracted Slave of Love, when his wealth had been seized,
was perplexed, and began to weep for himself, so as to
break his heart. He walked on, and ceased not on his
way to the close of day, suffering from excessive hunger and fatigue, until he arrived at a village, where he
entered a mosque,[1] and seated himself upon a round
mat, and he leaned his back against one of the walls of
the building, and then threw himself down, under the
influence of extreme hunger and weariness. There he
remained until the morning, his heart palpitating from
want of food; vermin attacked his body, his breath became fetid, and he was altogether changed; and the
people of that village, coming to perform the morning
prayers, found him lying there sick through want of food,
yet exhibiting evident traces of former affluence; and
when they approached him, they found him cold and
hungry. They clad him, therefore, with an old garment
having ragged sleeves, and said to him, Whence art thou,
O stranger, and what is the cause of thine infirmity? And

---

[1] Mosques are open, night and day, to all travellers.

Ganem opened his eyes, and looked at them, and wept; but he returned them no answer. Then one of them know-ing the violence of his hunger, went and brought him a saucer of honey and two cakes of bread, and he ate, while they sat around him until the sun rose, when they departed to their several occupations. In this state he remained among them for a month, and his infirmity and disease increased; so the people, commiserating him, consulted together respecting his case, and agreed to transport him to the hospital at Bagdad.

While they were thus conversing, lo, two women, beg-gars, came in to him, and they were his mother and sister; and when he beheld them, he gave them the bread that was at his head, and they slept by him the next night; but he knew them not. And on the following day the people of the village came to him, bringing a camel, and said to its owner, Convey this sick person on the camel, and when thou hast arrived at Bagdad, put him down at the door of the hospital : perhaps he may recover his health, and thou wilt receive a recompense. He answered them, I hear and obey. So they brought forth Ganem the son of Ayoub from the mosque, and placed him, with the round mat upon which he was sleeping, on the camel; and his mother and sister came to look at him among the other people ; but they knew him not. Then observing him at-tentively, they said, Verily he resembleth our Ganem! Can he be this sick person or not? But as to Ganem, he awoke not until he was mounted on the camel, and he be-gan to weep and moan ; and the people of the village saw his mother and sister weeping for him, though they did not know him. Then his mother and sister journeyed onward to Bagdad, while the camel driver also proceeded, without stopping, until he had deposited Ganem at the door of the hospital, when he took his camel and returned.

Ganem remained lying there until the morning, and when the people began to pass along the street, they beheld him. He had become so emaciated that his form resembled that of a toothpick, and the people ceased not to gaze at him until the sheikh of the market came and repelled them from him, and said, I will gain Paradise by means of this poor person ; for if they take him into the hospital they will kill him in one day.[1]   He then ordered his young men to carry him, and they conveyed him to his house, where he spread for him a new bed, and put for him a new cushion, and said to his wife, Serve him faithfully.   She replied, On the head : and she tucked up her sleeves, and, having heated for him some water, washed his hands, and feet, and body, and clothed him in a vest of one of her female slaves.   She then gave him to drink a cup of wine, and sprinkled rose-water upon him : so he recovered his senses ; and he remembered his beloved Kut-ul-Kulub, and his anguish increased.   Thus did it happen to Ganem.

Now as to Kut-ul-Kulub: when the caliph, incensed against her, had lodged her in the dark chamber, she remained there in the same state eighty days ; and it happened that the caliph passed one day by that place, and heard her reciting verses ; and when she had finished her recitation of them, she exclaimed, O my beloved ! O Ganem !   How kind art thou, and how chaste is thy disposition !   Thou hast acted with kindness unto him who hath injured thee, and hast guarded the honor of him who hath violated thine, and hast protected his harem, and he hath

[1] This hatred of the hospital, common in the East, may be observed among the ignorant in the West.

enslaved both thee and thy family ; but thou wilt assuredly
stand, and the Prince of the Faithful, before a Just Judge,
and thou wilt obtain justice against him on the day when
the Judge shall be God, and the witnesses the angels !
And when the caliph heard her words, and understood
her complaint, he knew that she was injured ; and he entered his palace, and sent the eunuch to her, and when
she came before him she hung down her head, with weeping eye and sorrowful heart ; and he said to her, O Kut-ul-
Kulub, I see that thou complainest of my oppression, and
accusest me of tyranny, and thinkest that I have injured
him who hath acted kindly unto me. Who then is he who
hath guarded my honor and I have violated his ; and who
hath protected my harem and I have enslaved his ? She
answered him, Ganem the son of Ayoub ; for he hath not attempted any dishonest action toward me, by thy beneficence,
O Prince of the Faithful ! Upon this the caliph exclaimed,
There is no strength nor power but in God ! and then
added, O Kut-ul-Kulub, desire of me what thou wilt, and I
will grant thy wish. So she replied, I desire of thee my
beloved, Ganem the son of Ayoub. And when he heard
her words, he said, I will cause him to be brought hither,
if it be the will of God, in honor. O Prince of the Faithful, she rejoined, when thou shalt have caused him to be
brought, wilt thou present me to him ? He answered,
When I have had him brought I will present thee to him,
the present of a generous man who will not revoke his
gift. So she said, O Prince of the Faithful, permit me to
search about for him : perhaps God may unite me with
him. And he replied, Do as thou wilt.

Upon this she rejoiced, and went forth, taking with her
a thousand pieces of gold, and visited the sheikhs, and gave

alms for the sake of Ganem ; and on the following day she
went to the market of the merchants, and gave to the chief
of the market some money, saying to him, Bestow it in alms
upon the strangers. Then again, in the following week, she
went forth, taking with her a thousand pieces of gold, and,
entering the market of the goldsmiths and jewellers, summoned the chief of the market, and he came, and she gave
him the thousand pieces of gold, and said to him, Bestow
it in alms upon the strangers : whereupon the chief, who
was the sheikh of the market before mentioned, looked at
her, and said to her, Wilt thou go with me to my house, to
look at a young stranger there, and see how elegant he is,
and how perfectly charming ? For it is probable that he is
Ganem the son of Ayoub, the Distracted Slave of Love.
But the chief had no knowledge of him, and imagined that
he was a poor person involved in debt, whose wealth had
been taken from him, or a lover parted from his beloved.
And when she heard his words, her heart beat, and her
affections were engrossed by him, and she answered, Send
with me some one to conduct me to thy house. So he sent
with her a young boy, who conducted her to the house
where the stranger was lodged, and she thanked him for
so doing; and when she entered the house, and saluted the
chief's wife, the latter arose and kissed the ground before
her; for she knew her. Then Kut-ul-Kulub said to her,
Where is the sick person who is with you ? And she wept,
and answered, Here he is, O my mistress; but he is of a
respectable family, and exhibiteth traces of former affluence. And Kut-ul-Kulub looked toward the bed upon
which he was lying, and regarding him narrowly, beheld
him as though he were Ganem himself; but his condition was changed, and he had become so emaciated that

he resembled a toothpick, and the truth of his case was disguised from her, so that she did not discover him to be the person whom she sought; but she was moved with compassion for him, and she wept, and exclaimed, Verily, strangers are objects of pity, though they be emirs in their own countries! She then ordered for him supplies of wine and medicines, and sat at his head awhile, and mounted, and returned to her palace; and she continued to go forth to every market for the purpose of searching for Ganem.

Soon after, the chief of the market brought the mother of Ganem, and his sister Fetnah, and went with them to Kut-ul-Kulub, and said to her, O most charitable lady, there have entered our city this day a woman and a girl of respectable origin, bearing evident traces of former affluence, but they are clad in garments of hair-cloth, and each of them hath a wallet hung to her neck, and their eyes are weeping, and their hearts sorrowful: so I have brought them unto thee, that thou mayest give them refuge, and preserve them from the disgrace of beggary; for they are not persons suited to ask alms of the sordid; and, please God, we shall enter Paradise by their means. By Allah, O my master, she replied, thou hast made me long to behold them! Where are they? Order them to come in. So, upon this, Fetnah and her mother came in to Kut-ul-Kulub, who, when she saw them, and observed that they were both distinguished by beauty, wept for them, and said, By Allah, they are persons of an affluent family, and traces of wealth are conspicuous in their appearance. O my mistress, replied the chief of the market, we love the poor and indigent for the sake of future recompense; and probably the extortioners have oppressed these two persons, and plundered them of their wealth, and ruined their houses. Then these two females wept violently, and, remembering Ganem the son of Ayoub, the Distracted Slave of Love, their wailing increased, and Kut-ul-Kulub wept with them; and the mother of Ganem exclaimed, We pray God to unite us with him whom we seek, and he is my son Ganem the son of Ayoub. When Kut-ul-Kulub, therefore, heard these words, she knew that this woman was the mother of her beloved, and that the other was his sister, and she wept until she fell down in a swoon; and when she recovered, she approached them, and said to them, Ye have nothing to fear; for this day is the first of your prosperity, and the last of your adversity; therefore grieve not. She then ordered the chief of the market to take them to his house, and to let his wife conduct them into the bath, and attire them in handsome clothing, and take care of them, and treat them with the utmost honor; and she gave him a sum of money.

Then on the following day, Kut-ul-Kulub mounted and went again to the house of the chief of the market, and went in to visit his wife, who rose to her, and kissed the ground before her, and thanked her for her charity; and she saw that the wife had conducted the mother of Ganem and his sister to the bath, and taken off their former clothes, and that the traces of their original affluence had become more conspicuous in consequence; and she sat awhile conversing with them; after which she asked the wife of the chief of the market respecting the sick person who was with her. She answered, He is in the same state. And Kut-ul-Kulub said, Arise, and let us look at him and visit him. So they both arose, with Ganem's mother and sister, and went in to him, and seated themselves by him;

and when Ganem the son of Ayoub, the Distracted Slave of Love, heard one of them mention Kut-ul-Kulub, emaciated as he was in body and limbs, his soul returned to him, and he raised his head from the pillow, and called out, O Kut-ul-Kulub! She looked at him, therefore, and knew him, and cried, saying, Yes, O my beloved! He then said to her, Draw near to me. And she asked him, Art thou Ganem the son of Ayoub, the Distracted Slave of Love? He answered her, Yes; I am he. And upon this she fell down in a swoon; and when his sister and his mother heard their words, they cried out, O our joy! and in like manner fainted. And when they recovered, Kut-ul-Kulub said to Ganem, Praise be to God who hath united us with thee and with thy mother and sister! Then approaching him, she related to him all that had happened to her with the caliph, adding, I said to him, I have declared to thee the truth, O Prince of the Faithful: and he believed my words, and approved thee; and he is now desiring to see thee. And she said to him, The caliph hath given me to thee: whereupon he was filled with the utmost joy: and Kut-ul-Kulub said to them all, Quit not this place until I come again.

She then arose immediately, and departed to her palace, and removed thence the chest that she had brought from Ganem's house, and took forth from it some pieces of gold, which she gave to the chief of the market, saying to him, Take these pieces of gold, and buy for each of them four complete suits of dress of the best kinds of stuff, and twenty handkerchiefs, and whatever else they require. And after this she conducted them to the bath, and gave orders to wash them, and prepared for them boiled meats, and infusion of galangal, and juice of apples, after they had come forth from the bath and dressed themselves. For three days she remained with them, feeding them with fowls and with boiled meats, and giving them sherbet of refined sugar to drink ; and after the three days their spirits returned to them. Then she conducted them again to the bath, and they came forth, and she changed their clothes, and, leaving them in the house of the chief of the market, went to the caliph, and kissed the ground before him, and related to him the story, telling him that her master, Ganem the son of Ayoub, the Distracted Slave of Love, had come, and his mother and sister had also arrived. When the caliph, therefore, heard these words of Kut-ul-Kulub, he said to the eunuchs, Bring hither to me Ganem. And Giafar went down with them to bring him ; but Kut-ul-Kulub had gone before him, and went in unto Ganem, and said to him, The caliph hath sent to thee to bring thee before him : have a care then to display eloquence of tongue and firmness of heart, and sweetness of speech. And she attired him in a magnificent dress, and gave him pieces of gold in abundance, saying to him, Bestow plentifully upon the domestics of the caliph as thou goest in to him. And lo, Giafar approached him, mounted upon his mule, and Ganem advanced to meet him, and greeted him with a prayer for long life, kissing the ground before him.

The planet of his prosperity had appeared, and the star of his glory had risen aloft, and Giafar took him, and they proceeded until they entered into the presence of the Prince of the Faithful ; and when Ganem came before him, he looked toward the viziers, and emirs, and chamberlains, and lieutenants, and the other officers of the court and the warriors, and, being eloquent of tongue, firm of heart, delicate in the style of his language, and pleasing in the allusions it conveyed, hung down his head toward the ground, and then looked toward the caliph, and addressed him in a series of complimentary verses. And when he had finished his recitation, the caliph was delighted with the graces of his person, and pleased with the eloquence of his tongue and sweetness of his speech; and he said to him, Approach me. He therefore approached him, and the caliph said to him, Explain to me thy tale, and acquaint me with the truth of thy history. So Ganem sat and related to the caliph all that had happened to him from beginning to end; and when the caliph knew that he spoke the truth, he bestowed upon him a dress of honor, and admitted him into his favor, and said to him, Acquit me of responsibility. And he did so, and said to him, O Prince of the Faithful, the slave and all that his hands possess belong to his master: and the caliph rejoiced. He then gave orders to appropriate a palace to him exclusively, and appointed him abundant pensions and allowances, and removed to him his mother and his sister. And the caliph, hearing that his sister Fetnah was in beauty (as her name imported) a temptation, demanded her of him in marriage. Ganem therefore replied, She is thy handmaid, and I am thy mamlouk. And the caliph thanked him, and gave him a hundred thousand pieces of gold, and summoned the cadi and witnesses, and they performed the marriage contract. Then he and Ganem visited their wives on the same day, the caliph going to Fetnah, and Ganem the son of Ayoub to Kut-ul-Kulub; and on the following morning the caliph ordered that all that had happened to Ganem, from first to last, should be committed to writing and inserted in the records, that his posterity might consider it, and wonder at the disposals of destiny, and commit their affairs unto the Creator of the night and the day.

THE STORY OF ALADDIN[1] ABUSHAMAT.

IT hath been told me, O happy king, that there was, in ancient times, a merchant in Cairo, named Shemseddin. He was one of the best and the most veracious in speech of all the merchants, and was possessor of servants and other dependants, and male black slaves, and female slaves, and mamlouks, and of great wealth, and was syndic of the merchants in Cairo. And there resided with him a wife whom he loved, and who loved him; but he had lived with her forty years, and had not been blessed with a daughter nor with a son by her. And he sat one day in his shop, and saw the other merchants, every one of them having a son, or two sons, and the greater number of these sons were sitting in shops like their fathers. That day was Friday: so this merchant entered the bath and performed the ablution of Friday; and when he came forth [from the inner apartment], he took the barber's looking-glass, and, looking at his face in it, said, I testify that there is no Deity but God, and I testify that Mohammed is God's Apostle. He then looked at his beard, and saw that the white eclipsed the black; and he reflected that hoariness was the monitor of death.

It was therefore great joy to him and to his wife, who

---

[1] The name in Arabic is Ala-al-Din. It is the same name so familiar to English readers as Aladdin. But this is not he of the lamp. The meaning of the name is "The Glory of the Faith."

had sorrowed with his sorrow, that in an auspicious hour a fine boy was born to them. The nurse charmed him by repeating the names of Mohammed and Ali, and she pronounced in his ear the tecbir and the adan, and wrapped him up and gave him to his mother, who nursed him, and he took his nourishment until he was satiated, and slept. The midwife remained with them three days, until they had made the sweetmeat to distribute on the seventh day; and then they sprinkled the salt for the infant. And the merchant went in and congratulated his wife on her safety, and said to her, Where is God's deposit? Whereupon she presented to him an infant of surprising loveliness, the work of the Ever-present Governor. He was an infant of seven days; but he who beheld him would say that he was a child a year old; and the merchant looked in his face, and saw that it was like a shining full moon, with moles upon the cheeks. He said to his wife, What hast thou named him? And she answered, Were it a girl, I had named her; but this is a boy: so no one shall name him but thyself. The people of that age used to name their children from an omen; and, while they were consulting upon the name of the merchant's son, lo, one said to his companion, O my master Aladdin. So the merchant said to his wife, We will name him Aladdin Abushamat. He commissioned the nurses to rear him, and the child drank the milk for two years; after which they weaned him, and he grew up, and walked upon the floor. And when he had attained the age of seven years, they put him in a chamber beneath a trapdoor, fearing the influence of the eye upon him, and his father said, This boy shall not come forth from beneath the trap-door until his beard groweth. The merchant appointed a slave girl and a male black slave to attend upon him: the slave girl prepared the table for him, and the black slave carried it to him. Then his father circumcised him, and made for him a magnificent banquet; and after this he brought to him a professor of religion and law to teach him; and the professor taught him writing, and the Koran, and science until he became skilful and learned.

But it happened that the black slave took to him the table one day, and inadvertently left the trap-door open; whereupon Aladdin came forth from it and went in to his mother. There was with her a party of women of rank; and while they were conversing with her, lo, he came in to them, resembling an intoxicated mamlouk, in the excess of his beauty. So when the women saw him, they covered their faces, and said to his mother, Allah requite thee, O such-a-one! How dost thou cause this strange mamlouk to come in to us? Dost thou not know that modesty is one of the points of the faith? But she said to them, Pronounce the name of Allah! Verily this is my son, and the darling of my heart, the son of the syndic of the merchants, and the child of the nurse, and the necklace, and the crust, and the crumb! They replied, In our lives we never saw such a son of thine. So she said, Verily his father feared for him from the influence of the eye, and therefore made as his nursery a subterranean chamber under a trap-door; and probably the eunuch hath inadvertently left the trap-door open and he hath in consequence come up from it; but it was not our desire that he should come out from it until his beard should grow. The women, therefore, congratulated her upon this. And the youth went forth from them into the court of the house, and then ascended into the upper room, and there seated himself; and while he was sitting there, the slaves entered the house with the mule of his father; whereupon Aladdin said to them, Where hath this mule been? They answered him, We have conducted thy father to the shop, mounted upon her, and brought her back. And he asked them, What is the trade of my father? Thy father, they answered him, is the syndic of the merchants in the land of Egypt, and he is sultan of the sons of the Arabs.

And upon this Aladdin went in to his mother, and said to her, O my mother, what is the trade of my father? She answered him, O my son, thy father is a merchant, and he is the syndic of the merchants in the land of Egypt, and sultan of the sons of the Arabs. His slaves consult him not respecting the sale of anything excepting that of which the smallest price is a thousand pieces of gold. As to the sale of a thing for nine hundred pieces of gold or less, they consult him not respecting it, but sell it of their own free will. And there cometh not merchandise from other parts, little or much, but it is submitted to him, and he disposeth of it as he willeth; and no merchandise is packed up and goeth to other parts, but it is under the disposal of thy father. God (whose name be exalted!) hath given to thy father, O my son, great wealth, that cannot be calculated. So he said to her, O my mother, praise be to God that I am the son of the sultan of the sons of the Arabs, and that my father is the syndic of the merchants! But for what reason, O my mother, do ye put me in a chamber beneath a trap-door, and leave me there imprisoned? She answered him, O my son, we put thee not in the chamber beneath the trap-door but in our fear for thee from the influence of the eyes of men; for "the influence of the eye is true,"[1] and most of the inhabitants of the

[1] A proverb of Mohammed.

graves are victims of the eye. But he said to her, O my mother, and where is a place of refuge from destiny? Caution preventeth not fate, and from that which is written there is no escape. Verily he who took my grandfather will not leave my father : so if he is alive to-day, he will not be alive to-morrow ; and when my father dieth, and I go forth and say, I am Aladdin the son of the merchant Shemseddin, not one of the people will believe me, and the aged will say, In our lives we never saw a son nor a daughter of Shemseddin : then the officers of the government treasury will come down and take my father's wealth. Allah have mercy upon him who said, The liberal-minded man dieth, and his wealth departeth, and the meanest of men taketh his women. Do thou, then, O my mother, speak to my father, that he may take me with him to the market street and open for me a shop, and I will sit in it with merchandise, and he shall teach me the art of selling and buying, and taking and giving. She replied, O my son, when thy father cometh I will acquaint him with thy wish.

And when the merchant returned to his house, he found his son Aladdin Abushamat sitting with his mother : so he said to her, Wherefore hast thou taken him forth from beneath the trap-door ? O son of my uncle, she answered, I did not take him forth ; but the servants inadvertently left the trap-door open, and, while I was sitting with a party of women of rank, lo, he came in to us. And she acquainted him with that which his son had said ; whereupon the merchant said to him, O my son, to-morrow, if it be the will of God (whose name be exalted!), I will take thee with me to the market street ; but, O my son, sitting in the market streets and shops requireth polite and accomplished manners under every circumstance.

So Aladdin passed the next night full of joy at the words of his father; and when the morning came, his father took him into the bath, and clad him in a suit worth a large sum of money. And after they had breakfasted, and drank the sherbet, the merchant mounted his mule, and put his son upon another mule, and, taking him behind him, repaired with him to the market street ; and the people of the market street saw the syndic of the merchants approaching, followed by a youth whose face was like the moon in its fourteenth night. It was customary, when the syndic came from his house in the morning and sat in his shop, for the chief of the market to approach the merchants and recite the opening chapter of the Koran to them ; whereupon they arose and came with him to the syndic of the merchants and recited the chapter to him, and wished him good morning: then each of them departed to his shop. But when the syndic of the merchants seated himself in his shop on that day according to his custom, the merchants came not to him as they were wont to do. So he called the chief (who was named the Sheikh Mohammed Simsim, and who was a poor man), and said to him, Wherefore have not the merchants come together according to their custom? The chief answered him, that they were disputing on the subject of the youth who was with him, wondering who he could be, and he said, Is he thy mamlouk, or is he related to thy wife? He is my son, said the syndic. The chief replied, In our lives we have never seen a son of thine. The syndic therefore said, In my fear for him from the influence of the eye, I reared him in a subterranean chamber beneath a trap-door, and it was my desire

that he should not come up from it until he could hold his
beard with his hand ; but his mother would not consent :
and he requested me to open a shop, and to give him merchandise, and teach him the art of selling and buying.   So
the chief went to the merchants, and acquainted them with
the true state of the case ; upon which all of them arose
and went with him to the syndic, and, standing before him,
recited the Koran, and congratulated him on his having this
youth for a son, and said to him, May our Lord preserve
the root and the branch!   But (they added) the poor among
us, when a son or a daughter is born to him, is required to
make for his brothers a saucepan of asidah,[1] and to invite
his acquaintances and relations, and yet thou hast not done
this.   So he said to them, I will give you the entertainment, and our meeting shall be in the garden.

Accordingly, when the next morning came, he sent his
servant to the saloon and the pavilion which were in the
garden, and desired him to spread the furniture in them.
He sent also the necessaries for cooking, as lambs and
clarified butter,[2] and such other things as the case required, and prepared two tables, one in the pavilion and
one in the saloon.   The merchant Shemseddin girded himself, and so did his son Aladdin, and the former said to the
latter, O my son, when the hoary man cometh in, I will
meet him, and seat him at the table which is in the pavilion ; and thou, O my son, when the beardless youth cometh
in, shalt take him and conduct him into the saloon, and seat

---

[1] *Asidah :* flour made consistent by boiling in water, with the addition of
clarified butter.

[2] *Samn,* and honey, more like pap than custard.   This is Captain Burton's note.   New England housekeepers may recognize a similarity to what they
call "soft custard."

him at the table there. His son said to him, Wherefore, O my father? What is the reason of thy preparing two tables, one for the men and one for the youths? O my son, answered the merchant, the beardless youth is ashamed to eat in the presence of men. So his son approved of this. And when the merchants came, Shemseddin met the men, and seated them in the pavilion; and his son Aladdin met the youths, and seated them in the saloon. Then the servants placed the food, and the party ate and drank, and enjoyed themselves and were delighted, and they drank the sherbet, and the servants gave vent to the smoke of the perfume; after which the aged men sat conversing upon science and tradition.

Meanwhile, the youths had seated Aladdin among them at the upper end of the chamber, and one of them said to his companion, O my master Hassan, acquaint me respecting the capital in thy possession, by means of which thou sellest and buyest, how it came to thee. He replied, When I grew up and attained to manhood, I said to my father, O my father, give me some merchandise; but he replied, O my son, I have none; go, however, and procure money from some merchant, and traffic with it, and learn the art of selling and buying, and taking and giving. So I repaired to one of the merchants, and borrowed of him a thousand pieces of gold, and, having bought some stuffs with it, I journeyed with them to Syria, where I obtained double the cost price. Then I took merchandise from Syria, and journeyed with it to Bagdad, where I sold it, and again obtained double the cost price; and I ceased not to traffic until my capital became about ten thousand pieces of gold. And each of the youths said to his companion the like of this until the turn to speak came round

to Aladdin Abushamat ; when they said to him, And thou,
O our master Aladdin. So he replied, I was reared in a
subterranean chamber beneath a trap-door, and came forth
from it this week, and I go to the shop and return from it
to the house. And upon this they said to him, Thou art
accustomed to remain in the house, and knowest not the
delight of travel, and travel is for none but men. He replied, I have no need to travel ; and is ease of no value ?
And one of them said to his companion, This is like the
fish : when he quitteth the water he dieth. They then
said to him, O Aladdin, the glory of the sons of the merchants consisteth in nothing but travel for the sake of
gain.

At these words Aladdin became enraged, and he went
forth from among the youths, with weeping eye and sorrowful heart, and, having mounted his mule, repaired to
the house. And his mother saw him in a state of excessive rage, and weeping : so she said to him, What maketh
thee weep, O my son ? He therefore answered her, All
the sons of the merchants have reproached me, and said to
me, The glory of the sons of the merchants consisteth in
nothing but travel for the sake of gaining pieces of silver
and gold. His mother said to him, O my son, dost thou
desire .to travel ? He answered, Yes. And she asked
him, To what country wouldst thou travel ? To the city
of Bagdad, he answered ; for there a man gaineth double
the cost price of his merchandise. His mother then said
to him, O my son, thy father hath great wealth ; but if he
prepare not merchandise for thee with his wealth, I will
prepare for thee some with mine. And he replied, The
best of favors is that which is promptly bestowed ; and if
there be kindness to be shown, this is the time for it. She

therefore summoned the slaves, and sent them to the persons who packed up stuffs, and, having opened a magazine,
took from it some stuffs for him, and they packed up for
him ten loads.

His father, in the mean time, looked around, and found
not his son Aladdin in the garden. So he inquired respecting him, and they told him that he had mounted his
mule, and gone to the house ; whereupon he mounted and
went after him ; and when he entered his abode, seeing the
loads packed up, he asked concerning them. His wife
therefore informed him of the manner in which the sons of
the merchants had acted toward his son Aladdin. And
upon this he said to him, O my son, malediction be upon
foreign travel ! for the Apostle of God (may God favor and
preserve him !) hath said, It is of a man's good fortune that
he be sustained in his own country ; and the ancients have
said, Abstain from travel, though it be but a mile's journey. Then he said to his son, Hast thou determined to
travel, and wilt thou not relinquish thy purpose ? His son
answered him, I must travel to Bagdad with merchandise,
or I will pull off my clothes, and put on the habit of the
dervises, and go forth a wanderer through the countries.
So his father said to him, I am not in need, nor destitute ;
but, on the contrary, I have great wealth. And he showed
him all the wealth, and merchandise, and stuffs that he
possessed, and said to him, I have stuffs and other merchandise suitable for every country. And he showed him,
of such goods, forty loads packed up, upon each of which
was written its price, a thousand pieces of gold. He then
said to him, O my son, take the forty loads, and the ten
loads which are given thee by thy mother, and journey
under the protection of God, whose name be exalted !

But, O my son, I fear for thee on account of a forest in thy way, called the Forest of the Lion, and a valley there called the Valley of the Dogs ; for lives are sacrificed in those two places without pity. IIow so, O my father? said his son. The merchant answered, By a Bedouin, an intercepter of the way, who is named Ejlan. But his son replied, The means of preservation are from God, and if I have any share in them left, no harm will happen to me.

Then he mounted with his father, and went to the market of the beasts of burden ; and lo, an akkam [1] dismounted from his mule, and, kissing the hand of the syndic of the merchants, said to him, By Allah, for a long time, O my master, thou hast not employed us in the transaction of mercantile business. The syndic replied, Every time hath its fortune and its men. O my master, it is none but this my son who desireth to travel. And the akkam said, God preserve him to thee ! The syndic then made a covenant between his son and the akkam that the former should be as the son of the latter, and gave the akkam a charge respecting Aladdin, and said to him, Take these hundred pieces of gold for thy young men. After which he bought sixty mules, and a covering for the grave of Abdel-Kader Gilani, [2] and said to his son, O my son, while I am absent, this akkam shall be thy father in my stead, and with whatever he saith to thee do thou comply. Then he returned, with the mules and the young men, and the next night they caused a recitation of the whole of the

[1] One who has charge of camels and tents, and other articles required in travelling.

[2] A celebrated saint of Bagdad of the twelfth century, who founded the order which bears his name. The reference gives a hint for fixing the date of the book.

Koran to be performed, and celebrated a festival in honor, of the Sheikh Abdel-Kader Gilani. And when the follow-ing morning came, the syndic of the merchants gave to his son ten thousand pieces of gold, saying to him, When thou enterest Bagdad, if thou find the stuffs of easy sale, sell them; but if thou find them not in request, expend of these pieces of gold.

They then loaded the mules, and bade one another fare-well and the party went forth from the city. They contin-ued their way over the deserts and wastes until they came in sight of Damascus, and from Damascus they proceeded un-til they entered Aleppo, and thence they continued their route until there remained between them and Bagdad one day's journey. Still they advanced till they descended into a valley, and Aladdin desired that they should halt there; but the akkam said, Halt ye not here: continue on your way and hasten in your pace: perhaps we may reach Bagdad before its gates be closed; for the people open them not nor close them but when the sun is up, in their fear lest the rejectors[1] should take the city and throw the books of science into the Tigris. Aladdin, however, re-plied, O my father, I came not with this merchandise unto this town for the sake of traffic, but for the sake of amus-ing myself by the sight of foreign countries. O my son, rejoined the akkam, we fear for thee and for thy property on account of the Arabs. But Aladdin said, O man, art thou a servant or a person served? I will not enter Bag-dad but in the morning, that the sons of Bagdad may see my merchandise, and may know me. So the akkam replied, Do what thou wilt; for I have advised thee, and thou canst

---

[1] These are the Persian schismatics (*shi'ah*), who cursed the first three caliphs.

judge for thyself. And Aladdin ordered them to take
down the burdens from the backs of the mules ; and they
did so, and pitched the pavilion, and remained until midnight.

Aladdin then went forth from the pavilion, and saw
something glittering in the distance. So he said to the
akkam, O my master, what is this thing that is glittering ?
And the akkam, looking attentively and with a scrutiniz-
ing eye, saw that what glittered was the points of spears and
the iron of Bedouin weapons and swords. And lo, they were
Arabs, whose chief was named the Sheikh of the Arabs
Ejlan Abou Naib ; and when these Arabs drew near them
and saw their packages, they said one to another, O night
of spoil ! As soon as the travellers heard them say this,
Kemaleddin, the akkam, exclaimed, Avaunt, O least of
Arabs ! But Abou Naib smote him with his spear upon
his breast, and it protruded glittering from his back ; whereupon he fell at the door of the tent, slain. Then the
water-carrier exclaimed, Avaunt, O basest of Arabs ! And
one of them struck him upon his shoulder with a sword,
and it passed forth glittering from his vitals, and he, also,
fell down slain. All this took place while Aladdin stood
looking on. The Arabs surrounded and fiercely assaulted
the caravan, and killed the attendants of Aladdin, not
sparing one of them ; after which they placed the loads
upon the backs of the mules, and retired. Aladdin then
said to himself, Nothing will occasion thy slaughter, but thy
mule and this thy dress. So he arose and pulled off the
dress, and threw it upon the back of his mule, remaining
in the shirt and drawers alone ; and, looking before him,
toward the door of the tent, he found a pool of blood flowing
from the slain ; and he rolled himself in it with the shirt

and the drawers, so that he appeared like one slain, drowned in his blood.

Meanwhile, the sheikh of the Arabs, Ejlan, said to his troops, O Arabs, was this caravan entering from Egypt, or going forth from Bagdad? They answered him, Coming from Egypt into Bagdad. And he said to them, Return to the slain; for I imagine that the proprietor of this caravan hath not died. So the Arabs returned to the slain, and proceeded to pierce and strike them again until they came to Aladdin. He had thrown himself among the slain; and when they came to him they said, Thou hast feigned thyself to be dead; so we will complete thy slaughter. And a Bedouin took his spear, and was about to thrust it into the breast of Aladdin; whereupon Aladdin said, O thy blessing, O my lord Abdel-Kader Gilani![1] And he saw a hand turn away the spear from his breast to the breast of Kemaleddin, the akkam; so that the Bedouin pierced the latter with it, and left Aladdin; after which the Arabs replaced the burdens on the backs of the mules and departed with them.

Aladdin then looked, and, seeing that the birds had flown with their spoils, arose and ran away. But lo, the Bedouin Abou Naib said to his companions, I saw a faint appearance of an object in the distance, O Arabs. One of them, therefore, came forth, and beheld Aladdin running; upon which he said to him, Flight will not profit thee while we are behind thee. And he struck his mare with his fist, and she hastened after him. Now Aladdin had seen before him a tank containing water, and by the side of it was a cistern: so he ascended to a window of the cistern, and there stretching himself along, feigned

[1] The saint referred to above.

himself asleep, and said, O kind Protector, cover me with
the veil of thy protection that cannot be removed! And
behold, the Bedouin stopped beneath the cistern, and
stretched forth his hand to seize Aladdin; whereupon the
latter said, O thy blessing, O my Lady Nefesa![1] This is
thy time! And lo, a scorpion stung the Bedouin in the
palm of his hand; and he cried out, and said, O Arabs,
come to me, for I am stung! And he alighted from the
back of his mare, and his companions, coming to him,
mounted him again, and said to him, What hath befallen
thee? He answered them, A scorpion hath stung me.
And they then took the property of the caravan and
departed.

Aladdin remained a while sleeping in the window of the
cistern. Then arising, he proceeded, and entered Bagdad.
The dogs barked behind him as he passed through the
streets, and in the evening, while he was walking on in
the dark, he saw the door of a mosque, and, entering its
vestibule, he concealed himself in it. And, lo, a light
approached him, and as he looked attentively at it, he
perceived two lanterns in the hands of two black slaves,
who were walking before two merchants. One of these
was an old man of comely countenance, and the other
was a young man; and he heard the latter say to the
former, By Allah, O my uncle, I conjure thee to restore
to me my cousin, thy daughter. To which the old man
replied, Did I not forbid thee many times, when thou
wast making divorce thy constant cry? Then the old
man looked to the right, and saw Aladdin, appearing
like a piece of the moon; and he said to him, Peace be

---

[1] Name of a celebrated female saint. She was buried in Cairo, and famed
for her miracles. Such miracles are called *kiramat.*

on thee! Aladdin, therefore, returned his salutation, and the old man said to him, O youth, who art thou? He answered him, I am Aladdin the son of Shemseddin the syndic of the merchants in Cairo. I requested my father to give me merchandise, and he prepared for me fifty loads of goods, and gave me ten thousand pieces of gold; and I journeyed until I arrived at the Forest of the Lion, when the Arabs came upon me and took my wealth and my packages; and I entered this city, not knowing where to pass the night: so, seeing this place, I concealed myself in it. The old man then said to him, O my son, what sayest thou of my giving thee a thousand pieces of gold, and a suit of clothing of the price of a thousand pieces of gold? For what purpose, said Aladdin, wilt thou give me these things, O my uncle? He answered him, This young man who is with me is the son of my brother, and his father hath no son but him; and I have a daughter, and have none but her, who is named Zobeide the Lute Player. She is endowed with beauty and loveliness, and I married her to him, and he loveth her; but she hateth him; and he swore an oath of triple divorcement, and scarcely had his wife heard it when she separated herself from him. And he employed all the people of his acquaintance to intercede with me that I should restore her to him: so I said to him, This will not be right unless by means of a mustahall¹ and I agreed with him that we should employ some foreigner as a mustahall, in order that no one might reproach him on account of this affair. Since, then, thou art a foreigner, come with us, that we may write thy con-

¹ A Mohammedan who has triply divorced his wife cannot take her again unless she be married and divorced by some other person: this person is termed a *mustahall.*

tract of marriage to her, and to-morrow thou shalt divorce
her, and we will give thee what I have mentioned. So
Aladdin said within himself, To do what he proposeth will
be better than passing the nights in the by-streets and
vestibules.

Accordingly, he went with the two men to the cadi. And
when the cadi saw him, his heart was moved with affection
for him, and he said to the father of the damsel, What is
your desire? The old man answered, It is our desire to
employ this person as a mustahall for our daughter; but
we will write a bond against him, stating that the portion
of the dowry to be paid in advance is ten thousand pieces
of gold; and if he divorce her to-morrow morning, we will
give him a dress of the price of a thousand pieces of gold,
and a mule of the same price, and a thousand pieces of gold
besides; but if he divorce her not, he will pay ten thousand
pieces of gold. So they settled the contract on this condition, and the father of the damsel received a bond to this
effect. He then took Aladdin with him, clad him with the
suit, and proceeded with him until they came to the house
of his daughter, when he stationed him at the door of the
house, and, going in to his daughter, said to her, Receive
the bond of thy dowry; for I have written thy contract of
marriage to a comely young man, named Aladdin Abushamat: so consider thyself under a most strict charge respecting him. And he gave her the bond, and repaired to his
house.

Now the damsel Zobeide had a female friend who frequently visited her, and her husband used to treat her with
beneficence; and he said to her, O my mother, if Zobeide
the daughter of my uncle see this comely young man, she
will not accept me after; so I desire of thee that thou con-

trive a stratagem to restrain the damsel from him. By the life of thy youth,[1] she replied, I will not suffer him to go near her. She then went to Aladdin, and said to him, O my son, I give thee good advice for the sake of God (whose name be exalted !) ; therefore do thou accept my advice, and approach not that damsel, but let her remain alone, and neither touch her nor draw near to her. Wherefore? said he. And she answered him, Verily her whole skin is affected with elephantiasis, and I fear for thee lest she communicate the disease to thy comely, youthful person. So he replied, I have no need of her. Then she went to the damsel, and said to her as she had said to Aladdin; and the damsel replied, I have no need of him ; on the contrary, I will leave him to remain alone, and in the morning he shall go his way. And she called a slave girl, and said to her, Take the table with the food, and give it to him that he may sup. The slave girl, therefore, carried to him the table with the food, and placed it before him, and he ate until he was satisfied, and then sat reciting a chapter of the Koran, with a charming voice; and the damsel, listening to him, found that his voice was like the sounds of the Psalms sung by the family of David. So she said within herself, Allah send trouble upon this old woman who told me that he was afflicted with elephantiasis ! for he who is in such a state hath not a voice of this kind. Surely this assertion is a lie against him. Then she took a lute made in India, and tuning the strings, sang to it in a voice so sweet that its music would stay the birds in the heart of heaven. And she began these two couplets:—

" I love a fawn with gentle white-black eyes
Whose walk the willow wand with envy kills:

---

[1] This is a woman's oath, not used by men.

Forbidding me he bids for rival mine,
'Tis Allah's grace who grants to whom He wills!"   •

And when he heard her chant these lines he ended his recitation of the chapter, and began also to sing: and thus repeated the following couplet:—

" My Salám to the Fawn in the garments concealed,
And to roses in gardens of cheek revealed."

The lady rose up when she heard this, — and she lifted the curtain, — and, when she drew near him, and there remained but two paces between them, he recited these two couplets:—

" She spread three tresses of unplaited hair,
One night, and showed me nights, not one, but four;
And faced the moon of Heaven with her brow,
And showed me two-fold moons in single hour."

And as she approached him he said to her, Retire from me, lest thou communicate thy disease to me. So she uncovered her wrist, which was beautifully formed, and its whiteness was like that of silver; after which she said to him, Retire from me; for thou art afflicted with elephantiasis, and perhaps thou wilt communicate the disease to me. He therefore asked her, Who informed thee that I was afflicted with elephantiasis? She answered him, The old woman acquainted me with it. And he replied, The old woman also informed me that thou wast afflicted with leprosy. Then he uncovered to her his arms, and she found that his skin was like pure silver. So she accepted him as her husband.

And on the following morning he said to her, Alas for joy that is not complete! The raven hath taken it and flown away! She therefore said, What is the meaning of these words? And he answered her, O my mistress, I have only this hour to remain with thee. Who saith so? she asked. Thy father, he answered her, wrote a bond against me, obliging me to pay ten thousand pieces of gold toward thy dowry; and if I produce it not this day, they imprison me for it in the house of the cadi; and now my hand is unable to advance a single half drachma of the sum of ten thousand pieces of gold. But she said to him, O my master, is the matrimonial tie in thy hand, or in their hands? He answered her, The tie is in my hand; but I have nothing in my possession. The affair, she rejoined, is easy; and fear nothing; but take these hundred pieces of gold. Had I more I would give thee what thou desirest. This, however, I cannot do; for my father, from the affection that he beareth for the son of his brother, hath transferred all his property from my hands to his house: even all my ornaments he took. But when they send to thee a sergeant from the court of justice this morning, and the cadi and my father say to thee, Divorce, do thou say to them, By what code is it ordained as proper that I should marry at nightfall and divorce in the morning? Then thou shalt kiss the hand of the cadi, and give him a present: and in like manner thou shalt kiss the hand of each witness, and give him ten pieces of gold. And all of them will speak with thee: and if they say to thee, Wherefore wilt thou not divorce, and receive a thousand pieces of gold, and the mule and the dress, according to the condition which we imposed upon thee? do thou answer them, Every hair of her head is, in my estimation, worth a thousand pieces of gold, and I will never divorce her, nor will I receive a dress or anything else. If the cadi then say to thee, Pay the dowry, reply, I am at present unable to pay. And thereupon the cadi and the witnesses will treat thee with benevolence, and will grant thee a delay.

Now while they were thus conversing, the sergeant of the cadi knocked at the door. So he went forth to him, and the sergeant said to him, Answer the summons of the effendi,[1] for thy father-in-law citeth thee. And Aladdin gave to him five pieces of gold, saying, O sergeant, by what code am I required to marry at nightfall and to divorce in the morning? He answered him, To do so is not held proper by us in any case; and if thou be ignorant of the law, I will act as thy deputy. And they proceeded to the court of justice, and the cadi said to Aladdin, Wherefore dost thou not divorce the woman, and receive what the contract hath prescribed for thee? And upon this he advanced to the cadi, and, kissing his hand, put into it fifty pieces of gold, and said to him, O our lord the cadi, by what code is it allowable that I should marry at nightfall and divorce in the morning by compulsion? The cadi therefore answered, Divorce by compulsion is not allowable by any of the codes of the Mohammedans. Then the father of the damsel said, If thou divorce not, pay me the dowry, ten thousand pieces of gold. Aladdin replied, Give me three days' delay. But the cadi said, Three days will not be a sufficient period of delay; he shall grant thee ten days. And to this they agreed, binding him, after the ten days, either to pay the dowry or to divorce.

On this condition, therefore, he went forth from them, and, having procured the meat, and rice, and clarified but-

---

[1] *Effendi:* This is a Turkish title of rank, corresponding, perhaps, to our title of Esquire. Captain Burton remarks that it is a late addition of some copyist.

ter, and other eatables that the case required, returned to
the house, and went in to the damsel and related to her all
that had happened to him. She replied, Between night
and day wonders take place ; and divinely gifted was he
who said,

Be mild when thou art troubled by rage, and be patient when calamity
befalleth thee ;
For the nights are pregnant with events, and give birth to every kind
of wonder.

She then arose, prepared the food, and brought the table,
and they ate and drank, and enjoyed themselves, and were
moved with merriment ; and he requested her to perform
a piece of music. So she took the lute, and performed a
piece in such a manner that a rock would have danced at
it as if with joy, the sounds of the chords vying with the
voice of David ; and she began the more rapid part of the
performance.

But while they were full of delight and jesting, and mirth
and gladness, the door was knocked. She therefore said
to him, Arise, and see who is at the door. Accordingly
he went down to the door, found four dervises standing
there, and he said to them, What do ye desire ? O my
master, answered one of them, we are foreign dervises :
the food of our souls consisteth in music and in the delicacies of poetry, and we desire to recreate ourselves with thee
this night, until the morning, when we will go our way ;
and thou wilt receive thy recompense from God (whose
name be exalted !) ; for we are passionately fond of music,
and there is not one among us who doth not retain in his
memory odes and other pieces of poetry and lyric songs.
Aladdin replied, I must consult. And he went up and informed the damsel ; and she said to him, Open the door to

them.   So he opened to them the door, and, having conducted them up, seated them, and welcomed them, and
brought them food.   But they declined eating, and one of
them said to him, O my master, verily our victuals are the
commemoration of God with our hearts, and the hearing of
songs with our ears ; and divinely was he gifted who said,

Our desire is for naught but the enjoyment of society; and eating is
naught but a characteristic of the brutes.

We just now heard some pleasant music in thine abode :
but when we came up it ceased ; and we would that we
knew whether she who was performing is a white or a
black slave girl, or a lady.   Aladdin replied, She is my wife.
And he related to them all that had happened to him, and
said to them, My father-in-law hath bound me to pay ten
thousand pieces of gold as her dowry, and they have given
me ten days' delay.   Upon this one of the dervises said to
him, Grieve not, nor anticipate anything but good fortune ;
for I am the Sheikh of the Convent, having under me forty
dervises over whom I exercise authority, and I will collect
for thee the ten thousand pieces of gold from them, and
thou shalt discharge the dowry that thou owest to thy
father-in-law.   But desire her (he added) to perform a piece
of music for us, that we may be rejoiced and enlivened;
for music is to some people like food ; and to some like a
remedy ; and to some like a fan.   Now these four dervises
were the Caliph Haroun Alrashid, and the vizier Giafar the
Barmecide, and Abou Nuwas Elhassan the son of Hani,[1]
and Mesrour the Executioner.   And the reason of their

[1] The reader has already met Giafar and Mesrour.   The fourth person in
this evening party is known as a poet of that time.   His name means "The
Father of Sidelocks," or "Hasan of the Ringlets," because he wore two long
pigtails hanging to his shoulders,

passing by the house was, that the bosom of the caliph was contracted ; so he said to the vizier, O vizier it is our desire to descend and to go about through the city ; for I experience a contraction of the bosom. They therefore clad themselves in the apparel of dervises, and went down into the city, and, passing by this house, they heard music, and desired to ascertain the cause. They passed the night there in happiness and good order, and in relating stories one after another, until the morning came, when the caliph put a hundred pieces of gold beneath the prayer carpet, and he and his companions took leave of Aladdin, and went their way.

When the damsel, therefore, lifted up the prayer carpet, she saw the hundred pieces of gold beneath it. And she said to her husband, Take these hundred pieces of gold that I have found under the prayer carpet ; for the dervises put them before they went, without our knowledge. So Aladdin took them, and, repairing to the market, bought the meat, and the rice, and the clarified butter, and all that he required. And on the following night he lighted the candles, and said to his wife, The dervises have not brought the ten thousand pieces of gold which they promised me ; but they are poor men. While they were talking, however, the dervises knocked at the door ; and she said to him, Go down and open to them. He therefore did so, and they came up, and he said to them, Have ye brought the ten thousand pieces of gold that ye promised me ? They answered him, Nothing of the sum hath been provided ; but fear no evil : if it be the will of God (whose name be exalted !), to-morrow we will perform an alchemical process for thee : and now do thou desire thy wife to gratify our ears by an excellent performance of music, that our hearts may be enlivened by it ; for we love music. So she performed a piece for them upon the lute, such as would make a rock to dance. And they passed the night in enjoyment, and happiness, and conversation, and cheerfulness, until the morning came and diffused its light ; whereupon the caliph again put a hundred pieces of gold beneath the prayer carpet, and he and his companions took leave of Aladdin, and departed from him and went their way.

Thus they continued to do for a period of nine nights ; the caliph every night putting beneath the prayer carpet a hundred pieces of gold, until the tenth night, when they came not ; and the cause of their ceasing their visits was this. The caliph sent to a great merchant, saying to him, Make ready for me fifty loads of stuffs, such as come from Cairo, each load of the price of a thousand pieces of gold, and write upon each the amount of its price ; and provide for me a male Abyssinian slave. So the merchant made ready for him all that he ordered him to provide, after which the caliph committed to the slave a basin and ewer of gold, and another present, and the fifty loads, and wrote a letter as from Shemseddin the syndic of the merchants in Cairo, the father of Aladdin, and said to the slave, Take these loads and the things that are with them, and repair with them to such a quarter, in which is the house of the syndic of the merchants, and say, Where is my master Aladdin Abushamat ? Then the people will direct thee to the quarter and to the house. The slave therefore took the loads and what was with them, and went as the caliph commanded him.

In the mean time, the damsel's cousin repaired to her father, and said to him, Come, let us go to Aladdin, that we may effect the divorce of my cousin. So the father descended and went with him to Aladdin; but when they arrived at the house, they found fifty mules, upon which were fifty loads of stuffs, attended by a black slave upon a mule; and they said to him, To whom belong these loads? He answered, To my master Aladdin Abushamat; for his father prepared for him merchandise, and despatched him on a journey to the city of Bagdad, and the Arabs came upon him, and took his wealth and his loads; and the news reached his father; wherefore he sent me to him with loads in their stead. He sent with me also a mule laden with fifty thousand pieces of gold, and a wrapper of clothes worth a large sum of money, and a furred robe of sable, and a basin and ewer of gold. Upon this the father of the damsel said, This person is my son-in-law, and I will show thee the way to the house.

And while Aladdin was sitting in the house in a state of violent grief, the door was knocked; and he said, O Zobeide, God is all-knowing; but it seemeth that thy father hath sent to me a sergeant from the cadi or from the judge. She replied, Go down and see what is the case. So he went down and opened the door, and beheld his father-in-law, who was the syndic of the merchants, the father of Zobeide; and he found there an Abyssinian slave of dark complexion and of pleasant countenance, mounted upon a mule. And the slave, having descended from the mule, kissed his hands; and he said to him, What dost thou desire? He answered, I am the slave of my master Aladdin Abushamat, the son of Shemseddin, the syndic of the merchants in the land of Egypt; and his father hath sent me to him with this deposit. He then gave him the letter ; and Aladdin took it, and opened it and read it, and found written in it these words :

After perfect salutations, and compliments, and respectful greetings, from Shemseddin to his son Aladdin Abushamat. Know, O my son, that the news of the slaughter of thy men, and the plunder of thy wealth and thy loads, hath reached me ; and I have therefore sent to thee, in their stead, these fifty loads of Egyptian stuffs, and the suit of dress, and the furred robe of sable, and the basin and ewer of gold. And fear no evil ; for the wealth is thy ransom, O my son ; and may grief never affect thee. Thy mother and the people of the house are well, in prosperity and health ; and they greet thee with abundant salutations. Moreover, O my son, news hath reached me that they have employed thee as a mustahall for the damsel Zobeide the Lute Player, and have imposed upon thee the payment of ten thousand pieces of gold as her dowry. Therefore fifty thousand pieces of gold will be brought to thee with the loads, attended by thy slave Selim.

As soon as Aladdin had finished reading the letter, he took possession of the loads, and, looking toward his father-in-law, said to him, O my father-in-law, receive the ten thousand pieces of gold, the amount of the dowry of thy daughter Zobeide : receive also the loads and dispose of them, and the profit shall be thine : only do thou restore to me the cost price. But he replied, Nay, by Allah, I will take nothing ; and as to the dowry of thy wife, do thou make an agreement with her respecting it. So Aladdin arose, together with his father-in-law, and they went into the house, after the loads had been brought in. And Zobeide said to her father, O my father, to whom belong these loads ? He answered her, These loads belong to

Aladdin thy husband. His father hath sent them to him in the place of those which the Arabs took from him ; and he hath sent to him fifty thousand pieces of gold, and a wrapper of clothes, and a furred robe of sable, and a mule, and a basin and ewer of gold : and as for thy dowry, it is for thee to decide respecting it. Then Aladdin arose, and, having opened the chest, gave her her dowry. The damsel's cousin said, O my uncle, let Aladdin divorce my wife for me. But the father of the damsel replied, This is a thing that now can by no means be, as the matrimonial tie is in his hand. And upon this the young man went away, grieved and afflicted, and laid himself down sick in his house, and there he died.

As to Aladdin, he went forth to the market, after he had received the loads, and, having procured what he desired of food, and drink, and clarified butter, made the same regular preparations as on each preceding night, and said to Zobeide, See, these lying dervises gave us a promise and broke it. She replied, Thou art the son of a syndic of the merchants, and yet thy hand was unable to produce a half drachma. What then is the case of the poor dervises? God (whose name be exalted !), he rejoined, hath rendered us independent of them, and I will not again open the door to them if they come to us. But she said to him, Wherefore, seeing that good fortune happened not unto us but in consequence of their coming ; for every night they put for us beneath the prayer carpet a hundred pieces of gold? It is absolutely necessary, then, that thou open the door to them if they come. And when the day departed with its brightness, and the night came, they lighted the candles, and Aladdin said to his wife, O Zobeide, arise, and perform a piece of music

for us. And immediately the door was knocked: so she
said to him, Rise, and see who is there. He descended,
therefore, and opened the door, and seeing the dervises, he
said, Oh! welcome to the liars! Come up. Accordingly,
they went up with him, and he seated them and brought
the table of food to them; and they ate and drank, and
enjoyed themselves and were merry. They then said to
him, O my master, verily our hearts have been troubled
respecting thee. What hath happened to thee with thy
father-in-law? God, he answered them, hath granted us a
recompense above our desires. And they said to him, By
Allah, we were in fear for thee, and nothing prevented our
coming to thee again but the inadequacy of our means to
procure the money. He replied, Speedy relief hath come
to me from my Lord, and my father hath sent to me fifty
thousand pieces of gold, and fifty loads of stuffs, each load
of the price of a thousand pieces of gold, and a suit of
dress, and a furred robe of sable, and a mule and a slave,
and a basin and ewer of gold: a reconciliation hath taken
place between me and my father-in-law, and my wife hath
become lawful to me; and praise be to God for this!

The caliph then arose and withdrew; and the Vizier
Giafar, inclining toward Aladdin, said to him, Impose
upon thyself the obligation of good manners: for thou
art in the company of the Prince of the Faithful. What
have I done, asked Aladdin, inconsistently with good
manners in the company of the Prince of the Faithful,
and which of you is the Prince of the Faithful? The
vizier answered him, He who was speaking to you, and
who hath just now retired, is the Prince of the Faithful,
Haroun Alrashid, and I am the Vizier Giafar, and this is
Mesrour, the caliph's executioner, and this is Abou Nuwas

Elhassan the son of Hani. Reflect then with thy reason, O Aladdin, and consider how many days are required for the journey from Cairo to Bagdad. He replied, Five and forty days. Then said Giafar, Thy loads were carried off only ten days ago; and how could the news reach thy father, and how could he pack up the other loads for thee, and these loads traverse a space of five-and-forty days' journey in ten days? O my master, said Aladdin, and whence came they unto me? The vizier answered him, From the caliph, the Prince of the Faithful, on account of his excessive affection for thee. And while they were thus conversing, lo, the caliph approached. So Aladdin arose, and kissed the ground before him, and said to him, God preserve thee, O Prince of the Faithful, and prolong thy life, and may mankind never be deprived of thy bounty and beneficence! And the caliph said, O Aladdin, let Zobeide perform for us a piece of music,[1] as a gratuity for thy safety. She therefore performed a piece on the lute of the most admirable kind, such as would make a rock to shake as with joy, and the sounds of the lute vied with the voice of David. They passed the night in the happiest manner until the morning, when the caliph said to Aladdin, To-morrow come up to the court. And Aladdin replied, I hear and obey, O Prince of the Faithful, if it be the will of God (whose name be exalted!), and mayest thou continue in prosperity.

Then Aladdin took ten trays, and put on them a costly present; and on the following day he went up with them to the court.

And Aladdin said, O Prince of the Faithful, verily the

---

[1] *Haldwak.* Such a sweetmeat as men give to their friends after sickness or a journey.

prophet (God favor and preserve him!) accepted a present; and these ten trays with what is upon them are a present from me unto thee. And the Prince of the Faithful accepted them from him. He gave orders also to invest him with a robe of honor, appointed him syndic of the merchants, and seated him in the council chamber. And while Aladdin was sitting there, lo, his father-in-law, the father of Zobeide, approached, and, finding him sitting in his place, and wearing the robe of honor, said to the Prince of the Faithful, O king of the age, wherefore is this person sitting in my place, and wearing this robe of honor? The caliph answered him, I have appointed him syndic of the merchants; and offices are conferred by investiture, not granted for perpetuity; and thou art displaced. And he replied, He is of our family and our connections, and excellent is that which thou hast done, O Prince of the Faithful. May God always make the best of us to preside over our affairs! And how many a small person hath become great! The caliph then wrote a diploma[1] for Aladdin, and gave it to the judge, and the judge gave it to the executioner, and he proclaimed in the court, None is syndic of the merchants but Aladdin Abushamat; and his word is to be heard, and respect is to be paid to him: he is entitled to honor, and reverence, and exaltation! And when the court was dissolved, the judge descended with the crier before Aladdin, and the crier proclaimed, None is syndic of the merchants but my master Aladdin Abushamat! And they went about with him through the great thoroughfare streets of Bagdad, the crier repeating the same proclamation.

[1] *Firman.* It was originally a command. The word is Persian. It now applies to an order given by the prime minister, as distinct from an order given by the sultan.

On the following morning, therefore, Aladdin opened a shop for the slave, and seated him in it to sell and buy, while he rode and took his place in the court of the caliph. And it happened that he was sitting in his place one day according to his custom, and as he sat, lo, a person said to the caliph, O Prince of the Faithful, may thy head long survive such-a-one, the boon companion; for he hath been admitted to the mercy of God (whose name be exalted!) and may thy life be prolonged! And the caliph said, Where is Aladdin Abushamat? So he presented himself before the caliph, who, when he saw him, bestowed upon him a magnificent robe of honor, appointed him his boon companion, and assigned him a monthly salary of a thousand pieces of gold; and Aladdin continued with him as his boon companion. And it happened again that he was sitting one day in his place according to his custom, in the service of the caliph, when an emir came up into the court with a sword and shield, and said, O Prince of the Faithful, may thy head long survive the reis-el-sittein; for he hath died this day. And the caliph gave orders to bring a robe of honor for Aladdin Abushamat, and appointed him reis-el-sittein in the place of the deceased. The latter had no son, nor daughter, nor wife; so Aladdin went down, and put his hand upon his wealth; and the caliph said to him, Inter him, and take all that he hath left of wealth, and male slaves, and female slaves, and eunuchs. Then the caliph shook the handkerchief,[1] and the court dispersed; and Aladdin departed, with the officer Ahmad El-Denef, the officer of the right division of the caliph's guard, attended by his forty followers, by his stirrup, on the right ; and on his left, Hassan Shuman, the officer of the left division of

---

[1] By shaking the handkerchief, he dismisses the assembly.

the caliph's guard, together with his forty followers. And Aladdin looked toward the officer Hassan Shuman, and his followers, and said to them, Be ye intercessors with Ahmad El-Denef, that he may accept me as his son by a covenant before God. And he accepted him, and said to him, I and my forty followers will walk before thee to the court every day.

After this Aladdin continued in the service of the caliph for many days. And it happened that he descended from the court one day and went to his house, and, having dismissed Ahmad El-Denef and his attendants, seated himself with his wife Zobeide, who, after she had lighted the candles, went into an adjoining chamber; and while he was sitting in his place, he heard a great cry. He therefore arose quickly to see who it was that cried, and beheld, in the person from whom the sound proceeded, the form of his wife Zobeide, lying extended upon the floor ; and he put his hand upon the bosom of the prostrate damsel, and found her dead. Her father's house was opposite to that of Aladdin, and he (the father) also heard her cry : so he came up, and said to her husband, What is the matter, O my master Aladdin ? The latter replied, May thy head, O my father, long survive thy daughter Zobeide; but now, O my father, we must pay respect to the dead by its burial. And when the following morning came, they interred the damsel's body ; and Aladdin and the father of Zobeide consoled each other. Aladdin put on the apparel of mourning, separated himself from the court, and continued with weeping eye and mourning heart.

So the caliph said to Giafar, O vizier, what is the reason of Aladdin's absenting himself from the court ? The vizier answered him, O Prince of the Faithful, he is mourning

for his wife Zobeide, and engaged in receiving the visits of
consolation for her loss. Upon this the caliph said, It is
incumbent on us to console him. And the vizier replied,
I hear and obey. The caliph, therefore, descended with
Giafar and some of the household attendants, and they
mounted, and repaired to the house of Aladdin. And as
he was sitting, lo, the caliph, and the vizier, and their
attendants approached him; whereupon he arose to meet
them, and kissed the ground before the caliph, who said to
him, May God compensate thee happily! Aladdin replied,
May God prolong thy life to us, O Prince of the Faithful!
And the caliph said, O Aladdin, what is the reason of thy
separating thyself from the court? He answered, My
mourning for my wife Zobeide, O Prince of the Faithful!
The caliph replied, Dispel anxiety from thy mind: for she
hath departed to receive the mercy of God (whose name be
exalted!), and mourning will never avail thee aught. But
Aladdin said, I will not cease to mourn for her until I die
and they bury me by her. The caliph rejoined, Verily
with God is a compensation for every loss, and neither
stratagem nor wealth will save one from death.

Aladdin then passed the night, and when the morning
came, he mounted and repaired to the court, and, going in
to the caliph, kissed the ground before him. And the caliph raised himself to him slightly from the throne, welcoming him and saluting him; and after he had desired him to
take the place belonging to him, he said to him, O Aladdin, thou art my guest this night. Then the caliph took
him into his palace, and called a slave girl named Kout
Elkuloub, and said to her, Aladdin had a wife whose name
was Zobeide, and she used to divert him from anxiety and
grief; but she hath departed to receive the mercy of God

(whose name be exalted!), and I desire that thou gratify his ears by a performance on the lute, of the most admirable kind, in order that he may be diverted from anxiety and sorrows. So the damsel performed an admirable piece of music; and the caliph said, What sayest thou, O Aladdin, of the voice of this slave girl? Verily, he answered, Zobeide had a better voice than hers; but she is eminently skilled in playing on the lute; for she would make a rock to dance. And the caliph said to him, Hath she pleased thee? He answered him, She hath pleased me, O Prince of the Faithful. Then said the caliph, By my head, and by the tombs of my ancestors, verily she is a present from me unto thee, with her female slaves also. And Aladdin imagined that the caliph was jesting with him. But when the caliph arose in the morning, he went to his slave girl Kout Elkuloub, and said to her, I have made thee a present to Aladdin. And she rejoiced at this; for she had seen him and loved him. He then went from the pavilion of the palace to the council chamber, and having summoned the porters, said to them, Remove the goods of Kout Elkuloub, and put her in the litter, and convey her, together with her female slaves, to the house of Aladdin. So they conveyed her, with her female slaves and her goods, to the house, and conducted her into the pavilion. And the caliph remained sitting in the hall of judgment until the close of the day, when the court broke up, and he retired to his pavilion.

Now as to Kout Elkuloub, when she had entered the pavilion of Aladdin, with her female slaves, who were forty in number, and the eunuchs also, she said to two of the eunuchs, One of you two shall sit on a chair on the right of the door, and the other shall sit on a chair on the left of it ; and when Aladdin cometh, kiss his hands, and say to him, Our mistress Kout Elkuloub requesteth thy presence in the pavilion ; for the caliph hath given her to thee, together with her female slaves. And they replied, We hear and obey. They then did as she commanded them. So when Aladdin arrived, he found the two eunuchs of the caliph sitting at the door, and he wondered at the event, saying within himself, Perhaps this is not my house ; or if it be, what hath occurred ? And when the eunuchs saw him, they rose to him, and kissed his hands, and said, We are of the dependents of the caliph, and the slaves of Kout Elkuloub, and she saluteth thee, and saith to thee, that the caliph ·hath given her to thee, together with her female slaves, and she requesteth thy company. Aladdin, however, replied, Say to her, Thou art welcome ; but as long as thou art in his abode, he will not enter the pavilion in which thou residest ; for it is not fit that what hath belonged to the master should become the property of the servant : and say to her, What was the amount of thy daily expenditure with the caliph ? They therefore went up to her, and said to her as he desired them ; and she replied, A hundred pieces of gold each day. So he said to himself, I have no need of the caliph's giving to me Kout Elkuloub, that I should expend in this manner upon her ; but I have no means of avoiding this.

She then remained in his abode many days, he assigning to her daily a hundred pieces of gold, until he absented himself one day from the court ; whereupon the caliph said, O Vizier Giafar, I gave not Kout Elkuloub to Aladdin but that she might divert him from mourning for his wife ; and what is the cause of his absenting himself from us ? The vizier answered, O Prince of the Faithful, he hath spoken truth who hath said, Whoso findeth his friends forgetteth his mere acquaintances. The caliph, however, replied, Probably nothing hath caused him to absent himself from us save some event that rendereth him excusable ; but we will visit him. Now, some days before this, Aladdin had said to the vizier, I complained to the caliph of the grief that I suffered for the loss' of my wife Zobeide the Lute Player, and he gave to me Kout Elkuloub. And the vizier said, If he did not love thee, he had not given her to thee. And hast thou visited her, O Aladdin ? He answered, No, by Allah ; nor do I know the difference between her height and breadth. And why so ? said the vizier. Aladdin answered, O vizier, what is suited to the master is not suited to the servant. Then the caliph and Giafar disguised themselves, and went to visit Aladdin : and they proceeded, without stopping, until they went in to him ; whereupon he recognized them, and arose and kissed the caliph's hands. And when the caliph saw him, he found the impress of mourning upon his countenance : so he said to him, O Aladdin, what is the cause of this mourning which thou sufferest ? Hast thou not visited Kout Elkuloub ? O Prince of the Faithful, he answered, what is suited to the master is not suited to the servant ; and, verily, to the present time I have not visited her, nor do I know the difference between her height and her breadth : therefore quit me of her. The caliph said, I desire an interview with her, that I may ask her respecting her state. And Aladdin replied, I hear and obey, O Prince of the Faithful. The caliph therefore went in to her ; and when she beheld him, she arose and kissed the ground before him ; and he said to her, Hath Aladdin visited thee ? She answered, No, O Prince of the Faithful : I sent to invite him ; but he would not. And the caliph gave orders for her return to the palace, and said to Aladdin, Absent not thyself from us. And he then went back to his palace.

So Aladdin passed that night, and in the morning mounted and repaired to the court, and seated himself in the place of the reis-el-sittein. And the caliph ordered the treasurer to give to the Vizier Giafar ten thousand pieces of gold. He therefore gave him that sum ; and the caliph said to the vizier, I require of thee that thou go down to the market of the female slaves, and that thou purchase a slave girl for Aladdin with the ten thousand pieces of gold. And the vizier obeyed the command of the caliph. He went down, taking with him Aladdin, and proceeded with him to the market of the female slaves.

Now it happened this day that the Judge of Bagdad, who held his office by the appointment of the caliph, and whose name was the Emir Kaled, went down to the market for the purpose of buying a slave girl for his son ; and the cause was this : He had a wife named Katoun, and he had by her a son of foul aspect, named Habazlam Bazaza, who had attained to the age of twenty years and knew not how to ride on horseback. But his father was bold, valiant, stout in defence, one who was practised in horse-manship, and who waded through the seas of night. And his mother said to his father, I desire that we marry him ; for he is now of a fit age. The emir, however, replied, He is of foul aspect, of disgusting odor, filthy, hideous : no woman will accept him. So she said, We will buy for him a slave girl. And it happened, in order to the accomplish-ment of an event which God (whose name be exalted !) had decreed, that on the same day on which the vizier and Aladdin went down to the market, the Emir Kaled, the

judge, went thither also, with his son Habazlam Bazaza.
And while they were in the market, lo, there was a slave
girl endowed with beauty and loveliness, and justness of
stature, in the charge of a broker; and the vizier said,
Consult, O broker, respecting a thousand pieces of gold
for her. But the broker passed with her by the judge, and
Habazlam Bazaza beholding her, the sight drew from him
a thousand sighs, and he was enamored of her, and love of
her took entire possession of him; so he said, O my father,
buy for me this slave girl. The judge therefore called the
broker, and asked the slave girl her name. She answered
him, My name is Jasmin. And the judge said to his son,
O my son, if she please thee, bid higher for her. Accordingly he said, O broker, what price hath been offered
thee? The broker answered, A thousand pieces of gold.
And Habazlam Bazaza said, Let her be mine for a thousand and one pieces of gold. So the broker went to Aladdin, and he bid for her two thousand; and every time that
the son of the judge bid one piece of gold more, Aladdin
bid a thousand. And the son of the judge was enraged at
this, and said, O broker, who outbiddeth me in the price of
the slave girl? The broker answered him, The Vizier Giafar desireth to buy her for Aladdin Abushamat. And at
last Aladdin bid for her ten thousand pieces of gold;
whereupon her master gave his assent, and received her
price; and Aladdin took her, and said to·her, I emancipate
thee for the sake of God, whose name be exalted! He
then wrote his contract of marriage to her, and repaired
with her to the house.

The broker returned with his brokerage; and the son of
the judge called him and said to him, Where is the slave
girl? He answered him, Aladdin hath purchased her for

ten thousand pieces of gold, and hath emancipated her, and written his contract of marriage to her. And upon this the young man was incensed ; his sighs were many, and he returned to the house in a state of infirmity in consequence of his love for the damsel, and threw himself upon the bed. He abstained from food, and his love and desire were excessive. So when his mother saw him in this state of debility, she said to him, Allah preserve thee, O my son ! What is the cause of thine infirmity ? He answered, Buy me Jasmin, O my mother. And his mother said, When the seller of sweet-scented flowers passeth by, I will buy for thee a pannier full of jasmine. He replied, What I mean is not the jasmine that people smell ; but a slave girl whose name is Jasmin, whom my father would not buy for me. So she said to her husband, Why didst thou not buy for him this slave girl ? He answered her, What is suited to the master is not suited to the servant ; and I have no power to take her ; for none purchased her but Aladdin, the reis-el-sittein.

In consequence of this, the illness of the young man · so increased that he abandoned sleep and food ; and his mother bound her head with the kerchiefs of mourning. And while she was sitting in her house, mourning for her son, lò, an old woman came in to her. She was the mother of Ahmad Kamakim the arch-thief ; and this arch-thief used to break through a middle wall, and to scale an upper one, and steal the kohl from the eye. He was distinguished by these abominable practices in the beginning of his career. Then they made him chief of the watch, and he stole a sum of money, and was discovered in consequence ; the judge came upon him suddenly, and took him and led him before the caliph, who gave orders to slay him in the place of blood. But he implored the protection of the vizier, whose intercession the caliph never rejected; and he interceded for him. The caliph said to him, How is it that thou intercedest for a viper, noxious to mankind? But he replied, O Prince of the Faithful, imprison him; for he who built the first prison was a wise man, since the prison is the sepulchre of the living, and a cause of the exaltation of the enemies over those who are confined in it. And upon this the caliph gave orders to put him in chains, and they engraved upon his chains, Appointed to remain until death: they shall not be loosed but on the bench of the washer of the dead. And they put him chained in the prison.

Now his mother used to frequent the house of Emir Kaled, the judge, and to go in to her son in the prison, and say to him, Did I not say to thee, Repent of unlawful deeds? And he used to reply, God decreed this to befall me; but, O my mother, when thou goest in to the wife of the judge, induce her to intercede for me with him. And when the old woman went in to the judge's wife, and found her with her head bound with the kerchiefs of mourning, she said to her, Wherefore art thou mourning? She answered, For the loss of my son Habazlam Bazaza. And the old woman said, Allah preserve thy son! What hath befallen him? The wife of the judge, therefore, related to her the story. And upon this the old woman said, What sayest thou of him who will achieve an extraordinary feat by which thy son shall be preserved? And what wouldst thou do? said the judge's wife. The old woman answered, I have a son named Ahmad Kamakim the archthief, and he is chained in the prison, and on his chains are engraved the words, Appointed to remain until death.

Do thou, therefore, attire thyself in the most magnificent apparel that thou hast, and adorn thyself in the best manner : then present thyself before thy husband with a cheerful and smiling countenance, and say to him, When a man requireth aught of his wife, he importuneth her until he obtaineth it from her ; but if the wife require aught of her husband, he will not perform it for her. And he will say to thee, What is it that thou wantest ? And do thou answer, When thou hast sworn, I will tell thee. But if he swear to thee by his head, or by Allah, say to him, Swear by thy divorce from me. And when he hath sworn to thee by divorce, do thou say to him, Thou hast in the prison a mukaddam, named Ahmad Kamakim, and he hath a poor mother, who hath had recourse to me, and urged me to conciliate thee, saying to me, Induce him to intercede for my son with the caliph, that my son may repent, and thy husband will be recompensed. And the judge's wife replied, I hear and obey.

Accordingly, when the judge came to his wife, she addressed him with the words which the old woman had dictated; and he swore to her by the oath of divorce. And on the following morning he performed the morning prayers, and, going to the prison, said, O Ahmad Kamakim, O arch-thief, wilt thou repent of thy conduct ? He answered, Verily I do turn unto God with repentance, and forsake my sins, and say from my heart and with my tongue, I beg forgiveness of God. So the judge released him from the prison, and took him with him to the court, still in his chains. Then advancing toward the caliph, he kissed the ground before him ; whereupon the caliph said to him, O Emir Kaled, what dost thou desire ?' And he led forward Ahmad Kamakim, swinging his arms in the chains as he advanced, before the caliph, who, on seeing him, said, O Kamakim, art thou still alive? O Prince of the Faithful, he answered, verily the life of the wretch is protracted. And the caliph said, O Emir Kaled, for what purpose hast thou brought him thither? The judge answered him, Verily he hath a poor, desolate mother, who hath no son but him, and she hath had recourse to thy slave, that he should intercede with thee, O Prince of the Faithful, and beg thee to release him from the chains, and he will repent of his former conduct ; and do thou appoint him head of the watch, as he was at first. Upon this the caliph said to Ahmad Kamakim, Dost thou repent of thy former conduct? And he answered him, I do turn unto God with repentance, O Prince of the Faithful. And the caliph gave orders to bring the blacksmith, and he unfastened his chains upon the bench of the washer of the dead.[1] The caliph then appointed him again head of the watch, and charged him to conduct himself well and uprightly. So he kissed the hands of the caliph, and descended with the robe of his investiture as head of the watch, and they proclaimed his appointment.

After this, when he had remained some time in his office, his mother went in to the wife of the judge, and the latter said to her, Praise be to God who hath released thy son from the prison, and that he is at present in health and safety ! But now, she added, why dost thou not tell him to contrive some means of bringing the damsel Jasmin to my son Habazlam Bazaza? The old woman answered, I will tell him. So she departed from her, and went in to her son, whom she found intoxicated ; and she said to him, O my son, no one was the cause of

---

[1] In order to keep his oath at the altar.

thy release from the prison but the wife of the judge, and she desireth of thee that thou contrive some means of killing Aladdin Abushamat, and that thou bring the damsel Jasmin to her son Habazlam Bazaza. He replied, This will be the easiest of things. I must contrive some means this night. Now that night was the first of the new month, and it was the custom of the Prince of the Faithful to pass it with the lady Zobeide, for the purpose of emancipating a female slave or a mamlouk, or with some similar intention. And it was his habit to take off the royal apparel, and to leave the rosary, and the dagger, and the royal signet, putting them all upon the chair in the sitting-room. The caliph had also a lamp of gold, to which were attached three jewels disposed upon a gold wire; and that lamp was dear in his estimation. He charged the eunuchs with the care of the suit of apparel, and the lamp, and the rest of the things, and entered the private apartment of the lady Zobeide. Then Ahmad Kamakim waited until the night was half spent, and Canopus shone, and mankind slept, and the Creator covered them with the curtain of darkness; when he drew his sword and took it in his right hand, and took his grappling instrument in his left, and, approaching the caliph's sitting-room, fixed his scaling-ladder. He threw his grappling instrument upon the sitting-room, and it caught hold upon it, and he mounted the ladder, ascended to the roof, lifted up the trap-door of the saloon, and descended into it, and found the eunuchs sleeping; and he administered some bhang to them,[1] took the caliph's suit of apparel, with the rosary and the dagger, and the handkerchief and the sig-

[1] The Arabs used such drugs for stupefaction long before we used ether or chloroform.

net, and the lamp that was adorned with jewels, and descended by the same way by which he had made his ascent. He then repaired to the house of Aladdin Abushamat, who was this night occupied with the damsel's wedding festivities, and who had retired to her. And Ahmad Kamakim the arch-thief descended into Aladdin's saloon, pulled up a slab of marble in its floor, and, having dug a hole beneath it, deposited there some of the things that he had stolen, retaining the rest in his possession. After this he cemented the marble slab with gypsum as it was before, and descended by the way he had ascended, and said within himself, I will sit and get drunk, and put the lamp before me, and drink the cup by its light. He then returned to his house.

Now when the morning came, the caliph went into the saloon (his sitting-room), and found the eunuchs stupefied with bhang. So he awoke them, and, putting his hand upon the chair, he found not the suit of apparel, nor the signet, nor the rosary, nor the dagger, nor the handkerchief, nor the lamp; whereupon he was violently enraged, and put on the apparel of anger, which was a suit of red,[1] and seated himself in the council chamber. And the vizier advanced, and, having kissed the ground before him, said, May God avert evil from the Prince of the Faithful! O vizier, replied the caliph, the evil is enormous. And the vizier said to him, What hath occurred? The caliph therefore related to him all that had happened. And, lo, the judge came up, with Ahmad Kamakim the arch-thief by his stirrup, and found the caliph in an excessive rage. And when the caliph saw the judge he said to him, O Emir

---

[1] A red dress is still the sign that an execution is to be ordered in many parts of the East.

Kaled, what is the state of Bagdad? He answered, Safe
and secure. The caliph replied, Thou liest. How so, O
Prince of the Faithful? said the judge. And the caliph
explained to him the affair, and said to him, I require thee
to bring to me all those things. The judge replied, O Prince
of the Faithful, the worms of the vinegar are of it and in
it: and a stranger can never obtain access to this place.
But the caliph said, If thou bring me not these things I will
put thee to death So the judge replied, Before thou slay
me, slay Ahmad Kamakim the arch-thief; for none knoweth
the robber and the traitor but the chief of the watch. And
upon this Ahmad Kamakim said to the caliph, Accept my
intercession for the judge, and I will be responsible to thee
for the thief, and I will trace him until I discover him : but
give me two persons on the part of the cadi, and two on
the part of the judge; for he who did this deed feareth not
thee, nor doth he fear the judge nor any one else. And
the caliph replied, Thou shalt have what thou hast desired ;
but the search shall be first made in my palace, and then
in the palace of the vizier, and in that of the reis-el-sittein.
Thou hast spoken rightly, O Prince of the Faithful, said
Ahmad Kamakim : probably he who did this deed is one
who hath been brought up in the palace of the Prince of the
Faithful, or in the palace of one of his chief officers. And
the caliph said, By my head, whosoever shall appear to have
done this deed shall surely be slain, though he be my son!

Then Ahmad Kamakim took what he desired, and received a written order authorizing him to force his entrance
into the houses, and to search them. Accordingly, he went
down, having in his hand a rod,[1] one third of which was of

[1] The American reader has probably seen divining-rods. Those who use
them among us sometimes make them with wire.

bronze, and one third of copper, and one third of iron ; and he searched the palace of the caliph, and that of the Vizier Giafar, and went about to the houses of the chamberlains and lieutenants, until he passed by the house of Aladdin Abushamat. And when Aladdin heard the clamor before his house, he arose from the presence of Jasmin his wife, and descending, opened the door ; whereupon he found the judge in the midst of a tumult. So he said to him, What is the matter, O Emir Kaled ? The judge therefore related to him the whole affair ; and Aladdin said, Enter my house and search it. The judge replied, Pardon, O my master : thou art surnamed Faithful ; and God forbid that the faithful should become treacherous. But Aladdin said, My house must be searched. The judge therefore entered, and the cadies and the witnesses ; and Ahmad Kamakim, advancing to the floor of the saloon, came to the slab of marble beneath which he had buried the stolen things ; when he let fall the rod upon the slab with violence, and the marble broke, and lo, something shone beneath it ; whereupon the chief exclaimed, In the name of Allah ! Wonderful is Allah's will ! Through the blessing attendant upon our coming, a treasure hath opened unto us ! Let me descend into this hoarding place, and see what is in it. And the cadi and witnesses looked into this place, and found the stolen things. So they wrote a paper stating that they had found the things in the house of Aladdin, and, after they had put their seals upon the paper, commanded to seize Aladdin ; and they took his turban from his head, and registered all his wealth and property.

Ahmad Kamakim the arch-thief then seized the damsel Jasmin, and gave her to his mother, saying to her, Deliver her to Katoun, the wife of the judge. The old woman therefore took Jasmin, and went in with her to the judge's wife; and when Habazlam Bazaza saw her, vigor returned to him, and he arose instantly, rejoicing excessively, and approached her. But she drew a dagger from her girdle, and said to him, Retire from me, or I will kill thee and kill myself! His mother Katoun exclaimed, O impudent wench, suffer my son to take thee as his wife! O brutish woman, said Jasmin, by what code is it allowed a woman to marry two husbands; and what shall admit the dogs to the abode of the lions? So the young man's desire increased, passion and distraction enfeebled him, and he again relinquished food, and took to the pillow. The wife of the judge said to Jasmin, O impudent wench, how is it that thou causeth me to sorrow for my son? Thou shalt surely be punished; and as to Aladdin, he will inevitably be hanged. But Jasmin replied, I will die in my love for him. And upon this the wife of the judge arose, and pulled off from her the ornaments and silken apparel that were upon her, and, having clad her in drawers of canvas and a shirt of hair-cloth, sent her down into the kitchen, and made her one of the menial slave girls, and said to her, Thy recompense shall be that thou break up the wood, and peel the onions, and put the fire under the cooking pots. Jasmin replied, I will consent to every kind of torment, but I will not consent to see thy son. God, however, moved the hearts of the female slaves with sympathy for her, and they worked in her stead in the kitchen. Such was the case of Jasmin.

As to Aladdin, they took him, together with the articles belonging to the caliph, and proceeded with him until they arrived at the council chamber; and while the caliph was sitting upon the throne, lo, they came up with Aladdin and the stolen things, and the caliph said, Where did ye find them? They answered him, In the midst of the house of Aladdin Abushamat. And upon this the caliph was enraged, and he took the things, but found not among them the lamp: so he said, O Aladdin, where is the lamp? He answered, I have not stolen, nor known, nor seen, nor have I any information. But the caliph said to him, O traitor, how is it that I draw thee near unto me and thou rejectest me, and that I confide in thee and thou actest toward me with treachery? And he gave orders to hang him. The judge therefore descended with him, and the crier proclaimed before him, This is the recompense, and the smallest recompense, of him who acteth treacherously toward the orthodox caliphs! And the populace collected at the gallows.

Meanwhile, Ahmad El-Denef, the chief of Aladdin, was sitting with his followers in a garden. And as they were seated there in joy and happiness, lo, a water-carrier, one of those belonging to the court, came in to them, and, kissing the hand of Ahmad El-Denef, said, O my master Ahmad, O Denef, thou art sitting in enjoyment, with the water running beneath thy feet, and hast thou no knowledge of that which hath happened? So Ahmad El-Denef said to him, What is the news? The water-carrier answered, Verily thy son by a covenant before God, Aladdin, they have taken down to the gallows. Upon this Ahmad El-Denef said, What stratagem hast thou to propose, O Hassan, O Shuman? He answered, Verily Aladdin is innocent, and this is a plot that hath been practised against him by some enemy. And what is thy advice? said Ahmad El-Denef. His deliverance, he answered, shall be accomplished by us, if the Lord will. Then

Hassan Shuman repaired to the prison, and said to the jailer, Give us some one who is deserving of being put to death. And he gave him one who was the nearest of men in resemblance to Aladdin Abushamat. And he covered his head, and Ahmad El-Denef [1] took him between him and Ali El-Zebak of Cairo. They had then brought forward Aladdin to hang him ; and Ahmad El-Denef advanced, and put his foot upon the foot of the executioner. The latter therefore said to him, Give me room, that I may perform my office. And Ahmad El-Denef replied, O accursed, take this man, and hang him in the place of Aladdin Abushamat; for he is unjustly accused, and we will ransom Ishmael with the ram. So the executioner took that man, and hanged him instead of Aladdin.

Then Ahmad El-Denef and Ali El-Zebak of Cairo took Aladdin and repaired with him to the saloon of Ahmad El-Denef, and Aladdin said to Ahmad, May God recompense thee well, O my chief. But Ahmad El-Denef said, O Aladdin, what is this deed that thou hast committed ? God have mercy upon him who hath said, Whoso confideth in thee, act not treacherously toward him, though thou be a traitor. The caliph established thee in his court, and surnamed thee the Trusty and the Faithful. How, then, couldst thou act toward him in this manner, and take his goods ? Aladdin replied, By the Most Great Name, O my chief, it was not my deed : I am not guilty of it ; nor do I know who did it. So Ahmad El-Denef said, Verily none committed this deed except a manifest enemy, and he who committeth a deed will be requited for it : but, O Aladdin, thou canst no longer reside in Bagdad ; for kings do not

---

[1] The two names mean " The Distressing Sickness," or " The Calamity " and The " Quicksilver " or " Mercury."

relinquish one object for another, and great is the fatigue of him of whom they are in quest. Whither shall I go, O my chief? said Aladdin. I will conduct thee, answered Ahmad El-Denef, to Alexandria; for it is a blessed place, and its threshold is green, and life there is agreeable. To this Aladdin replied, I hear and obey, O my chief. And Ahmad El-Denef said to Hassan Shuman, Be mindful, and if the caliph inquire respecting me, answer, He is gone to to make a circuit through the provinces.

He then took Aladdin, and went forth from Bagdad, and they proceeded without stopping until they arrived at the vineyards and gardens, where they found two Jews, of the caliph's collectors of the revenue, mounted on two mules; and Ahmad El-Denef said to them, Give me the blackmail. On what account, said they, shall we give thee the blackmail?[1] He answered them, I am the watchman of this valley. And upon this each of them gave him a hundred pieces of gold. After which Ahmad El-Denef slew them, and having taken the two mules, he mounted one of them, and Aladdin mounted the other, and they proceeded to the city of Ayas. There they put the mules in a khan, and passed the night in it; and when the morning came, Aladdin sold his mule, and charged the door-keeper with the care of the mule of Ahmad El-Denef. Then embarking in a ship in the harbor of Ayas, they proceeded to Alexandria. And Ahmad El-Denef landed with Aladdin, and they walked to the market; and lo, a broker was crying for sale a shop, within which was a suit of rooms, announcing the sum bidden to be nine hundred and fifty; whereupon Aladdin said, Let them be mine for a thousand. And the seller assented

---

[1] Such blackmail was still paid to the Bedouin of Ramleh, near Alexandria, till the bombardment of 1881.

to his offer for the property, which belonged to the government treasury; and Aladdin received the keys, and, opening
the shop and the suit of rooms, found the latter spread with
carpets, etc., and furnished with cushions. He saw there
also a magazine containing sails, and masts, and ropes, and
chests, and leather bags full of beads and shells, and stirrups, and battle-axes, and maces, and knives, and scissors,
and other things; for its owner was a dealer in second-hand
goods. So Aladdin seated himself in the shop, and Ahmad
El-Denef said to him, O my son, the shop and the suit of
rooms, and what they contain, have become thy property:
sit therefore in the shop, and sell and buy; and be not displeased; for God (whose name be exalted!) hath blessed
commerce. And he remained with him three days, and on
the fourth day he took leave of him, saying to him, Continue in this place until I have gone and returned to thee
with news of thy safety from the caliph, and seen who hath
practised this plot against thee. He then set forth on his
voyage, and proceeded until he arrived at Ayas, when he
took the mule from the khan, and went on to Bagdad, and,
meeting with Hassan Shuman and his followers, he said to
him, O Hassan, hath the caliph inquired respecting me?
No, answered Hassan; nor hast thou occurred to his mind.
    After this Ahmad El-Denef continued in the service of
the caliph, and endeavored to learn news [respecting the
case of Aladdin]. And he saw the caliph look toward
the Vizier Giafar one day, saying to him, See, O vizier,
how Aladdin hath acted toward me. The vizier replied,
O Prince of the Faithful, thou hast recompensed him with
hanging, and hath not his recompense been accomplished
upon him? O vizier, rejoined the caliph, I desire to go
down and see him hanging. And the vizier said, Do as

thou wilt, O Prince of the Faithful. So the caliph went down, accompanied by the Vizier Giafar, and proceeded to the gallows, and, raising his eyes, he saw that the body which was hanging there was not that of Aladdin, the Trusty and the Faithful. He said, therefore, O vizier, this is not Aladdin. How knowest thou, said the vizier, that it is not he? The caliph answered, Aladdin was short, and this is tall. The vizier replied, A person when hanged becomes lengthened. The caliph then said, Aladdin was fair, and the face of this person is black. But the vizier replied, Knowst thou not, O Prince of the Faithful, that death is followed by blackness? And the caliph gave orders to take down the body from the gallows; and when they had done so, he found written upon the heels of the corpse the names of the first two caliphs;[1] whereupon he said, O vizier, Aladdin was a Sunnee, and this was a heretic. So the vizier replied, Extolled be the perfection of God, who is omniscient with respect to the things that are hidden from the senses! We know not whether this be Aladdin or some other person. The caliph then gave orders to bury the body, and they buried it; and Aladdin became utterly forgotten.

Now as to Habazlam Bazaza, the son of the judge, his passion and desire were protracted until he died; and they interred him. And as to the damsel Jasmin, when she had accomplished her time of nine months after her marriage to Aladdin, she gave birth to a male child like the moon. The female slaves said to her, What wilt thou name him? And she answered, Were his father living he

---

[1] The Shi'ahs, who are considered as heretics by the Sunnees, are said to write the names of the first caliphs under their feet, that they may be trodden upon, in token of detestation.

had named him, but I will name him Aslan. She nursed him two successive years, and weaned him; and he crawled and walked. And it happened that his mother was occupied with the service of the kitchen one day, and the boy walked forth, and seeing the stairs of the upper rooms, he went up them. The Emir Kaled, the judge, was sitting there; and he took him and seated him in his lap, extolling the perfection of his Lord in respect of that which He had created and formed; and he looked at his face, and saw that he was the nearest of beings in resemblance to Aladdin Abushamat. Then his mother Jasmin searched for him, but found him not; so she went up into the upper room, and beheld the Emir Kaled sitting with the child playing in his lap; God having instilled an affection for the boy into the heart of the emir. And the child looked aside, and, seeing his mother, would have thrown himself upon her; but the Emir Kaled held him tightly in his lap, and said to his mother, Come hither, O slave girl. And when she had come, he said to her, Whose son is this child? She answered him, This is my son, and the darling of my heart. And who, said he, is his father? She answered, His father was Aladdin Abushamat; but now he˙hath become thy son. The emir replied, Aladdin was a traitor. But she said, Allah preserve him from the imputation of treachery! Allah forbid that it should ever be said that the Faithful was a traitor! And he said to her, When this boy groweth up, and saith to thee, Who is my father? do thou answer him, Thou art the son of the Emir Kaled, the judge, the chief of the police. So she replied, I hear and obey. Then the Emir Kaled circumcised the boy, and educated him carefully, and brought him a professor of religion and law, skilled in

caligraphy, who taught him the arts of writing and reading; and he read the Koran the first and second times,
and recited the whole of it; and as he grew up he used to
say to the Emir Kaled, O my father. The judge also used
to exercise his followers in the horse-course, collect the
horsemen, and descend and teach the youth the different
modes of battle, and thrusting and striking, until he became accomplished in horsemanship, acquired courage,
attained the age of fourteen years, and gained the rank of
an emir.

After this it happened that Aslan met one day with
Ahmad Kamakim the arch-thief, and they became companions. And Aslan followed him to the tavern, and lo,
Ahmad Kamakim took forth the lamp ornamented with
jewels, which he had taken from the things belonging to
the caliph, and, placing it before him, drank the cup by its
light, and intoxicated himself; and Aslan said to him, O
my master, give me this lamp. He replied, I cannot give
it thee. Why so? said Aslan. He answered, because
lives have been lost on account of it. Aslan therefore
said, What life hath been lost on account of it? And
Ahmad Kamakim answered him, There was a person who
came to us here and was made reis el-sittein, named Aladdin Abushamat, and he died on account of this lamp.
And what is his story? said Aslan, and what was the cause
of his death? Thou hadst a brother, answered Ahmad
Kamakim, named Habazlam Bazaza; and when he attained
a fit age for marriage, his father desired to purchase for
him a slave girl. Then Ahmad Kamakim proceeded, and
acquainted him with the story from beginning to end, informing him of the illness of Habazlam Bazaza, and of the
unmerited fate of Aladdin. So Aslan said within himself,

Probably that damsel is Jasmin, my mother, and none was my father but Aladdin Abushamat. And the youth Aslan went forth from him sorrowful, and he met Ahmad El-Denef, who, when he saw him, exclaimed, Extolled be the perfection of Him unto whom none is like! Upon this Hassan Shuman (being with him) said to him, O my chief, at what dost thou wonder? He answered, At the form of this youth Aslan; for he is the nearest of mankind in resemblance to Aladdin Abushamat. And he called him, saying, O Aslan! And Aslan having answered him, he said, What is the name of thy mother? He answered, She is named the slave girl Jasmin. So Ahmad El-Denef said to him, O Aslan, be of good heart and cheerful eye; for none was thy father but Aladdin Abushamat: but, O my son, go in to thy mother and ask her respecting thy father. And he replied, I hear and obey. Accordingly, he went in to his mother and asked her, and she answered him, Thy father is the Emir Kaled. But he replied, None was my father but Aladdin Abushamat. And his mother wept, and said to him, Who acquainted thee with this, O my son? He answered, The Chief Ahmad El-Denef. She therefore related to him all that had happened, and said to him, O my son, the truth hath appeared, and falsehood is withdrawn;[1] and know that thy father was Aladdin Abushamat. None, however, reared thee but the Emir Kaled, and he adopted thee. And now, O my son, when thou meetest with Ahmad El-Denef, say to him, O my chief, I conjure thee by Allah that thou take my revenge for me upon him who killed my father, Aladdin Abushamat.

[1] This is a quotation from Mohammed, who cried out, "Truth is come, and falsehood is vanished," when the idols fell to the ground in the Caaba.

So he went forth from her to Ahmad El-Denef, and
kissed his hand ; and Ahmad El-Denef said, What dost
thou want, O Aslan ? He answered, I have known of a
certainty that my father was Aladdin Abushamat, and I
request of thee that thou take my revenge for me upon
him who killed him. Ahmad El-Denef said, Who killed
thy father ? And Aslan answered him, Ahmad Kamakim
the arch-thief. And who, said Ahmad El-Denef, acquainted thee with this ? The youth answered, I saw in
his possession the lamp ornamented with jewels that was
lost with the other things belonging to the caliph, and I
said to him, Give me this lamp ; but he would not ; and he
replied, Lives have been lost on account of this. He told
me also that he was the person who descended into the
chamber of the caliph and stole the things, and that he deposited them in the house of my father. Upon this Ahmad El-Denef said to him, When thou seest the Emir
Kaleb attiring himself in the apparel of war, say to him,
Clothe me like thyself. And when thou goest up with
him, and performest some feat of valor before the Prince
of the Faithful, the caliph will say to thee, Request of me
what thou desirest, O Aslan. Thou shalt then reply, I request of thee that thou avenge my father for me upon him
who killed him. The caliph thereupon will say to thee,
Thy father is living, and he is the Emir Kaleb the judge.
And thou shalt reply, Verily my father was Aladdin
Abushamat ; and Kaleb the judge hath a claim upon me
only for his having reared me. Acquaint him also with all
that hath happened between thee and Ahmad Kamakim
the arch-thief ; and say to him, O Prince of the Faithful,
give orders to search him, and I will produce the lamp from
his pocket. So Aslan replied, I hear and obey.

He then went forth, and found the Emir Kaleb preparing himself to go up to the court of the caliph, and he said to him, I would that thou clothe me with the apparel of war like thyself, and take me with thee to the caliph's court. And he clad him, and took him to the court. The caliph then went down with the troops, without the city, and they pitched the pavilions and tents, and the ranks were formed, and they proceeded to play with the ball and the goff-stick, one of the horsemen striking the ball with the goff-stick, and another striking it back to him. Now there was among the troops a spy who had been incited to kill the caliph ; and he took the ball and struck it with the goff-stick, aiming it at the face of the caliph. But lo, Aslan warded it off from the caliph, and smote with it him who had impelled it, and it struck him between the shoulders: whereupon he fell on the ground, and the caliph exclaimed, God bless thee, O Aslan ! They then alighted from the backs of their horses, and seated themselves upon the chairs, and the caliph gave orders to bring the man who had struck the ball at him. And when he was brought before him, he said to him, Who incited thee to do this deed ; and art thou an enemy or a friend ? He answered, I am an enemy, and I was purposing to kill thee. For what reason ? said the caliph. Art thou not a Mohammedan ? No, he answered ; but I am a heretic. So the caliph gave the order to put him to death.

And he said to Aslan, Request of me what thou desirest. He therefore replied, I request of thee that thou avenge my father for me upon him who killed him. The caliph said to him, Thy father is living, and he is standing upon his feet. Who is my father ? said Aslan. The caliph answered him, The Emir Kaled, the judge. O Prince of the Faithful, re-

plied Aslan, he is not my father save in having reared me;
and none was my father but Aladdin Abushamat. The
caliph said, Thy father was a traitor. But Aslan replied,
O Prince of the Faithful, God forbid it should be said that
the Faithful was a traitor! And in what, said he, did he
act treacherously toward thee? The caliph answered, He
stole my suit of apparel, and the things that were with it.
O Prince of the Faithful, replied Aslan, God forbid it should
be said that my father was a traitor! But, O my lord, he
added, when thy suit of apparel was lost and returned to
thee, didst thou see the lamp brought back to thee also?
The caliph answered, We found it not. Then said Aslan,
I saw it in the possession of Ahmad Kamakim, and begged
it of him; but he would not give it me; and he said, Lives
have been lost on account of this. And he told me of the
illness of Habazlam Bazaza, the son of the Emir Kaled, and
his passion for the damsel Jasmin, and his own release from
the chains, and informed me that he was the person who
stole the suit of apparel and the lamp. Do thou, therefore,
O Prince of the Faithful, avenge my father for me upon
him who killed him. So the caliph said, Seize Ahmad
Kamakim. And they did so. And he said, Where is the
Chief Ahmad El-Denef? He therefore came before him;
and the caliph said to him, Search Kamakim. And he put
his hands into his pocket, and took forth from it the lamp
ornamented with jewels; whereupon the caliph said, Come
hither, O traitor. Whence came to thee this lamp? He
answered, I bought it, O Prince of the Faithful. But the
caliph said to him, Whence didst thou buy it; and who
could possess himself of such a thing, that he should sell
it to thee? They then beat him; and he confessed that he
was the person who stole the suit of apparel and the lamp.

And the caliph said to him, Wherefore didst thou these deeds, to destroy Aladdin Abushamat, who was the Trusty and Faithful? And he commanded to seize him, and the judge also. But the judge said, O Prince of the Faithful, I am injured. Thou gavest me the order to hang him, and I had no knowledge of this plot; for the thing was contrived by the old woman, and Ahmad Kamakim, and my wife, and I had no information of it. I implore thy protection, O Aslan. So Aslan interceded for him with the caliph. The Prince of the Faithful then said, What hath God done with the mother of this youth? The judge answered, She is in my house. And the caliph said, I command that thou order thy wife to attire her in her apparel and ornaments, and to restore her to her rank of a lady, and that thou take off the seals that are upon the house of Aladdin, and give to his son his possessions and wealth. The judge replied, I hear and obey. And he descended, and gave the orders to his wife, who attired Jasmin in her apparel; and he took off the seals from the house of Aladdin, and gave Aslan the keys.

The caliph then said, Request of me what thou desirest, O Aslan. Aslan replied, I request that thou unite me with my father. And the caliph wept, and said, It is most probable that thy father was the person who was hanged, and died; but, by my ancestors, whosoever bringeth me the good news of his being alive, I will give him all that he shall require. So upon this Ahmad El-Denef advanced, and, having kissed the ground before him, said to him, Grant me indemnity, O Prince of the Faithful. The caliph replied, Thou hast indemnity. And Ahmad El-Denef said, I give thee the good news that Aladdin Abushamat, the Trusty and Faithful, is well, and still living. The caliph said to him, What is it thou assertest? He answered, By thy head, my words are true; for I ransomed him by substituting another, from among such as deserved to be put to death, and conducted him to Alexandria, where I opened for him a shop of a dealer in second-hand goods. So the caliph said, I require thee to bring him. He replied, I hear and obey. And the caliph commanded to give him ten thousand pieces of gold, and he departed on his way to Alexandria.

But as to Aladdin Abushamat, he sold all that he had in the shop, excepting a few articles, and a leathern bag. And he shook this bag, and there dropped from it a bead, large enough to fill the hand, attached to a chain of gold, and having five faces, whereon were names and talismans like the tracks made by the creeping of ants. And he rubbed the five faces; but no one answered him. So he said within himself, Probably it is a bead of onyx. He then hung it up in the shop. And lo, a consul[1] passed along the street, and, raising his eyes, saw the bead hung up; whereupon he seated himself at Aladdin's shop, and said to him, O my master, is this bead for sale? Aladdin answered him, All that I have is for sale. And the consul said to him, Wilt thou sell it to me for eighty thousand pieces of gold? Aladdin answered, May God open a better way to dispose of it. The consul then said, Wilt thou sell it for a hundred thousand pieces of gold? And he answered, I sell it thee for a hundred thousand pieces of gold: so pay me the coin. But the consul

---

[1] That is, a well-to-do Frank. — *Burton.* The reference to a "consul" is evidently modern, so is the mention of "cannon." Either the tale is more recent than the rest of the series, or additions have been made in repetitions or by copyists.

replied, I cannot carry the sum ; and in Alexandria are robbers and sharpers : do thou therefore come with me to my ship, and I will thee give the price, together with a bale of Angora wool, and a bale of satin, and a bale of velvet, and a bale of broadcloth. So Aladdin arose and closed the shop, after he had delivered to him the bead ; and he gave the keys to his neighbor, saying to him, Keep these keys in thy charge while I go to the ship with this consul and bring the price of my bead ; but if I remain long away from thee, and the chief Ahmad El-Denef who established me in this place come to thee, give him the keys, and acquaint him with this circumstance.

He then repaired with the consul to the ship ; and when he went on board with him, the consul put him in a chair, and seated him upon it, and said, Bring the money. And having paid him the price, and given him the four bales which he had promised him, he said to him, O my master, I desire that thou refresh my heart by taking a mouthful of food, or a draught of water. Aladdin replied, If thou have water, give me to drink. And the consul gave orders to bring sherbet ; and there was bhang in it. So when he had drank, he fell down on his back. And they took away the chairs, and put by the poles, and loosed the sails, and the wind favored them until they advanced into the midst of the sea. The captain then gave orders to bring up Aladdin from the cabin ; and they brought him up, and made him smell the antidote of bhang ; so he opened his eyes, and said, Where am I ? The captain answered, Thou art here with me, bound and in custody ; and hadst thou said again, May God open a better way to dispose of it, I had increased my offer to thee. And what, said Aladdin, is thy occupation ? He answered, I am a captain, and I desire to take thee to the beloved of my heart.

Now while they were talking, there appeared a ship, on board of which were forty Mohammedan merchants; and the captain attacked them, fixed the grappling-irons in their ship, and boarding her with his men, they plundered her, and took her, and proceeded with her to the city of Genoa. The captain with whom Aladdin was a prisoner then went to a door of a palace opening upon the sea : and lo, a damsel came down, drawing a veil before her face, and said to him, Hast thou brought the bead and its owner? He answered her, I have brought both. And she said to him, Give me the bead. So he gave it to her. And after this he returned to the port, and fired the guns to announce his safe return ; and the king of the city, becoming acquainted with his arrival, came forth to welcome him, and said to him, How hath been thy voyage? He answered, It hath been very prosperous, and I have captured, in the course of it, a ship containing forty-one Mohammedan merchants. The king then said to him, Bring them forth into the port. And he brought them forth in irons, with Aladdin among them ; and the king and the captain mounted and made the prisoners walk before them until they arrived at the council chamber, when they seated themselves, and caused the first of the prisoners to be led forward ; and the king said to him, Whence art thou, O Mohammedan? He answered, From Alexandria. And the king said, O executioner, slay him. The executioner therefore struck him with the sword, and severed his head from his body. Thus was done to the second also, and the third, and to their companions successively, until forty had been put to death. Aladdin remained to the last : so he drank their sighs, and

he said to himself, The mercy of God be on thee, O Aladdin! Thy life hath expired! Then the king said, And
from what country art thou? He answered, From Alexandria. And the king said, O executioner, strike off his
head.

The executioner, accordingly, raised his hand with the
sword, and was about to strike off the head of Aladdin;
but lo, an old woman, of venerable appearance, advanced
before the king; whereupon he rose to her, to show her
honor; and she said, O king, did I not say to thee, When
the captain cometh with the captives, remember to supply
the convent with a captive or two to serve in the church?
O my mother, he answered, would that thou hadst come a
little earlier; but take this captive that remaineth. And
the old woman, looking toward Aladdin, said to him, Wilt
thou serve in the church, or shall I suffer the king to slay
thee? He answered her, I will serve in the church. So
she took him, and, going forth with him from the council
chamber, repaired to the church; and Aladdin said to her,
What service am I to perform? She answered, Thou shalt
arise early in the morning, and take five mules, and repair
with them to the forest, cut dry fire-wood, and break it up,
and bring it to the kitchen of the convent. After that
thou shalt take up the carpets, and sweep and wipe the
stone and marble pavements, and spread the carpets again
as they were. And thou shalt take half an ardebb [1] of
wheat, and sift it, and grind it, and knead it, and make it
into cakes for the convent; and thou shalt take a bushel
of lentils, and grind them with the hand-mill, and cook
them. Then thou shalt fill the tanks of the four fountains
with water, and convey it in barrels, and fill three hundred

[1] About two bushels.

and sixty-six wooden bowls, and crumble the cakes into
them, and pour into them some of the lentil porridge, and
take in to each monk or patriarch his bowl. To this Aladdin replied, Return me to the king and let him slay me ;
for death will be easier to me than this work. She said to
him, If thou work, and perform the service that is required
of thee, thou wilt escape slaughter ; and if thou perform it
not, I will cause the king to put thee to death. So Aladdin sat full of trouble. And there were in the church ten
blind and impotent men, who employed him in the most
degraded of services. Then the old woman came, and
said to him, Wherefore hast thou not done the work in
the church ? How many hands have I, said he, that I
should be able to accomplish this work ? Thou fool, she
replied, I brought thee not but to work. She then said,
Take, O my son, this rod (and it was of brass, with a cross
at the top), and go forth into the great thoroughfare street ;
and when the judge of the town approaches thee, say to
him, I summon thee to the service of the church. And
he will not disobey thee. So make him take the wheat,
and sift it, and grind it, and pass it through the second
sieve, and knead it, and bake cakes of it ; and whoever
shall disobey thee, beat him, and fear not any one. So he
replied, I hear and obey. He did as she had told him, and
ceased not to compel great and small to work, gratuitously,
for the space of seventeen years.

After this as he was sitting in the church, lo, the old
woman came in to him, and said to him, Go without the
convent. Whither shall I go ? said he. She answered
him, Pass this night in a tavern, or in the house of one of
thy companions. He said, Wherefore dost thou send me
away from the church ? And she answered, The beautiful

Mary, the daughter of the King John,[1] the king of this city, desireth to pay a visit to the church, and it is not proper that any one should be in her way. So he professed his assent to her order, and arose, pretending to her that he was going out from the church ; but he said within himself, I wonder whether the daughter of the king is like our women, or more beautiful than they. I will not go, therefore, until I have gratified myself by the sight of her. Accordingly, he concealed himself in a closet which had a window looking into the church. And while he was looking thence into the church, lo, the daughter of the king approached, and he directed at her a glance which occasioned him a thousand sighs ; for he found her to be like the full moon when it appeareth from behind the clouds : and with her was a damsel, to whom she was saying, Thou hast cheered me by thy society, O Zobeide. And Aladdin, looking intently at that damsel, saw that she was his wife Zobeide the Lute Player, who (as he supposed) had died. The king's daughter then said to Zobeide, Perform for us now a piece of music on the lute. But Zobeide replied, I will not perform it for thee until thou accomplish for me my desire, and fulfil thy promise to me. What have I promised thee ? said the daughter of the king. Zobeide answered her, Thou promisedst me to reunite me with my husband Aladdin Abushamat, the Trusty and the Faithful. And the king's daughter said to her, O Zobeide, be of good heart and cheerful eye, and perform for us a piece of music

---

[1] Captain Burton gives a careful note on the origin of the word " John." The Jewish spelling, as he renders it in English characters, is " Yochanan," which he derives from the Chaldean " Euahanes." The Jewish word means, " Whom Jehovah has blessed." The Greeks made it " Joannes" ; the Arabs, " Johanna," which is contracted to " Hanna."

as a gratuity for our union with thy husband Aladdin. So Zobeide said, And where is he? Verily, answered the king's daughter, he is in this closet, hearing our words. And upon this Zobeide performed a piece of music upon the lute, such as would make a rock to dance; and when Aladdin heard it, longing desires were excited in his heart, and he went forth from the closet, and, rushing upon them, took his wife Zobeide in his bosom, and she recognized him.

They embraced each other, and fell down upon the floor senseless; and the Princess Mary came, and sprinkled some rose-water upon them, and recovered them, and said, God hath united you! Aladdin replied, Through thy kindness, O my mistress. Then looking toward his wife, he said to her, Thou wast dead, O Zobeide, and we buried thee in the grave. How, then, didst thou return to life, and come unto this palace? O my master, she answered, I died not; but one of the Genii carried me off, and flew with me to this place: and as to her whom ye buried, she was a Fairy, who assumed my form and feigned herself dead, and after ye had buried her she clove open the grave and came forth from it, and betook herself to the service of her mistress Mary, the daughter of the king. But as to myself, I was possessed,[1] and, opening my eyes, I saw that I was with Mary, the king's daughter, who is this lady; and I said to her, Wherefore hast thou brought me hither? She answered me, I am predestined to marry thy husband Aladdin Abushamat. And she said, Wilt thou accept me, O Zobeide, as thy fellow-wife? I answered her, I hear and obey, O my mistress; but where, said I, is my husband?

[1] Epilepsy, or falling sickness, which is always regarded, in these writings, as possession by evil spirits.

And she said, Upon his forehead is written what God hath decreed to happen unto him, and when he hath experienced the accomplishment of events that are written upon his forehead, he cannot fail to come unto this place; but thou shalt console thyself for his separation by melodious sounds, and playing upon musical instruments, until God unite us with him. So I remained with her during this period, till God united me with thee in this church.

Then the beautiful Mary looked toward him and said to him, O my master Aladdin, wilt thou accept me as a wife, and be to me a husband? O my mistress, said he, I am a Mohammedan, and thou art a Christian: how, then, should I marry thee? But she replied, God forbid that I should be an infidel! Nay, I am a Mohammedan, and for eighteen years I have held fast the religion of the Prophet, and I am guiltless of following any religion that is at variance with his. He then said to her, O my mistress, I desire to return to my country. And she replied, Know that I have seen written upon thy forehead events of which thou must experience the accomplishment, and thou shalt attain thy wish. Be rejoiced, also, O Aladdin, by the information that a son of thine hath made his appearance, whose name is Aslan, and he is now sitting in thy place in the court of the caliph, and hath attained the age of eighteen years. Know, too, that the truth hath appeared, and falsity is withdrawn, and our lord hath removed the veil of his protection from him who stole the goods of the caliph: he is Ahmad Kamakim the arch-thief and traitor; and he is now in prison, confined and chained. Know, moreover, that I am the person that sent to thee the bead, and caused it to be put for thee in the leathern bag in the shop; and I am the person who sent to thee the captain who brought thee and the bead. And know that this captain is enamoured of me, and desireth to possess me; but I would not yield to him, and I said to him, I will not grant thy request unless thou bring to me the bead and its owner. And I gave him a hundred purses, and sent him in the garb of a merchant, though he was a captain. Then, when they had brought thee forward to slay thee, after the slaughter of the forty captives with whom thou wast, I sent unto thee the old woman. So Aladdin said to her, May God recompense thee for me with every blessing! Then the beautiful Mary renewed to him her profession of conversion to the Mohammedan faith; and when he was convinced of the truth of her avowal, he said to her, Acquaint me with the virtue of this bead, and tell me whence it came.

She replied, This bead is from the charmed treasure, and possesseth five virtues, which will profit us in the time when we need them. My grandmother, the mother of my father, was an enchantress, who solved mysteries, and carried off treasures, and from a treasure this bead came into her possession. And when I had grown up, and attained the age of fourteen years, I read the Gospels and other books, and saw the name of Mohammed (God favor and preserve him!) in the four books, the Pentateuch, and the Gospels, and the Psalms, and the Koran: so I believed in Mohammed, and became a Mohammedan, and was convinced in my mind that none is to be worshipped in truth but God (whose name be exalted!), and that the Lord of mankind approveth of no faith but that of Mohammed. My grandmother, when she fell sick, made me a present of this bead, and acquainteth me with the five virtues that it possesseth. And before my grandmother died, my father said to her, Perform for me an operation of geomancy, and see the end of my history, and what will happen to me. And she said to him, Verily, thou wilt die slain by a captive who will come from Alexandria. So my father swore that he would put to death every captive that should come from that city, and acquainted the captain with his vow, and said to him, Thou must attack the vessels of the Mohammedans, and whomsoever thou seest from Alexandria, thou must kill him, or bring him unto me. The captain therefore complied with his command until he had slain a number as many as the hairs of his head. Then my grandmother perished; and I performed an operation of geomancy, considering in my mind and saying, I would know who will marry me. And it was revealed to me that none would marry me but one named Aladdin Abushamat, the Trusty and Faithful; whereat I wondered; and I waited until the time came and I met with thee.

Aladdin then married her and said to her, I desire to return to my country. She replied, If the case is so, come with me. And she took him and concealed him in a closet in her palace, and went in to her father, who said to her, O my daughter, I am to-day suffering from excessive oppression of spirits : sit, therefore, that I may intoxicate myself with thee. So she sat; and he called for the wine-table; and she proceeded to fill and to hand to him until he became insensible, when she put some bhang into his cup, and he drank the cup, and fell down upon his back. She then came to Aladdin, and, taking him forth from the closet, said to him, Thine adversary is laid prostrate upon his back; so do with him what thou wilt; for I have intoxicated him, and stupefied him with bhang. Aladdin therefore went in, and beheld him stupefied with bhang; and he bound his hands tightly behind him, and chained him ; after which he gave him the antidote of bhang, and he recovered his senses, and found Aladdin and his daughter sitting on his bosom. So he said, O my daughter, dost thou act thus toward me ? She replied, If I am thy daughter, embrace the Mohammedan faith ; for I have done so. The truth hath become manifest to me, and I have followed it, and falsity I have abandoned ; and I have humbled my face unto God, the Lord of all creatures, and am guiltless of following any religion that is at variance with the religion of Mohammed in this world and in that which is to come. If, then, thou become a Mohammedan, we will treat thee with affection and honor ; but if not, thy slaughter will be better than thy life. Then Aladdin also admonished him. But he refused and was obstinate : so Aladdin drew forth a dagger, and cut his throat from one jugular vein to the other, and, having written a paper stating what had happened, put it upon his forehead.

After this they took what was light to carry and great in value, and went forth from the palace, and repaired to the church. She then brought out the bead, and, putting her hand upon one of the faces of it, whereon was engraved a couch, she rubbed it ; and lo, a couch was placed before her. And she mounted with Aladdin and his wife Zobeide the Lute Player upon this couch, and said, By virtue of the names, and talismans, and scientific characters that are inscribed upon this bead, rise with us, O couch ! And the couch rose with them, and conveyed them to a valley wherein was no vegetation. Then she turned up the other four faces of the bead toward the sky, turning downward the face whereon the couch was figured, and it descended with them to the earth. And she turned round a face upon which was figured the form of a pavilion,

and rubbed it, saying, Let a pavilion be set up in this valley. Whereupon the pavilion was set up, and they seated
themselves in it. Now that valley was a waste, destitute
alike of vegetation and water: so she turned four faces of
the bead toward the sky, and said, By virtue of the names
of God, let trees spring up here, with a large river by their
side! And the trees sprang up immediately, and by them
ran a large murmuring river, agitated with waves; and
they performed the ablution with its water, and prayed
and drank. The king's daughter then turned round the
three faces yet undescribed, until she came to a face upon
which was represented a table of viands, and said, By virtue
of the names of God, let the table be spread! And lo, a
table was spread, whereon were all kinds of rich viands;
and they ate and drank. and were full of joy and merriment.

Meanwhile, the king's son went in to wake his father,
and found him slain; and he found also the paper which
Aladdin had written; so he read it, and became acquainted
with its contents. He then searched for his sister, and,
not finding her, he repaired to the old woman in the
church, and inquired of her respecting her; and she
answered, Since yesterday I have not seen her. He
therefore returned and betook himself to the troops, and
said to them, To horse, O riders! And he acquainted
them with that which had happened : whereupon they
mounted their horses, and proceeded until they drew near
to the pavilion, when the Princess Mary turned her eyes,
and saw that the dust had obstructed the view of the adja-
cent tracts; and after it had risen high and spread, it dispersed, and there appeared beneath it her brother and the
troops, who were calling out, Whither will ye go when we

are behind you? So the damsel said to Aladdin, How is thy stability in war and combat? And he answered her, As that of the stake in bran; for I am not acquainted with war and battle, nor with swords and spears. She therefore took forth the bead, and rubbed a face upon which were figured a horse and rider; and lo, a horseman appeared from the desert, and ceased not to smite with the sword among them until he had routed and repelled them.

The king's daughter then said to Aladdin, Wilt thou journey to Cairo or to Alexandria? He answered, To Alexandria. So they mounted the couch, and, after she had pronounced a spell upon it, it conveyed them to Alexandria in the twinkling of an eye; and Aladdin, having taken them into a cavern, went to the city, and brought them thence apparel, with which he clad them. He then conducted them to the shop and the suit of rooms, and went forth to procure dinner for them; and lo, the Chief Ahmad El-Denef approached, arriving from Bagdad. Aladdin saw him in the street, and he met him with open arms, saluting him and welcoming him; and Ahmad El-Denef gave him good news of his son Aslan, telling him that he had attained the age of twenty years; after which Aladdin related to him all that had happened to him from first to last, and took him to the shop and the suit of rooms; and Ahmad El-Denef wondered extremely at his story. They passed the next night, and when they arose in the morning, Aladdin sold the shop, and put its price with the rest of his money. Then Ahmad El-Denef informed him that the caliph desired his presence. But Aladdin replied, I am going to Cairo, to salute my father and mother, and the other members of my family. So they mounted the couch, all together, and repaired to the fortunate city of Cairo, and alighted in the Darb El-Asfar ;[1] for the house of Aladdin's family was in that quarter ; and he knocked at the door ; whereupon his mother said, Who is at the door after the loss of the beloved ? He answered her, I am Aladdin. And on hearing this the family came down and embraced him. He then sent his two wives, and the property that he had brought with him, into the house, and entered himself, accompanied by Ahmad El-Denef, and they rested three days ; after which he desired to depart to Bagdad. His father said to him, O my son, remain with me. But he replied, I cannot endure the separation from my son Aslan. And he took his father and his mother with him, and they journeyed to Bagdad.

Then Ahmad El-Denef went in to the caliph, and imparted to him the happy news of the arrival of Aladdin ; on hearing which the caliph went forth to meet him, taking with him his son Aslan, and they met and embraced him. And the caliph gave orders to bring Ahmad Kamakim, the arch-thief, and, when he came before him, said, O Aladdin, avenge thyself upon thine adversary. So Aladdin drew his sword, and, smiting Ahmad Kamakim, severed his head. The caliph then made a magnificent entertainment for Aladdin, after he had summoned the cadies and witnesses, and written Aladdin's contract of marriage to the Princess Mary. He also appointed his son Aslan to the office of reis-el-sittein, and bestowed upon both of them sumptuous robes of honor ; and they passed a most comfortable and agreeable life until they were visited by the terminator of delights, and the separator of companions.

---

[1] That is, the street called Yellow in the old, or northern part of Cairo.

THE STORY OF ABON HASSAN THE WAG, OR THE SLEEPER AWAKENED.

———◦◦◦———

THERE was a merchant of Bagdad in the reign of the Caliph Haroun Alrashid, and he had a son named Abon Hassan the Wag. And this merchant died, leaving to his son his vast wealth; whereupon Abon Hassan divided his property into two equal portions, one of which he laid aside, and of the other he expended. He took as his familiar friends a number of the sons of the merchants, and others, and gave himself up to the delights of good drinking and good eating, until all the wealth that he had appropriated to this purpose was consumed. And upon this he repaired to his associates, and relations, and boon-companions, and exposed to them his case, showing them how little property remained in his possession; but none of them paid any regard to him, or uttered a word in reply. So he returned to his mother with a broken heart, and told her of the treatment that he had experienced from his associates, that they would neither do him justice nor even reply to him. But she said, O Abon Hassan, thus are the sons of this age : as long as thou hast anything, they draw thee near to them ; and when thou hast nothing, they cast thee off. She was grieved for him, and he sighed and wept.

He then sprang up, and went to the place in which was deposited the other half of his wealth, and upon this he lived agreeably. He took an oath that he would not thenceforth associate with any one of those whom he knew, but only with the stranger, and that he would not associate with any person but for one night, and on the following morning would not recognize him. Accordingly, every night he went forth and seated himself on the bridge, and when a stranger passed by him, he invited him to an entertainment, and took him to his house, where he caroused with him that night, until the morning : he then dismissed him ; and after that he would not salute him if he saw him. Thus he continued to do for a whole year ; after which, as he was sitting one day upon the bridge as usual, to see who might come toward him, Alrashid and certain of his domestics passed by in disguise ; for the caliph had experienced a contraction of the bosom, and come forth to amuse himself among the people. So Abon Hassan laid hold upon him, and said to him, O my master, hast thou any desire for a repast and beverage ? And Alrashid complied with his request, saying to him, Conduct us. And Abon Hassan knew not who was his guest. The caliph proceeded with him until they arrived at Abon Hassan's house : and when Alrashid entered, he found in it a saloon, such that if thou beheldest it, and lookedst towards its walls, thou wouldst behold wonders ; and if thou observedst its conduits of water, thou wouldst see a fountain incased with gold. And after he had seated himself there, Abon Hassan called for a slave girl, like the twig of the Oriental willow, who took a lute and sang. And when Alrashid heard her, he said, Thou hast performed well. God bless thee ! Her eloquence pleased him, and he wondered at Abon Hassan and his entertainment.

He then said to Abon Hassan, O young man, who art

thou? Acquaint me with thy history, that I may requite thee for thy kindness. But Abon Hassan smiled, and replied, O my master, far be it from me that what hath happened should recur, and that I should be in thy company again after this time! And why so? said the caliph ; and why wilt thou not acquaint me with thy case? So Abon Hassan told his story, and when the caliph heard it, he laughed violently, and said, By Allah, O my brother, thou art excusable in this matter. Then a dish of roast goose was placed before him, and a cake of fine bread ; and Abon Hassan sat, and cut off the meat, and put morsels into the mouth of the caliph, and they continued eating until they were satisfied; when the basin and ewer were brought, with the kali; and they washed their hands. After this Abon Hassan lighted for his guests three candles and three lamps, spread the wine cloth, and brought clear, strained, old, perfumed wine, the odor of which was like fragrant musk, and, having filled the first cup, said, O my boon-companion, bashfulness is dismissed from us, with thy permission. Thy slave is by thee. May I never be afflicted by the loss of thee! And he drank the cup, and filled the second, which he handed to the caliph, waiting upon him as a servant. And the caliph was pleased with his actions, and the politeness of his words, and said within himself, By Allah, I will certainly requite him for this! Abon Hassan then, after he had kissed the cup, handed it to the caliph, who accepted it from his hand, kissed it and drank it, and handed it back to him. Abon Hassan still continued serving him, saying, Drink, and may it be attended with health and vigor. And they drank and caroused until midnight.

After this the caliph said to his host, O Abon Hassan,

is there any service that thou wouldst have performed, or any desire that thou wouldst have accomplished? And Abon Hassan answered, In our neighborhood is a mosque to which belong an imam and four sheikhs, and whenever they hear music or any sport, they incite the judge against me, and impose fines upon me, and trouble my life, so that I suffer torment from them. If I had them in my power, therefore, I would give each of them a thousand lashes, that I might be relieved from their excessive annoyance.

Alrashid replied, May Allah grant thee the accomplishment of thy wish! And without his being aware of it, he put into a cup a lozenge of bhang, and handed it to him; and as soon as it had settled in his stomach, he fell asleep immediately. Alrashid then arose and went to the door, where he found his young men waiting for him, and he ordered them to convey Abon Hassan upon a mule, and returned to the palace, Abon Hassan being intoxicated and insensible. And when the caliph had rested himself in the palace, he called for his vizier Giafar, and Abdallah the son of Tahir, the Judge of Bagdad, and certain of his chief attendants, and said to them all, In the morning when ye see this young man (pointing to Abon Hassan) seated on the royal couch, pay obedience to him, and salute him as caliph, and whatsoever he commandeth you, do it. Then going to his female slaves, he directed them to wait upon Abon Hassan, and to address him as Prince of the Faithful: after which he entered a private closet, and, having let down a curtain over the entrance, slept.

So when Abon Hassan awoke, he found himself upon the royal couch, with the attendants standing around, and kissing the ground before him; and a maid said to him, O our lord, it is the time for morning prayer. Upon which he laughed, and, looking round about him, he beheld a pavilion whose walls were adorned with gold and ultramarine, and the roof bespotted with red gold, surrounded by chambers with curtains of embroidered silk hanging before their doors; and he saw vessels of gold, and China-ware, and crystal, and furniture, and carpets spread, and lighted lamps, and female slaves, and eunuchs, and other attendants; whereat he was perplexed in his mind, and said, By Allah, either I am dreaming, or this is Paradise, and the Abode of Peace. And he closed his eyes. So a eunuch said to him, O my lord, this is not thy usual custom, O Prince of the Faithful. And he was perplexed at his case, and put his head into his bosom, and then began to open his eyes by little and little, laughing, and saying, What is this state in which I find myself? And he bit his finger; and when he found that the bite pained him, he cried, Ah! and was angry. Then raising his head, he called one of the female slaves, who answered him, At thy service, O Prince of the Faithful! And he said to her, What is thy name? She answered, Cluster of Pearls. And he said, Knowest thou in what place I am, and who I am? Thou art the Prince of the Faithful, she answered, sitting in thy palace, upon the royal couch. He replied, I am perplexed at my case; my reason hath departed, and it seemeth that I am asleep: but what shall I say of my yesterday's guest? I imagine nothing but that he is a devil, or an enchanter, who hath sported with my reason.

All this time the caliph was observing him from a place where Abon Hassan could not see him. And Abon Hassan looked toward the chief eunuch, and called to him. So he came, and kissed the ground before him, saying to him, Yes, O Prince of the Faithful. And Abon Hassan said to

him, Who is the Prince of the Faithful? Thou, he answered. Abon Hassan replied, Thou liest. And addressing another eunuch, he said to him, O my chief, as thou
hopest for Allah's protection, tell me, am I the Prince of
the Faithful? Yea, by Allah, answered the eunuch ; thou
art at this present time the Prince of the Faithful, and the
caliph of the Lord of all creatures. And Abon Hassan,
perplexed at all that he beheld, said, In one night do I become Prince of the Faithful! Was I not yesterday Abon
Hassan ; and to-day am I Prince of the Faithful? He remained perplexed and confounded until the morning, when
a eunuch advanced to him, and said to him, May Allah
grant a happy morning to the Prince of the Faithful! And
he handed to him a pair of shoes of gold stuff, reticulated
with precious stones and rubies ; and Abon Hassan took
them, and after examining them a long time, put them into
his sleeve. So the eunuch said to him, These are shoes to
walk in. And Abon Hassan replied, Thou hast spoken
truth. I put them not into my sleeve but in my fear lest
they should be soiled. He therefore took them forth, and
put them on his feet. And shortly after, the female slaves
brought him a basin of gold and a ewer of silver, and poured
the water upon his hands ; and when he had performed the
ablution, they spread for him a prayer carpet; and he
prayed ; but knew not how to do so. He continued his
inclinations and prostrations until he had performed twenty
rekahs ; meditating and saying within himself, By Allah, I
am none other than the Prince of the Faithful, in truth ;
or else this is a dream, and all these things occur not in a
dream. He therefore convinced himself, and determined
in his mind that he was the Prince of the Faithful ; and he
pronounced the salutations, and finished his prayers. They

then brought him a magnificent dress, and, looking at himself as he sat upon the couch, he retracted, and said, All
this is an illusion, and a machination of the Genii.
And while he was in this state, lo, one of the mamlouks
came in and said to him, O Prince of the Faithful, the
chamberlain is at the door, requesting permission to enter.
Let him enter, replied Abon Hassan. So he came in,
and, having kissed the ground before him, said, Peace be
on thee, O Prince of the Faithful! And Abon Hassan
rose, and descended from the couch to the floor; whereupon the chamberlain exclaimed, Allah! Allah! O Prince
of the Faithful! Knowest thou not that all men are thy
servants, and under thy authority, and that it is not proper
for the Prince of the Faithful to rise to any one? Abon
Hassan was then told that Giafar the Barmecide, and
Abdallah the son of Tahir, and the chiefs of the mamlouks, begged permission to enter. And he gave them
permission. So they entered, and kissed the ground before him, each of them addressing him as Prince of the
Faithful. And he was delighted at this, and returned
their salutation; after which he called the judge, who
approached him, and said, At thy service, O Prince of
the Faithful! And Abon Hassan said to him, Repair
immediately to such a street, and give a hundred pieces
of gold to the mother of Abon Hassan the Wag, with my
salutation; then take the imam of the mosque, and the
four sheikhs, inflict upon each of them a thousand lashes;
and when thou hast done that, write a bond against them,
confirmed by oath, that they shall not reside in the street,
after thou shalt have paraded them through the city,
mounted on beasts, with their faces to the tails, and hast
proclaimed before them, This is the recompense of those

who annoy their neighbors. And beware of neglecting that which I have commanded thee to do. So the judge did as he was ordered. And when Abon Hassan had exercised his authority until the close of the day, he looked toward the chamberlain and the rest of the attendants, and said to them, Depart.

He then called for a eunuch who was near at hand, and said to him, I am hungry, and desire something to eat. And he replied, I hear and obey; and led him by the hand into the eating chamber, where the attendants placed before him a table of rich viands; and ten slave girls, high-bosomed virgins, stood behind his head. Abon Hassan, looking at one of these, said to her, What is thy name? She answered, Branch of Willow. And he said to her, O Branch of Willow, who am I? Thou art the Prince of the Faithful, she answered. But he replied, Thou liest, by Allah, thou slut! Ye girls are laughing at me. So she said, Fear Allah, O Prince of the Faithful; this is thy palace, and the female slaves are thine. And upon this he said within himself, It is no great matter to be effected by God, to whom be ascribed might and glory! Then the slave girls led him by the hand to the drinking chamber, where he saw what astonished the mind; and he continued to say within himself, No doubt these are of the Genii, and this person who was my guest is one of the kings of the Genii, who saw no way of requiting and compensating me for my kindness to him but by ordering his slaves to address me as Prince of the Faithful. All these are of the Genii. May Allah then deliver me from them happily! And while he was thus talking to himself, lo, one of the slave girls filled for him a cup of wine; and he took it from her hand and drank it; after which, the slave girls

plied him with wine in abundance; and one of them threw
into his cup a lozenge of bhang; and when it had settled
in his stomach, he fell down senseless.

Alrashid then gave orders to convey him to his house;
and the servants did so, and laid him on his bed, still in
a state of insensibility. So when he recovered from his
intoxication, in the latter part of the night, he found himself in the dark; and he called out, Branch of Willow!
Cluster of Pearls! But no one answered him. His mother,
however, heard him shouting these names, and arose and
came, and said to him, What hath happened to thee, O my
son, and what hath befallen thee? Art thou mad? And
when he heard the words of his mother, he said to her,
Who art thou, O ill-omened old woman, that thou addressest the Prince of the Faithful with these expressions?
She answered, I am thy mother, O my son. But he replied
Thou liest: I am the Prince of the Faithful, the lord of
the countries and the people. Be silent, she said, or else
thy life will be lost. And she began to pronounce spells,
and to recite charms over him, and said to him, It seemeth,
O my son, that thou hast seen this in a dream, and all this
is one of the ideas suggested by the devil. She said to
him, I give thee good news, at which thou wilt be rejoiced.
And what is it? said he. She answered, The caliph gave
orders yesterday to beat the imam and the four sheikhs,
and caused a bond to be written against them, confirmed
by oath, that they shall not transgress henceforth against
any one by their impertinent meddling; and he sent me a
hundred pieces of gold, with his salutation. And when
Abon Hassan heard these words from his mother, he
uttered a loud cry, with which his soul almost quitted
the world; and he exclaimed, I am he who gave orders to

beat the sheikhs, and who sent thee the hundred pieces of gold, with my salutation, and I am the Prince of the Faithful.

Having said this, he rose up against his mother, and beat her with an almond stick, until she cried out, O ye faithful. And he beat her with increased violence, until the neighbors heard her cries and came to her relief. He was still beating her, and saying to her, O ill-omened old woman, am I not the Prince of the Faithful? Thou hast enchanted me! And when the people heard his words, they said, This man hath become mad. And not doubting his insanity, they came in and laid hold upon him, bound his hands behind him, and conveyed him to the mad-house. There every day they punished him, dosing him with abominable medicines, and flogging him with whips, making him a madman in spite of himself. Thus he continued, stripped of his clothing, and chained by the neck to a high window, for the space of ten days ; after which his mother came to salute him. And he complained to her of his case. So she said to him, O my son, fear God in thy conduct : if thou wert Prince of the Faithful, thou wouldst not be in this predicament. And when he heard what his mother said, he replied, By Allah, thou hast spoken truth. It seemeth that I was only asleep, and dreamed that they made me caliph, and assigned me servants and female slaves. So his mother said to him, O my son, verily Satan doeth more than this. And he replied, Thou hast spoken truth, and I beg forgiveness of God for the actions committed by me.

They therefore took him forth from the mad-house, and conducted him into the bath ; and when he recovered his health, he prepared food and drink, and began to eat. But

eating by himself was not pleasant to him ; and he said to
his mother, O my mother, neither life nor eating by myself
is pleasant to me.   She replied, If thou desire to do according to thy will, thy return to the mad-house is most
probable.   Paying no attention, however, to her advice, he
walked to the bridge to seek for himself a cup-companion.
And while he was sitting there, lo, Alrashid came to him
in the garb of a merchant ; for, from the time of his part-
ing with him he came every day to the bridge, but found
him not till now.   As soon as Abon Hassan saw him, he
said to him, A friendly welcome to thee, O King of the
Genii !   So Alrashid said, What have I done to thee ?
What more couldst thou do, said Abon Hassan, than thou
hast done to me, O filthiest of the Genii ?   I have suffered
beating, and entered the mad-house, and they pronounced
me a madman.   All this was occasioned by thee.   I
brought thee to my abode, and fed thee with the best of
my food ; and after that thou gavest thy devils and thy
slaves entire power over me, to make sport with my reason
from morning to evening.   Depart from me, therefore, and
go thy way.

'   The caliph smiled at this, and, seating himself by his
side, addressed him in courteous language, and said to him,
O my brother, when I went forth from thee, I inadvertently left the door open, and probably the devil went in to
thee.   Abon Hassan replied, Inquire not respecting that
which happened to me.   And what possessed thee, he
added, that thou leftest the door open, so that the devil
came in to me, and that such and such things befell me ?
And he related to the caliph all that had happened to him
from first to last, while Alrashid laughed, but concealed
his laughter : after which the caliph said to him, Praise be

to God that He hath dispelled from thee that which thou hatest, and that I have seen thee again in prosperity ! But Abon Hassan replied, I will not take thee again as my boon-companion, nor as an associate to sit with me ; for the proverb saith, He who stumbleth against a stone and returneth to it, is to be blamed and reproached : and with thee, O my brother, I will not carouse, nor will I keep company with thee: since I have not found thy visit to be followed by good fortune to me. The caliph, however, said, I have been the means of the accomplishment of thy desire with regard to the imam and the sheikhs. Yes, re-plied Abon Hassan. And Alrashid added, Perhaps some-thing will happen to thee that will rejoice thy heart more than that. Then what dost thou desire of me ? said Abon Hassan. My desire, answered Alrashid, is to be thy guest this night. And at length Abon Hassan said, On the condition that thou swear to me by the inscription on the seal of Solomon the son of David (on both of whom be peace !) that thou wilt not suffer thy Afrites to make sport with me. And Alrashid replied, I hear and obey.

So Abon Hassan took him to his abode, and put the food before him and his attendants, and they ate as much as satisfied them ; and when they had finished eating, the servants placed before them the wine and exhilarating bev-erages, and they continued drinking and carousing until the wine rose into their heads. Abon Hassan then said to the caliph, O my boon-companion, in truth I am perplexed respecting my case. It seemeth that I was Prince of the Faithful, and that I exercised authority, and gave and bestowed : and truly, O my brother, it was not a vision of sleep. But the caliph replied, This was the result of con-fused dreams. And having said this, he put a piece of bhang into the cup, and said, By my life, drink this cup. Verily I will drink it from thy hand, replied Abon Hassan. So he took the cup, and when he had drank it his head fell before his feet. The caliph then arose immediately, and ordered his young men to convey Abon Hassan to the palace, and to lay him upon his couch, and commanded the female slaves to stand around him; after which he concealed himself in a place where Abon Hassan could not see him, and ordered a slave girl to take her lute and strike its chords over Abon Hassan's head, and desired the other slave girls to play upon their instruments.

It was then the close of the night, and Abon Hassan, awaking, and hearing the sounds of the lutes, and tambourines, and flutes, and the singing of the slave girls, cried out, O my mother! Whereupon the slave girls answered, At thy service, O Prince of the Faithful! And when he heard this, he exclaimed, There is no strength nor power but in God, the High, the Great! Come to my help this night; for this night is more unlucky than the former! He reflected upon all that had happened to him with his mother, and how he had beaten her, and how he had been taken into the mad-house, and he saw the marks of the beating that he had suffered there. Then looking at the scene that surrounded him, he said, These are all of them of the Genii, in the shapes of human beings! I commit my affairs unto Allah! And looking toward a mamlouk by his side, he said to him, Bite my ear, that I may know if I be asleep or awake. The mamlouk said, How shall I bite thine ear, when thou art the Prince of the Faithful? But Abon Hassan answered, Do as I have commanded thee, or I will strike off thy head. So he bit it until his teeth met together, and Abon Hassan uttered a loud shriek.

Alrashid (who was behind a curtain in a closet), and all who were present, fell down with laughter, and they said to the mamlouk, Art thou mad, that thou bitest the ear of the caliph? And Abon Hassan said to them, Is it not enough, O ye wretches of Genii, that hath befalleth me? But ye are not in fault: the fault is your chief's, who transformed you from the shapes of Genii into the shapes of human beings. I implore help against you this night by the Verse of the Throne, and the Chapter of Sincerity, and the two Preventives! Upon this Alrashid exclaimed from behind the curtain, Thou hast killed us, O Abon Hassan! And Abon Hassan recognized him, and kissed the ground before him, greeting him with a prayer for the increase of his glory and the prolongation of his life. Alrashid then clad him in a rich dress, gave him a thousand pieces of gold, and made him one of his chief boon-companions.

Abon Hassan, after this, became a greater favorite with the caliph than all the other boon-companions, so that he sat with the caliph and his wife the Lady Zobeide, the daughter of Kasim, and he married her female treasurer, whose name was Nouzatalfuad. With this wife he resided, eating, and drinking, and enjoying a delightful life, until all the money that they possessed had gone; whereupon he said to her, O Nouzatalfuad! And she answered, At thy service. I desire, said he, to practise a trick upon the caliph, and thou shalt practise a trick upon the Lady Zobeide, and we will obtain from them immediately two hundred pieces of gold, and two pieces of silk. Do what thou desirest, replied she: and what, she asked, is it? He answered, We will feign ourselves dead. I will die before thee, and lay myself out: then do thou spread over me a napkin of silk, and unfold my turban over me, and tie my toes, and put upon my stomach a knife and a little salt: after which, dishevel thy hair, and go to thy Lady Zobeide, and tear thy vest, and slap thy face, and shriek. So she will say to thee, What is the matter with thee? And do thou answer her, May thy head long survive Abon Hassan the Wag; for he is dead! Whereupon she will mourn for me, and weep, and will order her female treasurer to give thee a hundred pieces of gold, and a piece of silk, and will say to thee, Go, prepare his corpse for burial, and convey it forth to the grave. So thou shalt receive from her the hundred pieces of gold, and the piece of silk, and come hither. And when thou comest to me, I will rise, and thou shalt lay thyself down in my place, and I will go to the caliph, and say to him, May thy head long survive Nouzatalfuad! And I will tear my vest and pluck my beard; upon which he will mourn for thee, and will say to his treasurer, Give to Abon Hassan a hundred pieces of gold, and a piece of silk: and he will say to me, Go, prepare her corpse for burial, and convey it forth to the grave. So I will come to thee. And Nouzatalfuad was delighted with this, and replied, Truly this is an excellent stratagem!

She forthwith closed his eyes, and tied his feet, covered him with the napkin, and did all that her master told her; after which she tore her vest, uncovered her head, and dishevelled her hair, and went in to the Lady Zobeide, shrieking and weeping. When the Lady Zobeide, therefore, beheld her in this condition, she said to her, What is this state in which I see thee, and what hath happened unto thee, and what hath caused thee to weep? And Nouzatalfuad wept and shrieked, and said, O my mistress, may thy head long survive Abon Hassan the Wag; for he is dead! And the Lady Zobeide mourned for him, and said, Poor

Abon Hassan the Wag! Then, after weeping for him a while, she ordered the female treasurer to give to Nouzatalfuad a hundred pieces of gold and a piece of silk, and said, O Nouzatalfuad, go, prepare his body for burial, and convey it forth. So she took the hundred pieces of gold and the piece of silk, and, returning to her abode full of joy, went in to Abon Hassan, and acquainted him with what had happened to her; upon which he arose and rejoiced, and girded his waist and danced, and took the hundred pieces of gold, with the piece of silk, and laid them up.

He then extended Nouzatalfuad, and did with her as she had done with him; after which he tore his vest, and plucked his beard, and disordered his turban, and ran without stopping until he went in to the caliph, who was in his hall of judgment; and in the condition above described, he beat his bosom. So the caliph said to him, What hath befallen thee, O Abon Hassan? and he wept, and said, Would that thy boon-companion had never been, nor his hour come to pass! The caliph therefore said to him, Tell me. He replied, May thy head long survive, O my lord, Nouzatalfuad! And the caliph exclaimed, There is no deity but God! and struck his hands together. He then consoled Abon Hassan, and said to him, Mourn not: I will give thee a slave in her stead. And he ordered his treasurer to give him a hundred pieces of gold, and a piece of silk. The treasurer therefore did as he was commanded, and the caliph said to Abon Hassan, Go, prepare her corpse for burial, and convey it forth, and make a handsome funeral for her. And he took what the caliph gave him, and went to his abode joyful, and going in to Nouzatalfuad, said to her, Arise; for our desire is accomplished. She therefore arose, and he put before her the hundred pieces of gold and the piece of silk. So she rejoiced; and they put these pieces of gold on the other pieces, and the piece of silk on the former one, and sat conversing, and laughing at each other.

But as to the caliph, when Abon Hassan parted from him, and went with the pretence of preparing the corpse of Nouzatalfuad for burial, he mourned for her, and, having dismissed the council, arose and went in, leaning upon Mesrour his executioner, to console the Lady Zobeide for the loss of her slave girl. He found her, however, sitting weeping, and waiting for his arrival, that she might console him for the loss of Abon Hassan the Wag. The caliph said, May thy head long survive thy slave girl Nouzatalfuad! But she replied, O my lord, Allah preserve my slave girl! Mayest thou long survive thy boon-companion Abon Hassan the Wag; for he is dead! And the caliph smiled, and said to his eunuch, O Mesrour, verily women are of little sense. By Allah, was not Abon Hassan just now with me? Upon this the Lady Zobeide said, after uttering a laugh from an angry bosom, Wilt thou not give over thy jesting? Is not the death of Abon Hassan enough, but thou must make my slave girl to be dead, as though we had lost them both, and thou must pronounce me of little sense? The caliph replied, Verily Nouzatalfuad is the person who is dead. And the Lady Zobeide rejoined, In truth he was not with thee, nor didst thou see him; and none was with me just now but Nouzatalfuad, who was mourning and weeping, with her clothes rent in pieces; and I exhorted her to have patience, and gave her a hundred pieces of gold, and a piece of silk; and I was waiting for thee, that I might console thee for the loss of thy boon-companion Abon Hassan the Wag; and I was going to send for thee. On hearing this the caliph laughed, and said, None is dead but Nouzatalfuad. And the Lady Zobeide said, No, no, O my lord ; none is dead but Abon Hassan. But the caliph now became enraged ; the vein between his eyes, which was remarkable in members of the family of Hashim, throbbed, and he called out to Mesrour the Executioner, saying to him, Go forth and repair to the house of Abon Hassan the Wag, and see which of the two is dead.

Mesrour, therefore, went forth running. And the caliph said to the Lady Zobeide, Wilt thou lay me a wager? She answered, Yes, I will, and I say that Abon Hassan is dead. And I, replied the caliph, lay a wager, and say that none is dead but Nouzatalfuad ; and our wager shall be, that I stake the Garden of Delight against thy pavilion, the Pavilion of the Pictures. And they sat waiting for Mesrour to return with the information. Now as to Mesrour, he ran without ceasing until he entered the by-street in which was the house of Abon Hassan the Wag. Abon Hassan was sitting reclining against the window, and, turning his eyes, he saw Mesrour running along the street. So he said to Nouzatalfuad, It seemeth that the caliph, after I went forth from him, dismissed the court, and hath gone in to the Lady Zobeide to console her, and that she, on his arrival, hath arisen and consoled him, and said to him, May God largely compensate thee for the loss of Abon Hassan the Wag! whereupon the caliph hath said to her, None is dead but Nouzatalfuad. May thy head long survive her! And she hath replied, None is dead but Abon Hassan the Wag, thy boon-companion. And he hath said again to her, None is dead but Nouzatalfuad. So they have become obstinate, and the caliph hath been enraged, and they have laid a wager, in consequence of which Mesrour the Executioner hath been sent to see who is dead. It is therefore the more proper that *thou* lay thyself down, that he may see thee, and go and inform the caliph, who will thereupon believe my assertion.

Accordingly, Nouzatalfuad extended herself, and Abon Hassan covered her with her veil, and seated himself at her head, weeping. And lo, Mesrour the eunuch came up into the house of Abon Hassan, and saluted him, and saw Nouzatalfuad stretched out ; upon which he uncovered her face, and exclaimed, There is no deity but God ! Our sister Nouzatalfuad is dead ! How speedy was the stroke of fate ! May Allah have mercy upon her, and acquit thee of responsibility ! He then returned, and related what had happened before the caliph and the Lady Zobeide, laughing as he spoke. So the caliph said to him, O thou accursed, this is not a time for laughing. Tell us which of them is dead. He therefore replied, By Allah, O my lord, verily Abon Hassan is well, and none is dead but Nouzatalfuad. And upon this the caliph said to Zobeide, Thou hast lost thy pavilion in thy play. And he laughed at her, and said, O Mesrour, relate to her what thou sawest. So Mesrour said to her, In truth, O my mistress, I ran incessantly until I went in to Abon Hassan in his house ; whereupon I found Nouzatalfuad lying dead, and Abon Hassan sitting at her head, weeping ; and I saluted him, and consoled him, and seated myself by his side ; and, uncovering the face of Nouzatalfuad, I beheld her dead, with her face swollen : I therefore said to him, Convey her forth presently to the grave, that we may pray over her. And he replied, Yes. And I came, leaving him to prepare her corpse for burial, in order to inform you. Upon this the caliph laughed, and said, Tell it again and again to thy mistress, the person of little sense. But when the Lady Zobeide heard the words of Mesrour, she was enraged, and said, None is deficient in sense but he who believeth a slave. And she abused Mesrour, while the caliph continued laughing; and Mesrour was displeased, and said to the caliph, He spoke truth who said that women are deficient in sense and religion.

The Lady Zobeide then said, O Prince of the Faithful, thou sportest and jestest with me, and this slave deceiveth me for the purpose of pleasing thee; but I will send, and see which of them is dead. The caliph replied, Do so. And she called to an old woman, a confidential slave, and said to her, Repair quickly to the house of Nouzatalfuad, and see who is dead, and delay not thy return. And she threw money to her. So the old woman went forth running, the caliph and Mesrour laughing. The old woman ran without ceasing until she entered the street, when Abon Hassan saw her and knew her; and he said to his wife, O Nouzatalfuad, it seemeth that the Lady Zobeide hath sent to us to see who is dead, and hath not believed what Mesrour hath said respecting thy death : wherefore she hath sent the old woman to ascertain the truth of the matter. It is therefore more proper now for *me* to be dead, that the Lady Zobeide may believe thee.

Then Abon Hassan laid himself along, and Nouzatalfuad covered him, and bound his eyes and his feet, and seated herself at his head, weeping. And the old woman came in to Nouzatalfuad, and saw her sitting at the head of Abon Hassan, weeping, and enumerating his merits; and when Nouzatalfuad saw the old woman, she shrieked, and said to her, See what hath befallen me! Abon Hassan hath died and left me single and solitary! Then she shrieked again, and tore her clothes in pieces, and said to the old woman, O my mother, how good he was! The old woman replied, Truly thou art excusable; for thou hadst become habituated to him, and he had become habituated to thee. And knowing how Mesrour had acted to the caliph and the Lady Zobeide, she said to Nouzatalfuad, Mesrour is about to cause a quarrel between the caliph and the Lady Zobeide. And what is this cause of quarrel, O my mother? said Nouzatalfuad. The old woman answered, O my daughter, Mesrour hath come to them and told them that thou wast dead, and that Abon Hassan was well. O my aunt, replied Nouzatalfuad, I was just now with my lady, and she gave me a hundred pieces of gold and a piece of silk; and see thou my condition, and what hath befallen me. I am perplexed; and what shall I do, single and solitary? Would that I had died, and that he had lived! Then she wept, and the old woman wept with her, and advancing, and uncovering the face of Abon Hassan, saw his eyes bound, and swollen from the bandage. And she covered him, and said, Truly, O Nouzatalfuad, thou hast been afflicted for Abon Hassan. And she consoled her, and went forth from her running until she went in to the Lady Zobeide, when she related to her the story; on hearing which, the Lady Zobeide laughed, and said, Tell it to the caliph who hath pronounced me of little sense, and caused this ill-omened, lying slave to behave arrogantly toward me. But Mesrour said, Verily this old woman lieth; for I saw Abon Hassan in good health, and it was Nouzatalfuad who was lying dead. The old woman replied, It is thou who liest, and thou desirest to excite a quarrel between the caliph and the Lady Zobeide. Mesrour rejoined, None lieth but thou, O ill-omened old woman, and thy lady believeth thee, for she is disordered in mind. And upon this the Lady Zobeide cried out at him, enraged at him and at his words ; and she wept.

At length the caliph said to her, I lie, and my eunuch lieth, and thou liest, and thy female slave lieth. The right course, in my opinion, is this, that we four go together to see who among us speaketh truth. So Mesrour said, Arise with us, that I may bring misfortunes upon this ill-omened old woman, and bastinade her for her lying. O thou imbecile in mind! exclaimed the old woman : is thy sense like mine? . Nay, thy sense is like that of the hen. And Mesrour was enraged at her words, and would have laid violent hands upon her ; but the Lady Zobeide, having pushed him away from her, said to him, Immediately will her veracity be distinguished from thine, and her lying from thine. They all four arose, laying wagers with each other, and went forth and walked from the gate of the palace until they entered the gate of the street in which dwelt Abon Hassan the Wag : when Abon Hassan saw them, and said to his wife Nouzatalfuad, In truth, everything that is slippery is not a pancake, and not every time the jar is struck doth it escape unbroken. It seemeth that the old woman hath gone and related the story to her lady, and acquainted her with our case, and that she hath contended with Mesrour the eunuch, and they have laid wagers respecting our death : so the caliph, and the eunuch, and the Lady Zobeide, and the old woman have all four come to us. And upon this Nouzatalfuad arose from her extended position, and said, What is to be done? Abon Hassan answered her, We will both feign ourselves dead, and lay ourselves out and hold in our breath. And she assented to his proposal.

They both stretched themselves along, bound their feet, closed their eyes, and held in their breath, lying with their heads in the direction of the kebla, and covered themselves with the veil. Then the caliph, and Zobeide, and Mesrour, and the old woman entered the house of Abon Hassan the Wag, and found him and his wife extended as if they were dead. And when the Lady Zobeide saw them, she wept, and said, They continued to assert the death of my female slave until she actually died ; but I imagine that the death of Abon Hassan so grieved her that she died after him in consequence of it. The caliph, however, said, Do not prevent me with thy talk and assertions ; for she died before Abon Hassan, because Abon Hassan came to me with his clothes torn in pieces, and with his beard plucked, and striking his bosom with two clods ; and I gave him a hundred pieces of gold, with a piece of silk, and said to him, Go, prepare her body for burial, and I will give thee a concubine better than her, and she shall serve in her stead : and it appears that her loss was insupportable to him ; so he died after her. I have therefore overcome thee, and gained thy stake. But the Lady Zobeide replied in many words, and a long dispute ensued between them.

The caliph then seated himself at the heads of the two pretended corpses, and said, By the tomb of the Apostle of Allah (God favor and preserve him !), and by the tombs of my ancestors, if any one would acquaint me which of them died before the other, I would give him a thousand pieces of gold. And when Abon Hassan heard these words of the caliph, he quickly rose and sprang up, and said, It was I who died first, O Prince of the Faithful.

Give me the thousand pieces of gold, and so acquit thyself
of the oath that thou hast sworn. Then Nouzatalfuad
arose and sat up before the caliph and the Lady Zobeide,
who rejoiced at their safety. But Zobeide chid her female
slave. The caliph and the Lady Zobeide congratulated
them both on their safety, and knew this pretended death
was a stratagem for the purpose of obtaining the gold : so
the Lady Zobeide said to Nouzatalfuad, Thou shouldst
have asked of me what thou desiredst without this proceeding, and not have tortured my heart on thine account. I
was ashamed, O my mistress, replied Nouzatalfuad. But
as to the caliph, he was almost senseless from laughing,
and said, O Abon Hassan, thou hast not ceased to be a
wag, and to do wonders and strange acts. Abon Hassan
replied, O Prince of the Faithful, this stratagem I practised
in consequence of the dissipation of the wealth that I received from thy hand ; for I was ashamed to ask of thee a
second time. When I was alone, I was not tenacious of
wealth; but since thou hast married me to this female
slave who is with me, if I possessed all thy wealth I should
make an end of it. And when all that was in my possession was exhausted, I practised this stratagem, by means
of which I obtained from thee these hundred pieces of gold
and the piece of silk, all of which are an alms of our lord.
And now make haste in giving me the thousand pieces
of gold, and acquit thyself of thine oath.

At this the caliph and the Lady Zobeide both laughed ;
and after they had returned to the palace, the caliph gave
to Abon Hassan the thousand pieces of gold, saying to
him, Receive them as a gratuity on account of thy safety
from death. In like manner, also, the Lady Zobeide gave
to Nouzatalfuad a thousand pieces of gold, saying to her

the same words.   Then the caliph allotted to Abon Hassan an ample salary and ample supplies, and he ceased not to live with his wife in joy and happiness, until they were visited by the terminator of delights and the separator of companions, the devastator of palaces and houses, and the replenisher of the graves.

www.ingramcontent.com/pod-product-compliance
Lightning Source LLC
Chambersburg PA
CBHW030905270326
41929CB00008B/586